R OGER C ONNOR

ROGER CONNOR

Home Run King of 19th Century Baseball

Roy Kerr

McFarland & Company, Inc., Publishers
Jefferson, North Carolina, and London

LIBRARY OF CONGRESS CATALOGUING-IN-PUBLICATION DATA

Kerr, Roy, 1947–
    Roger Connor : home run king of 19th century baseball /
Roy Kerr.
        p.   cm.
    Includes bibliographical references and index.

    ISBN 978-0-7864-5958-2
    softcover : 50# alkaline paper ∞

    1. Connor, Roger, 1857–1931. 2. Baseball players —
United States — Biography. 3. Baseball — Records — United
States. 4. Home runs (Baseball) I. Title.
GV865.C6716K47   2011
796.357092 — dc23
[B]   3011034669

BRITISH LIBRARY CATALOGUING DATA ARE AVAILABLE

Front cover: Roger Connor of the Troy City team, circa 1882
(National Baseball Hall of Fame Library, Cooperstown, New York)

Manufactured in the United States of America

McFarland & Company, Inc., Publishers
    Box 611, Jefferson, North Carolina 28640
    www.mcfarlandpub.com

For my home team:
Annie and Ed

Table of Contents

Acknowledgments   ix

Preface   1

Prologue: September 11, 1886   3

1. The Manchild   7

2. The Apprentice   23

3. The Veteran   49

4. The Brotherhood Rebel   95

5. The Journeyman   109

6. The Squire of Waterbury   138

7. The Forgotten Star   155

8. The Past Recaptured   166

Epilogue: The Giants of New York   177

Appendix A: Connor's Nicknames   181

*Appendix B: Connor's Major and
Minor League Statistics*   183

Notes   185

Bibliography   196

Index   199

Acknowledgments

Many people helped make this book possible. Ed Borsoi and Leon Lyday patiently reviewed and critiqued the text with care and insight. Richard A. Puff got me started on my Troy, New York, odyssey by graciously providing me with a photocopy of his out-of-print *Troy's Baseball Heritage*. Mark Rucker's 19th-century baseball photographs, as well as those supplied by the National Baseball Hall of Fame Library at Cooperstown, and by the Library of Congress, provided marvelous visual additions to the text. Howard P. Ohlous, of Rensselaer Polytechnic Institute, graciously permitted me to use his photographs of Troy, New York's Baseball Monument.

I am most grateful to Nora Galbraith at Florida Southern College's Roux Library and to the Society for American Baseball Research's microfilm lending service for the invaluable assistance they provided me on this project. I express my sincere gratitude to Emmett McSweeney, Director of the Silas Bronson Library in Waterbury, Connecticut, for his kind assistance, and most especially, to Bronson Library specialist Anita Bologna, who took time from her hectic schedule to insure that Roger Connor's clipping file was made available to me. I likewise gratefully acknowledge the assistance of the talented librarians at the Troy, New York, Public Library and the New York State Library in Albany, who facilitated my research in so many ways. Volunteer librarians Pat Woods and John Murphy at the History Room of the Holyoke, Massachusetts, Library, went out of their way to accommodate my review of essential microfilm for the study of Roger Connor's 1879 season.

I am most grateful to Connor family members Gary Laios, Gerry Laios and Mark Connor, for their support and concerted efforts to assist me, and I most especially thank Gerry and Gary, whose clipping, letter, and photograph files were essential to the completion of this project.

Finally, I express my deepest thanks and appreciation to Bill Jenkinson, baseball historian and friend for more than a half-century, who reviewed the manuscript, provided me access to his historical home run log and to important clippings and documents, and enthusiastically supported my research.

Preface

"The pitcher was lazy. The catcher was a bum. But here comes Roger to hit a home run."
— Connor-era children's rhyme, Waterbury, Connecticut,
Waterbury Republican-American, May 30, 2002

We forget the past. Intrepid navigators of the Information Age, we are regularly overwhelmed by the volume of data that constantly assaults our senses. Our only recourse is to jettison some of the old to make room for the incoming tide of the new. Nowhere is this process more evident than in the realm of popular culture, where "significant" events and "celebrity" status are, in the words of an old saying, here today and gone tomorrow. Who can remember the name of their great-grandparents' favorite song or most-admired silent-film star?

So it is also with baseball. Tracking back through the generations, how many stars from our fathers' era can we recall? How many from our grandfathers' era? Collective amnesia has relegated the majority of these players and their accomplishments to the dusty corridors of history.

Most baseball fans today have never heard of Roger Connor. The few that have, know him as "the Babe Ruth of the 1880's"—a title that, while appropriate, unfortunately confers upon him a one-dimensional status as a player and a man.

Who knew that the tape-measure–home-run hitter with the Paul Bunyan–sized body possessed a sweet tenor voice and liked nothing better than to sing to his daughter's piano accompaniment or to bounce his grandchildren on his knee? Who knew that he could lay down a sacrifice bunt with the best of them, or switch-hit against left-handed pitching and

1

slug home runs from the right side of the plate? Who knew that the great hitter was an accomplished first baseman who led the league in fielding four times, including his last full season in the major leagues, when he was 39 years old? Who knew that he was still agile and swift enough at age 53 to be stealing bases in a semi-pro league?

Such discoveries, and the correction of factual errors that have crept into the literature about Roger Connor's life and career, are some of the pleasures of recovering fragments of baseball's past. Of the many unexpected finds in Connor's case, none is more intriguing and illuminating than the more than three dozen colorful nicknames invented by the press to express wonder or admiration for Connor's size, strength, gentlemanly nature, or personal integrity — a quantity and variety of epithets arguably exceeded only by those applied to one other player in baseball history — Babe Ruth. Catalogued by date and source in Appendix A of this book, these condensed verbal portraits offer convincing proof of the Victorian-era baseball fans' fascination with, and admiration for the "King of First Basemen," the "Hercules of the New York team," the "Squire of Waterbury," who was one of the most talented and beloved players of his day.

—ɯ—

"The dead are soon forgotten, and some people don't have to wait that long."
                     — Roger Connor, *Sporting Life*, September 1, 1908

Prologue:
September 11, 1886

"Roger Connor ... Who he?"
—Red Smith, *New York Times*, September 5, 1973

It was a splendid Saturday in New York City, 115 years before the day's date, September 11, would forever after be associated with treachery and tragedy. After an August cool spell, warm weather had returned to Manhattan, with temperatures climbing to the mid–80s. Two weeks before the official beginning of fall, the city basked in the golden glow of Indian summer.

Nature had not been so kind to other parts of the country. The ravages of a severe Midwest drought had inflicted grievous damage to the grain crop. On the evening of August 31, an earthquake so pronounced that it was felt as far north as Massachusetts and as far west as Indiana leveled much of Charleston, South Carolina.

Despite such trials, the country's overall mood was upbeat, and President Grover Cleveland, who took office a year earlier, was enjoying widespread popularity. The recent surrender of Apache Chief Geronimo signaled the end of Indian uprisings in the West. As if in ironic counterpoise, Buffalo Bill Cody's "Wild West Show" was playing to packed houses and rave reviews on Staten Island. Construction of the Statue of Liberty in New York harbor was entering its final phase, and dedication ceremonies were set for October. Out beyond the harbor on this day, the New York Yacht Club's *Mayflower* defeated the English cutter *Galatea* in their second heat, securing a victory for the United States in the seventh America's Challenge Cup race.

3

Just before Independence Day, the *New York Herald* had become the first city newspaper to publish a linotype edition, a wondrous innovation that permitted an entire line of text to be set simply by typing on a keyboard. Overnight, printed news became quicker to assemble and distribute. Down in Atlanta at the beginning of the baseball season, pharmacist John Stith-Pemberton invented a dark, sweet, effervescent beverage, and christened it with an unusual name: "Coca Cola." Part Three of a new translation of Tolstoy's *War and Peace*, priced at 20 cents, made its appearance in bookstores in September, along with H. Rider Haggard's new adventure saga, *King Solomon's Mines*, a copy of which cost a quarter. The Cunard shipping line offered passage from New York to Liverpool, England, for 50 dollars, and the *New York Times* advertised a three-story home rental on Fifth Avenue near 131st Street for the princely sum of $1,000 a year. A.J. Commeyer's Sixth Avenue bargain store announced a more down-to-earth offer: a pair of fashionable ladies' hand-sewn shoes could be purchased for three dollars.

Forty-one years earlier in the city, a young bookstore owner, Alexander J. Cartwright, drew up a set of baseball rules for use by his local amateur club, the Knickerbockers. In the ensuing decades, while Cartwright's adventuresome spirit was leading him first to California for the 1849 Gold Rush, and ultimately to the far shores of Hawaii, his standardized "Knickerbocker Rules," as they came to be known, helped to transform baseball from a simple gentlemen's leisure activity to a professional sport — one that would capture the imagination of generations of Americans. Along the way, the game would offer a select, talented group of humble immigrants' sons a means to escape a working-class life as a farmer, miner, factory worker or mill hand, and to rise to the middle class. On this September Saturday in 1886, one of these men would perform a feat on a New York baseball diamond that would never be equaled.

Until 1880, athletic events at the original Polo Grounds, located just north of Central Park at 112th Street and Fifth Avenue, were limited to the sport that gave the site its name. On September 30 of that year it officially became a baseball field, hosting a game between two independent professional teams, the New York Metropolitans and the Washington Nationals. In the succeeding seven years the country's leading "batsmen," as hitters were then called, all had tried unsuccessfully to knock a ball over the fence at the Grounds. Attendance at today's National League contest between the Bostons and the New Yorks was less than one-quarter of the 12,000 present here on opening day, April 29, when the home squad bested

Boston, 5–4. Both teams at this juncture were statistically out of the hotly contested pennant race between the reigning champions, the White Stockings of Chicago, and the upstart Detroit Wolverines. Chicago would win the battle, but the Wolverines would claim the title the following year.

The Giants, New York's National League team, were making their first appearance at home since mid–August, having just returned from a disastrous road trip that included seven consecutive losses to the league leaders, Chicago and Detroit. Boston's ace, Charley "Old Hoss" Radbourn, son of an immigrant English butcher, was in the pitching box (there was as yet no "pitching mound") in the first inning as a tall, powerfully built left-handed Giants hitter who hailed from Waterbury, Connecticut, strode to the plate. Game accounts report that Radbourn gave the towering batsman a "good ball," which was met squarely, and then "it soared upward with the speed of a carrier pigeon. All eyes were turned on the tiny sphere as it flew over the head of Buffinton, in right field, and when it finally disappeared over the fence a shout of joy went up from the 2,600 spectators."[1] It was the only ball ever hit out of the original Polo Grounds, sailing over "an eight foot wall surmounted by a sixteen foot fence,"[2] and landing in a field on 112th Street. The Giants slugger "trotted the circuit around the bases, and when he finally reached the home base he looked at the fence and appeared happy. The members of the team shook the hand of the successful batsman, and he was gazed upon in wonderment by Radbourn and the other members of the Boston team."[3]

The mighty Giant's other contributions to the win against Boston that day, however, were forgotten in the excitement of the moment. He fielded flawlessly at first base, registering nine putouts and an assist, and after the record-setting home run in the first inning, contributed a double, a single, a walk, and another four-bagger to the 10–3 victory.

Over the years, a similar preference for foregrounding the accounts of this Giant's spectacular power-hitting displays has tended to obscure the fact that he was, by every measure, not just a home-run hitter, but a complete player, as worthy of election to the Hall of Fame for his other playing talents as he was for his home run production. Besides being the nineteenth century's home run king, he ranked first in that era in triples, second in walks, fourth in doubles and in runs scored, and second in fielding. Stolen bases were not counted officially until his seventh major league season, but subsequently, in the last decade of his career, between the ages of 30 and 40, he averaged over 20 per season. Not bad for a player who stood 6' 3" and weighed 230 pounds.

After the Polo Grounds hero of September 11, 1886, finished his major league career in 1897, he went home to Connecticut, and his baseball exploits soon were forgotten. He died in 1931, and for seven decades lay buried in an unmarked grave.

Who was he? Fans, sportswriters, and teammates of his era knew him by admiring or endearing nicknames. For them, he was the "giant of the Giants," or "dear old Roger." He was "the Oak of New York," or the "Gentleman of the Diamond." He was the "Rajah of Waterbury."

His name was Roger Connor.

1

The Manchild

"Baseball was to him, even in those juvenile days, everything."
—Margaret Colwell, Roger Connor's granddaughter,
Waterbury Sunday Republican, August 8, 1976

Nurtured by the confluence of numerous small streams, Connecticut's Naugatuck River rises in the state's northwestern Litchfield County and pursues a winding, 65-mile southern course, passing through the towns of Torrington, Thomaston, Waterbury, Naugatuck, and Ansonia. Upon reaching the tiny city of Derby, its waters blend with those of the Housatonic River and then continue south until they empty into Long Island Sound. The meandering Naugatuck carved scenic vistas through the surrounding granite hills over the centuries, but the river's narrow, swampy valley, poor in soil quality and susceptible to flooding, hindered the development of a traditional agricultural economy.

Fortunately for the region, the river's potential as a power source, its valley's proximity to New York's markets, and the enterprising efforts of some of its early metalworkers succeeded in providing an alternative income source in the form of manufacturing. Skilled tinsmiths Edward and William Pattison began the manufacture of tin mugs, pans, and plates in the Naugatuck Valley in 1746.[1] After the Revolutionary War, the Grilley brothers, Samuel, Silas, and Henry, manufactured tin buttons in Waterbury, switching to brass as the raw material for their product before the end of the 18th century.[2] In that era, brass was produced by combining precise amounts of copper and zinc, using a formula that had been patented in England in 1781. Enterprising Waterbury metalworkers soon circumvented the need to buy their finished brass products from Britain. They

7

melted down local scrap copper, purchased the needed zinc abroad, and rolled out their own brass sheets. The first fruits of these labors, brass buttons, proved to be a great revenue source during both the War of 1812 and the Civil War (the Confederacy bought its Connecticut-made buttons through a circuitous European route). Over time, other products complemented the button trade, including brass rings, buckles, tubing, door and furniture knobs, and in later years, ammunition shell casings and blank brass disks for the minting of U.S. one cent and nickel coins.

In 1855, Naugatuck Valley mills produced 2,000 tons of brass annually, and by 1900 Connecticut ranked first in the nation in total production of brass articles.[3] Waterbury was the locus of this activity. Incorporated in 1853 and proud of its manufacturing success, it officially proclaimed itself "The Brass City," and adopted the Latin phrase *"Quid aere perennius"* ("What is more lasting than bronze?") for its motto. Clock manufacturing, a spinoff of the brass industry, began in 1854 with the founding of the Waterbury Clock Company, whose name in time would change to Timex Corporation. As production increased and markets expanded, the Brass City's industries required more and more laborers. Fleeing their country's Great Famine of the 1840s, the Irish were the first to answer the call.

In September of 1852, 24-year-old Mortimer Connor of Tralee, County Kerry, on Ireland's southwest coast, arrived in New York on the passenger ship *Irvine*, made his way to the Naugatuck Valley and found work in a Waterbury brass mill. By the end of the following year he had married another County Kerry immigrant, Catherine Sullivan, who was five years his junior, and the couple had celebrated the birth of their first child, Hannah, named after Catherine's mother, Johanna Slattery Sullivan. The rapidity with which Mortimer settled in Waterbury, found a job, married and fathered his first child strongly suggests that he had relatives or friends in the area prior to his arrival, perhaps including members of the Sullivan family, who assisted him in establishing his new life in America.

Catherine and Mortimer arrived in Connecticut at the height of anti–Irish immigration sentiment in the United States. By 1854, the American Party, running on a platform of ending Catholic immigration and limiting public office jobs to native-born Americans, had won elections in Boston, Salem, and other New England cities, as well as in parts of Illinois, California, and Ohio. Nicknamed the "Know Nothing" party due to the fact that when asked about their organization's secret activities, members responded, "I know nothing," the American Party's national political influence was short-lived, but the anti–Irish sentiment it promoted lingered for decades.

Waterbury was not exempt from this prejudice, for while its industrialists welcomed Irish labor, its polite society did not. The newcomers there, as in cities across the nation, lived in poor, out-of-the way locations, termed "Irish Towns" or "Shanty Towns," within or just outside the city's limits. Irish Town in Waterbury was located in the Abrigador district, a series of streets to the west of a rocky granite hill, now known as Pine Hill, which overlooked the brass mills. A cleft in the promontory had given rise to its original Native American name *abrigador*, "from *abigad* or *abignat*, meaning 'shelter.'"[4] A half-mile long, a quarter-mile wide, and almost 600 feet high, the Abrigador for decades served as both a physical and symbolic barrier between Waterbury's Irish Town and the rest of the city.

In the late 1850s, the Connor family took up residence in the Abrigador at the end of Stone Street, a short cul de sac that ascends partially up the southwest side of the hill. Although today Interstate 84 cuts between the neighborhood and the location of the old brass mills, in Mortimer's era he could walk the half-mile distance from home to work, down the Abrigador in the morning, and back up in the evening after his 12-hour shift.

By 1860, three Connor children had come into the world: Hannah, age seven, Mary, four, and Roger, three. A decade later, Catherine had given birth to four more of her eventual total of 11 children. Two of the 11 would not survive childhood. It was a difficult life. Mortimer's meager wages were woefully insufficient to support the growing Connor family, and his children one-by-one took their place in the work world. The 1870 census lists 17-year-old Hannah a dress maker and 13-year-old Mary as a button factory worker. Twelve-year-old Roger was listed as still "at school,"[5] but soon joined his father at the brass works. At home, Mortimer Connor supplemented his income by raising chickens, growing vegetables in the rocky soil, and boarding horses in the ramshackle barns behind the house. There Roger made and repaired harnesses and learned how to shoe horses, skills that his father had acquired in Ireland. The family was so poor that in winter the children had to "contrive wrappings for their feet in lieu of shoes so that they could work around the barns and garden in all kinds of weather."[6] Although by his early teens Roger could easily do the work of a grown man both at home and at work, all his energies and attention had been captured by a less practical activity — baseball. His work ethic was steady and sure during the winter, but "come spring, summer, and autumn — Roger was no help to the family,"[7] for he spent all his time on the ball field.

In the dozen years that transpired between the 1845 publication of the "Knickerbocker Rules" and Roger Connor's birth, adult amateur baseball "began to spread among people in all walks of life"[8] and to all areas of the country. By 1857, clubs had formed as far west as Detroit and the Minnesota Territory. A year later teams were playing ball in California. The New York City area alone was home to over 50 clubs, including the premier Knickerbockers, Gothams, Eagles and Empires in Manhattan, and the Excelsiors, Putnams, Atlantics and Eckfords in Brooklyn. Before the decade ended, the Excelsiors, led by their star pitcher, Jim Creighton, became the first team to take a road trip, racking up more than a thousand miles by train and competing in exhibition matches against teams in upstate New York, Baltimore, and Philadelphia. Besides returning home to Brooklyn undefeated, the Excelsiors' tour helped to develop tremendous interest in baseball on the east coast. In 1867, the Washington Nationals performed a similar service to the game by spending the month of July on a more extended exhibition tour through Ohio, Kentucky, Missouri and Illinois, sowing the seeds of baseball fever wherever they played.

In 1858, club representatives met in New York to found the National Association of Base Ball Players, or NABBP ("base ball" would not become one word until the 20th century). Although all the teams involved were amateurs, rules standardization, increasing skill level of players, and greater opportunities to hone these skills on the field against an increasing number of opponents inexorably led to increased competition between teams. Given these circumstances, clubs soon resorted to borrowing "ringers," or star players, from other teams in order to secure a victory. Baseball, to use historian David Quentin Voigt's elegant terms, was now in a conflict between the "ethic of sportsmanship" and the "ethic of victory."[9] The era of professionalism was at hand.

Opinions vary on the effect of the Civil War on baseball's growth and popularity. The traditional view, fostered initially by Albert G. Spalding's 1911 *The National Game*, is that returning soldiers who had learned the "Knickerbocker Rules" game during leisure hours in between battles, brought it home with them at war's end. Peter Morris, on the other hand, while acknowledging some historical accounts that support the Spalding thesis, notes that "in virtually every region of the country the onset of the war eradicated thriving clubs."[10] Those veterans who returned home "decided to move on to other phases of their lives. The need to accept new responsibilities was the most pressing reason for their departure from the game. But it was undoubtedly complemented by the difficulty of returning to an innocent game after going through the horrors of war."[11]

Regardless of one's position on this issue, the inescapable fact is that in the post-war years, Voigt's "ethic of victory" had supplanted the "ethic of sportsmanship" on the field, and competitive professional baseball not only improved the level of play, but attracted an increasing number of fans willing to pay to watch a game. In 1871, the NABBP was supplanted by another organization, one whose name signaled its new purpose: the National Association of *Professional* Base Ball Players, the first major league. By the early 1870s therefore, the concept of professional baseball had advanced to the stage that it could convince a tall, gangly lad from Connecticut in his early teens to leave home in hopes of earning a living on a professional team.

Mortimer Connor, a practical man struggling to support a large family, had no sympathy for his eldest son's frivolous fixation on a game. Late in life, Connor recalled the harsh retribution that his father exacted for being away from one's job or chores: "The Lord help the one who disobeyed; the punishment was quick and severe."[12] The day arrived, however, when the threat of such punishment did not chasten the strapping teenager. Around the age of 14 he had enough. Taking off on his own, Huck Finn style, Connor headed in the general direction of New York City, the baseball Mecca of the era, working odd jobs and trying to catch on with junior ball teams, always looking for an opportunity to play ball for a living. A left-handed third baseman who at this stage was still batting right-handed, he did not yet possess the skills to do so. Late in life, he confirmed that his earliest organized baseball experience did not begin until he had returned from his adolescent wanderings: "I can still recall my first days of amateur ball as vividly as if they were but a week ago. Way back in 1876 were my first days at the game and I played with the [Waterbury] Monitors about the vicinity."[13] Not until he joined the Monitors did Connor wear a baseball uniform. "I remember the time distinctly, the Monitors of Waterbury years ago purchased their new baseball uniforms and were very proud of them. We all went up to Watertown to play against a swell set from New York city [*sic*]. It was there I wore my first baseball uniform."[14]

Having proven himself as a man if not as a ballplayer during his extended "walkabout," Connor headed home to Waterbury as the 1874 Christmas season approached. The news he received on arrival was both joyous and tragic: his mother had given birth to her last child, Joseph, but his father Mortimer had died unexpectedly before Joe's birth. Stricken with guilt and remorse, Connor's adventuresome adolescence was over, and he returned to full-time work at the brass mill to support his family. For the rest of his life, however, he would serve as a protective big brother and surrogate father to his youngest sibling Joe, who was 17 years his junior.

Other than Connor's personal assertions to his granddaughter, there is scant historical evidence to document his adolescent "walkabout." However, such a story was not as unusual then as it would be today. A decade later, another son of Irish immigrants to New York State would leave home at age 13 to avoid his father's frequent beatings, making a hardscrabble living doing odd jobs while pursuing a baseball career. He would go on to become an outstanding player with Baltimore and the manager of the New York Giants. His name was John McGraw.[15]

When younger sister Nelly joined the family work force of Roger, Hannah, and Mary, the Connor family's financial situation gradually improved, and once again Roger could revisit the dream of being a professional ballplayer. At 18 he joined the Waterbury Monitors, one of two town teams, for the 1876 season.

As Roger Connor embarked on his quarter-century baseball career, the profession itself was beginning its own quarter-century transformation from what has been described as its "stone age,"[16] both in terms of its organizational structure and in the evolution of its on-field rules and regulations. "Big Roger" was a member of a small group of players who managed to adapt and adjust to such momentous changes while remaining productive athletes throughout the period. His individual achievements on the diamond, therefore, must be placed within their continuously shifting cultural context in order to be fully understood and appreciated.

The promise of the first professional league, the National Association of Professional Base Ball Players (1871–1875), did not bear fruit. Wildly unbalanced skill levels of the Association's teams (Boston captured four of the five Association pennants), poor attendance, gambling, fixing or throwing games, and a complete lack of central organization led to the demise of this first attempt to develop a player-controlled professional baseball league. Its 1876 replacement, the National League of Professional Base Ball Clubs, or National League, divested the players of any control over their individual ability to market their services to the highest bidder. In the Connor era this led to two unsuccessful attempts by the players to regain control of their own professional destinies through the establishment of player-organized leagues — the Union Association (1884), and the Players'

League (1890). In the latter struggle, Connor cast his lot with the players, a decision that exacted financial penalties, and after it failed, initiated an unsettling period in the twilight of his career during which he would play for three different clubs (Phillies, Giants, St. Louis Browns) in three years.

The players were not the only ones to challenge the National League's monopoly. A successful alternate league, the American Association, was formed in 1882, and offered fans some enticing options that the National League disdained: Sunday baseball, 25-cent admission (half that of its rival), and liquor sales at the game. The Association's success forced the League to recognize its rival as an equal in 1883, while still decrying it as the "beer and whiskey" league. In 1892 the leagues merged.

There would be no respite, however, for the new amalgam — a cumbersome 12-team affair known officially as the League Association. In 1901, Byron "Ban" Johnson, owner of a financially successful minor league organization, challenged the League Association's monopoly with his new American League, and succeeded. Two years later, the year of Roger Connor's retirement from professional baseball, the first modern World Series took place, between the Bostons of the American League and the Pittsburghs of the National. More than a century later, the National/American bipartite structure remains the essential organizing principle of major league baseball.

When Roger Connor began his career, there were no "minor" leagues as we know them today. By the late 1870s, there were more than 50 professional clubs and numerous regional associations competing with the National League. Many regional teams handily defeated National League squads in the League's early years. On such occasions, however, League teams often signed the best of their opponent's players to lucrative contracts after their contest. In order to protect their rosters from these raiding parties, most regional leagues eventually signed on to an 1883 pact (the National Agreement) between the National League and the American Association that required all parties to respect each other's reserve contracts. In signing, the regional leagues, de facto, accepted their classification as second or "minor" level organizations in comparison to the League and the Association. At this juncture, the minor and major leagues became a reality. In 1901, the leagues adopted a classification system (A through D) which, in a slightly altered form, still exists today.

In Connor's early playing days, however, organized baseball below the National League and the regional professional league level of play in his home state remained a fluid enterprise until the establishment of the

Connecticut State League in the 1880s. Towns and cities fielded their own clubs, and they issued written challenges to all comers from around the state and elsewhere in New England. Scheduling was haphazard and reports in local newspapers were irregular. Game venues were primitive, and as the following Waterbury notice indicates, contests often were not played in the best of locations: "The Monitors will play the Stars of New Haven, Thursday afternoon. The game will be played at the Monitors' new grounds, which can easily be reached by crossing the ditch near the gas works."[17]

Batting for the Waterbury Monitors in 1876, Roger Connor faced a pitcher who stood a mere 45 feet away from him. Five years later, while he was playing for Troy's National League team, this distance was moved back five feet. Under both of these circumstances the pitcher threw from a six-foot-square "pitcher's box," which was level with the rest of the field (i.e., no raised pitcher's mound), and he was allowed free movement within the box before delivering the pitch. Starting in 1887, the pitcher was required to keep one foot on the back line of a smaller pitcher's box, a distance of 55'6", until completing his delivery. Finally, in 1893, pitchers were required to keep one foot in contact with a 12-inch (later 24 inch) rubber slab placed at a distance of 60'6" from home plate.

Pitchers were compensated for the increasing distance between themselves and home plate by rule changes regarding the manner in which they could deliver the ball. From 1876 to 1882, they were required to throw underhanded. This rule was largely overcome, however, as "all the top pitchers used an underhand snap like that employed in fast pitch softball."[18] Sidearm delivery was allowed in 1883, and overhand delivery in 1884.

By the 1870s the curve ball had been added to the underhand pitcher's repertoire, which, when combined with a good change-up and fastball, could frequently stymie the best hitter. The most advantageous era for the pitcher — and conversely the most daunting for the hitter — was the period 1884–1886. During these three seasons, helmetless batters faced overhand hurlers who could move about freely in the pitcher's box and whose release point was often less than 50 feet from home plate. Getting hit by a pitch didn't earn you first base either — that wouldn't come until 1887. All you got for your pain was a called ball.

With the exception of the 1887 season, during which batters had an extra strike to make a hit, three strikes was the norm for a strike out. The number of balls for a walk, in contrast, ranged from nine in 1880 to the modern day four in 1889. Until 1887, batters had the right to call for a low or high pitch from the hurler. One thrown out of that range was considered a ball.

Although by the mid–1870s some catchers and pitchers were protecting their hands with skin-tight gloves, often with the fingers cut out, other position players fielded barehanded. The majority would continue to do so until the early 1890s. One umpire and one ball were assigned per game, regardless of how frayed the former's nerves became, or how dilapidated the latter's condition was. Initially a catcher's only protection was a rubber mouth guard. During Connor's career years, masks and chest protectors became standard equipment for catchers. Leg protection for catchers did not appear until Giant Roger Bresnahan strapped on a pair of cricket shin guards on opening day, 1907. Although in the early, unprotected era a catcher normally positioned himself far behind the plate, "with runners on, he had to move up and take his chances. Likewise with two strikes on the batter, it was prudent to move close to the bat to catch the third strike before it hit the ground. Wild pitches, foul tips, and errant throws all exacted their pound of flesh."[19]

During Connor's first year in organized ball, news of his team in the local newspaper took a distant second place to the newsworthiness of the exploits of a club from 30 miles up the road. The Hartford Dark Blues had garnered national attention in 1874 by securing a place in the National Association professional league. After finishing seventh that year under hard-hitting player-manager Lipman "Lip" Pike, believed to be the first Jewish player and/or manager in professional baseball,[20] the Dark Blues finished in second place in the Association's last year of existence, thanks in large part to the work of two pitchers: Irish-born Tommy Bond and diminutive (5' 4") Arthur "Candy" Cummings, the putative inventor of the curve ball. Cummings taught his Irish teammate how to throw the curve, which when combined with Bond's blazing fast ball, allowed him to accomplish a feat that no other pitcher in history has managed. In each of three consecutive seasons (1879–1881) while pitching for the Boston Nationals, Bond won more than 40 games. Hartford's player-manager, light-hitting third baseman Bob Ferguson, was so adept at catching anything hit to him in the air that he earned the cumbersome but unique nickname "Death to Flying Things."[21] In a few years Ferguson would manage a young third baseman from Waterbury, Roger Connor, during Connor's three years with Troy's National League entry (1880–1882).

The Dark Blues' second-place National Association finish in 1875 earned them a spot in the newly-formed National League in 1876, despite the fact that Hartford's population of 40,000 fell far below the League's minimum 75,000 population requirement for franchises. Although Hartford lasted only a year in the new league, its national notoriety guaranteed it first billing in the pages of the *Waterbury American* in 1876.

That year, Waterbury fielded two teams, the Monitors and the Rose Hills. The first report on either was published on May 10: "The Monitors play a picked nine at the Riverside Park tomorrow at 2:00."[22] The team's first box score of the season appeared on July 21, noting that the Monitors defeated the New Haven Stars, 5–2, and that Roger Connor, playing third base and batting third, went hitless, made six putouts, had two assists, and committed four errors. The account of this uninspiring performance is the first official press mention of Connor by name in his long career. Near the end of July, he scored two runs and played errorless ball in an 8–2 win against the Gerards of New Haven. In an early August rematch with New Haven's Stars, he went 1-for-5 and committed three errors at third in a 10–4 victory. The game summary provides the first account of Connor's performance beyond a simple box score: "in the eighth after one man was out and Connor had secured first base on an error of third base, Hayes [the Monitors' center fielder] made a two base hit but they were left on base as the next two strikers went out in order."[23]

The season ended with accounts of only two more Monitors contests reported: a 9–7 win against the hometown rival Rose Hills in mid–August, in which Connor went 2-for-5, including a double, and played errorless ball, and a 19–2 pounding by a Rhode Island team in which he managed one hit but made four of a team's 16 errors.

In addition to the account of this August massacre by the Rhode Island team, the August 19 *Waterbury American* makes reference to another local sport whose significance to the history of the development of ball and bat sports in the United States is noteworthy. Included on this date alongside the baseball score is an account of a series of wicket matches between Waterbury and Wolcottsville. Presumably derived from cricket, wicket differs from its probable English progenitor in that "the wickets were wider and much lower to the ground, and the ball was literally bowled on the ground, not pitched through the air."[24] The most striking difference between the two sports, however, was that wicket teams totaled 30 players on a side compared to cricket's 11. In many small towns, this could enable "virtually the entire community to take part."[25] In his groundbreaking *Baseball Before We Knew It: A Search for the Roots of the Game*, David Block conjectures that "when wicket all but vanished at the end of the 1850s, it may have been the result of some inherent shortcoming, such as the difficulty of fielding 30-player teams. A more likely explanation, however, is that the game's demise was an inexorable consequence of baseball's explosion in popularity at that very moment in history."[26] The presence of wicket scores beside baseball scores in an 1876 number of the *Waterbury American* suggests that while baseball indeed was making headway toward being acknowledged officially as the "National Pastime," wicket's demise in Connecticut was far more protracted than originally thought.

Nine Monitors games received Waterbury newspaper coverage in 1877. Of these contests against teams from Norwalk, New Haven, Meriden and other nearby towns, the home team won five, lost three, and tied one. For unknown reasons, Roger Connor did not play in three of these games, and on one occasion, a 6–2 loss to a team named the Jeffersons, he was not the only regular absent. The club that day was "without the services of Connor, Harrison, and Casey."[27] In the three contests in which Connor's stats were recorded (out of six games total), he had two hits, scored a run, and committed eight errors at third base. The 1876 Rose Hills had changed their name to the Waterburys in 1877, and they defeated their hometown rivals in mid–August, 9–4, giving them an 8–1 season record. Connor's Monitors came back a week later and defeated the Waterburys, 3–1 in the season's final contest.

While the available statistics for Roger Connor's first two years (seven games, five hits, three runs, 16 errors) are meager and obviously inconclusive, they suggest that he was at this point a fair hitter but a poor-fielding third baseman, even considering the era, when gloveless players who could field in the low .900 range were considered great defenders. Both the offensive and defensive aspects of his game would improve in dramatic fashion the following year.

In Waterbury's 1878 opener against Trinity, a close 7–6 win, "Connor distinguished himself, not only at third base but by his splendid base running."[28] He also "made a home run on three strikes [presumably, on what would have been the third strike]."[29] This brief notice is the first recorded account of a Roger Connor home run. In a July victory against the New Haven Haymakers, "The feature of the game was a neat home run by Connor, who batted the ball clear down to the fence."[30] In a follow-up 16–8 win against the same team a few days later, Connor scored three runs and banged out a remarkable seven hits: "Connor made a clean hit every time he went to the bat, scoring a total of 14 bases and bringing McElligott home three times."[31] Connor's new-found slugging power continued later in the month in a 6–4 win against a Bridgeport team. He "came to the rescue with a beauty far out of the center fielder's reach on which Connor easily made third."[32] By August, a passing reference to his hitting prowess in a game against New Haven's Haymakers gives indication that his success had earned him a new role on the Monitors team. "Captain Connor"[33] played shortstop in the game, pounding out four hits and scoring two runs. In mid-month the Monitors played and won an exhibition game against Waterbury for charity. Fifteen hundred fans attended, drawn by the natural town team rivalry, and, in all probability, by the gossip about the power-hitting Connor, who contributed a hit to the 11–2 win.

Other teams had taken notice of the sudden offensive explosion by the young Waterbury captain, as confirmed by a news item in the September 6 number of the *Waterbury American*. "Roger Connor went to Springfield this morning to play with the Holyokes against the Springfields."[34] Connor would finish the season with Holyoke and spend the next season with them also. He would not return to Waterbury as a player for more than two decades, when he came home to play minor league ball after his long major league career.

What prompted Connor's offensive explosion in 1878? The answer cannot be found in a box score or a game account from his Waterbury years. It was only revealed 20 years later in a *Sporting Life* portrait of a then-famous New England baseball man.

In April of 1878, prior to the start of the Waterbury Monitors season, Connor was given a two-week trial as a first baseman by Manager Frank "Banny" Bancroft of the New Bedford Whalers of the International Association. The Association, founded in 1877, was one of the three earliest regional professional leagues. Although "Banny" Bancroft is forgotten today, he was the "Charles Finley"[35] of his day. Too young to enlist in the Union army at the start of the Civil War, he signed on as a drummer boy, and by war's end had fought in many campaigns as a cavalryman. An amateur player in his home state but an entrepreneur at heart, he owned theaters and an opera house, and established a successful hotel in New Bedford. Instrumental in winning an International Association franchise for the town, he was named the team's manager. Bancroft went on to manage four National League teams and one American Association club in the 1880s After the 1879 season, he arranged for his Worcester International Association team to make a brief tour of Cuba, and Worcester thus became only the second professional club to play abroad. Banny's light-hitting 1884 Providence Grays club won the National League pennant behind

Hoss Radbourn's record 59 victories and 441 strikeouts. Bancroft then became the first manager to win a "World's Series," after Radbourn pitched and won all three games of a three-game set against the American Association champion New York Metropolitans. Two of the wins were shutouts.

A May 1897 Bancroft profile in *Sporting Life* revealed that after Roger Connor's two-week trial with the New Bedford Whalers in 1878, he was

> released because he could not bat. Roger batted right-handed in those days and turned around and practiced batting left-handed and blossomed out as one of the great hitters of the age. Bancroft, many times afterward, regretted the day he released Connor and always since says it was one of the greatest errors he made in the business.[36]

A few weeks after releasing Connor in April of 1878, the temperamental Bancroft abruptly pulled his New Bedford team out of the International Association, leading them instead on a successful 130-game barnstorming tour as an independent team. During his brief stay with the Whalers, young Connor practiced with the team's regular shortstop that year, Jim Mutrie, who was completing his first and last full season as a player in organized baseball. In 1885, Mutrie would manage New York's new National League team. Soon to be nicknamed the "Giants," the team would win consecutive pennants and World's Series in 1888 and 1889. Mutrie's first-baseman during those years was Roger Connor.

Having been let go by New Bedford, Connor returned to the Waterbury Monitors, whose season opened on May 3, 1878, and he proceeded, as we have seen, to tear up the league offensively. While it is highly improbable that he would have blossomed into a deadly left-handed power hitter overnight, it is clear that this gradual batting shift, occasioned by his failure in the New Bedford trial, eventually led to a long, successful major league career. Perhaps of equal importance is the fact that Frank Bancroft, normally "a shrewd judge of talent,"[37] had moved the error-prone, left-handed third baseman to first base during his two-week trial. Between 1879 and 1885, Connor would play just one full season at first base (1881, at Troy). Instead, he was constantly moved around, playing portions of the seasons at third, at shortstop, and in the outfield. Only after making a permanent transfer to first base would he blossom into a consistent, great hitter. He would adapt to his new position well thereafter, leading the league four times in fielding percentage (1887, 1890, 1892, 1896), including his last full season, and three times in total chances (1887, 1890, 1893).

Connor's switch to first base, as suggested by Frank Bancroft, eventually paid him enormous dividends both defensively and offensively.

Offensively, however, he never completely abandoned swinging from the right side of the plate, a fact that generally is not recognized today. Throughout his career, he occasionally hit right-handed against an opposing left-handed pitcher; "Roger Connor is a left-handed batsman but can turn around and hit successfully right-handed."[38] On some of those occasions, as we shall see, he proved that as a major leaguer, he could be as powerful a slugger as a right-hander as he was from the left side.

The 1879 Holyokes played in a league that at its inception in 1877 was called the International Association, since it included two Canadian and five U.S. teams. The Tecumsehs of London, Ontario, and the Maple Leafs of Guelph, Ontario, were the Canadian squads who competed against the Alleghenys of Pittsburgh, the Live Oaks of Lynn, Massachusetts, the Buckeyes of Columbus, Ohio, the Hop Bitters of Rochester, New York, and a New Hampshire team from Manchester, which was the only league team that had no nickname. The Association "was really only a weekend enterprise, since games appear to have been played only on Saturdays and Sundays."[39] The Canadian entries dropped out at the end of the Association's second season, and the league reorganized and chose a new name that was really an old name, one that harkened back to the beginning of the decade: the National Association. Nine teams from three New England states and the District of Columbia made up the "new" Association. Its ambitious lineup included the Nationals of Washington, D.C., Utica, Albany and Rochester (the "Hop Bitters") squads from New York State, Worcester, Holyoke, Springfield and New Bedford teams from Massachusetts, and the Manchesters from New Hampshire.

As professional baseball struggled through its adolescent years, the status of such regional organizations was fluid. The reserve clause had not yet filtered down fully to such leagues, and therefore the best talent frequently was siphoned off to the National League. In order to garnish their meager paychecks, teams from this short-lived, second-generation National Association often played as many exhibition games with college, state league or semi-pro teams as they played in league competition. Many former and future National League, National Association, and American Association players passed through the new league either on the way up or down in their careers. Lipman "Lip" Pike, for example, the great slugger from the earliest years of the original National Association and the National League, played 53 games for Holyoke, Albany and Springfield of the new Association in 1879, his last full year in professional baseball. Bob Ferguson, who played for Hartford's early National Association and National League teams, played briefly for Springfield of the new Association in 1879 before moving on to manage Roger Connor at Troy. Springfield pitcher Larry Corcoran, who spent the last week of the 1879 season at Holyoke, went on to pitch a half-dozen years for the National League Chicago White Stockings, where he would serve up multiple home runs to his former Holyoke teammate Roger Connor. Jim Mutrie, shortstop on the Worcester club, later managed Connor on the Giants. Mickey Welch, Connor's team-mate at Holyoke in 1879, joined the slugger both at Troy and New York. Tim Keefe, pitcher for the New Bedfords, eventually joined Connor and Welch on the Giants. Worcester's left-handed ace, Lee Richmond, pitched the first National League perfect game, and after Worcester's Ruby Legs joined the National League in 1881, he became the first pitcher to win 20 games for a last-place team. Holyoke outfielder Jerry Dorgan played on Worcester's National League team in 1880, and later on three other clubs in the American Association and the National League.

Poor attendance at many franchises and the high cost of team travel spelled an early demise for the reconstituted National Association. Utica, Rochester and Manchester disbanded in July, and Springfield followed suit in September. Albany ended the season in first place, with Worcester and Holyoke close behind, but the standings were rendered meaningless by the steady disintegration of the league, which itself folded at the end of the season.

At Holyoke, Roger Connor played third base and established his "iron man" reputation. In his first year of professional baseball, he was the only member of the team to play in every exhibition and league game. Holyoke played over 90 contests, about evenly divided between league games and exhibitions. Connor would play through the 1879, 1880 and 1881 seasons without missing a game. He started the season at Holyoke as team captain, as he had been in Waterbury, but found the leadership role not to his liking, and in August resigned the post. He would not take a similar post for another 17 years, when he briefly served as captain/manager for the St. Louis Browns.

The Holyokes opened the 1879 campaign in April with an exhibition contest against Yale University at Hamilton Park in New Haven, where "Connor batted right handed to avoid driving the ball against the wind."[40] Selective switch-hitting was already part of his offensive repertoire. Connor faced his old Waterbury Monitors squad in the last pre-season match and put on a one-man show, banging out six hits, including a home run, and scoring three runs. In the Holyokes' first two-game series against Worcester,

Connor slugged four hits, including a double, in nine plate appearances, and scored two runs. Worcester's manager, Frank Bancroft, who had released Connor the previous year at New Bedford due to his inability to hit, was already lamenting his decision. The pitching delivery of Holyoke ace and future Hall of Famer Mickey Welch caused controversy in the National Association: "Welch's pitching is illegal and unless he lowers his arm there will be trouble with other clubs."[41] Like other pitchers of the era, Welch was challenging the requirement that balls be pitched from below the waist. In a few years (1882) baseball would accept the inevitable and legalize the sidearm throw. A year later overhand pitching was approved.

Connor's defense was still inconsistent: "Connor's play at third base was a fine exhibition"[42]; "Connor distinguished himself by catching a difficult foul."[43] In contrast, his four errors in a September contest against Worcester contributed to Holyoke's 10–7 loss. Of his offensive prowess, however, there was no question. In the 54 1879 league games covered by *Holyoke Transcript* reports, Connor registered 93 hits, scored 59 runs, and hit eight doubles, five triples, and two home runs. This record includes three four-hit games, eight three-hit games, and 18 two-hit games. In the 16 Holyoke games played against non-league opponents for which records exist, Connor had 30 hits, including a home run, and he scored 30 runs.

In a late July contest against Albany in which Connor contributed a triple in a losing cause, the *Holyoke Transcript* reported that the *Albany Argus* "calls Connor 'the giant third baseman.'"[44] This is the first of over three dozen nicknames that would be applied to the Waterbury slugger during the course of his long career.

Springfield's switch-hitting Bob Ferguson had numerous opportunities to observe Connor's skills before being called up late in 1879 by Troy's National League team to serve as player/manager. Connor collected 12 hits in Holyoke's nine games against arch-rival Springfield. Ferguson clearly liked what he saw. The young slugger was one of the first players signed by Ferguson for the 1880 Troy City National League team.

2

—〰—

The Apprentice

"Connor's honorable and straightforward conduct and affable and courteous demeanor towards all with whom he is brought into contact have won him deserved popularity on and off the ball field."
—*New York Clipper*, October 2, 1880

Most modern-day baseball fans would react with disbelief to the assertion that Troy, New York, played a significant role in the history of major league baseball. The assertion, nonetheless, is accurate.

Founded as a part of New Netherlands by Dutch settlers in the 17th century and first known as Vanderheyden, Troy is situated on the east bank of the Hudson River just a few miles upstream from Albany. Its favorable location led to success as a distribution center for goods traveling up and down the Hudson. River schooners carried New England fruits and vegetables south through Troy to New York and returned north bearing manufactured goods. After the Erie Canal was completed in 1823, the proximity of its eastern terminus at Cohoes, just across the Hudson from Troy, also enabled the city to become a center for east-west trade. Coal extracted from Pennsylvania mines was barged through the Erie Canal to Troy to provide fuel for the city's successful iron and steel industry. "Troy excelled in the production of cast-iron stoves, pig [iron], ironware, iron and steel products, wire, nails, spikes, bloom and bar [large bars of steel formed directly from ingots] and railroad iron."[1] In the city's industrial heyday, 100,000 cast-iron bells for churches and city bell towers were forged in local foundries.[2] The latest production techniques for such products were designed and developed nearby at Rensselaer Polytechnic Institute, established in 1824 through the financial support of one of the region's last Dutch *patroons*, Stephen van Rensselaer.

Although iron and steel production declined in the late 19th century after industrialists moved their operations closer to the Pennsylvania coal fields, another city industry was waiting in the wings to take up the slack.

In 1827, Troy's Hannah Lord Montague, frustrated with cleaning her husband's dirty shirt collars and cuffs, cut them off his shirts, bound their edges, and attached strips (soon replaced by buttons) to hold them in place when they were reattached to the shirt. Cuff, collar, and shirt production soon became the focus of an industry so important to Troy that its nickname today remains "The Collar City." By 1900, "Ninety out of every one hundred collars worn in America were made in the city."[3] Popularity of the detachable collar led to the introduction of a now well-known expression: "Wearing a detached white collar gave rise to a new working social class, the 'white collar worker,' who differentiated themselves from the no collar or 'blue collar' worker."[4] As we shall see, the presence of the shirt and collar industry in Troy during Roger Connor's tenure with the Troy Trojans would have an unexpectedly profound effect on his future personal life.

Troy baseball history is linked to two towns that eventually became one: Troy and Lansingburg, a small village north of Troy proper that was annexed by its larger neighbor in 1898. In 1860, two years after the founding of the amateur National Association of Baseball Players, Troy's team, the Victories, gained admission to the organization. In July of that year the Victories played Brooklyn's Excelsiors during the latter's historic barnstorming tour, falling victim to the Brooklyns, 13–7. By 1866, the Lansingburg Unions were the top local team, supported both by their own town folk and those from Troy. That fall the Unions sailed down the Hudson to New York City to test their mettle against several legendary amateur city clubs. They were overwhelmed in their first contest against the Atlantics, 46–11, but on the following day, to the shock of New York's baseball world, the Unions defeated the powerful Mutuals, 15–13. An embarrassed city press expressed its contempt for these upstart, upstate hayseeds by christening them with a derogatory nickname: the Haymakers. Undismayed, the team adopted their new appellation with gusto, brandishing pitchforks in their team portraits and celebrating their new moniker in verse:

> Come all you jolly Haymakers and fill your glasses up
> Success to all who toss the ball, that be our parting cup....
>
> Amid the valleys of the East are brothers true and tried
> Who stretch a hand to welcome us across the stretches wide....

Now let us show the lads we meet we play a noble game
That we have mowed our fields and theirs for fun as well as fame....[5]

The Haymakers apparently fell short of their avowed intent to play a "noble game," for they were plagued by allegations of betting on games and "hippodroming" [losing games on purpose]. The most notorious of these charges surfaced after a game against the mighty Cincinnati Red Stockings in August 1869. The Red Stockings, baseball's first openly acknowledged professional team, had just returned home after a magnificent barnstorming tour in which they won 39 consecutive games, including a close 32–30 victory in May against the Haymakers in Lansingburg while on the first leg of their tour. Skippered by the legendary Harry Wright, who would manage Roger Connor in Philadelphia two decades later, Cincinnati was the first professional team to tour, following in the footsteps of their amateur predecessors, Brooklyn's Excelsiors and Washington's Nationals.

1867 Lansingburg (North Troy, New York) Unions, predecessors of the Troy National League teams of 1879–82. Referred to disparagingly in the New York City press as country-bumpkin "Haymakers," the Unions embraced the nickname and were proudly photographed with pitchforks (courtesy Transcendental Graphics/theruckerarchive.com).

In the Haymakers' second and final encounter with the Red Stockings, on this occasion in Cincinnati, the score was tied at 17–17 in a contest in which "each close play somehow was given to the Red Stockings."[6] In the sixth inning, Haymakers president James McKeon, apparently infuriated by yet another unfavorable call, requested a new umpire. When the request was denied, McKeon pulled his team off the field and the game was declared a 9–0 forfeit in favor of Cincinnati. In reality, the withdrawal appeared to be prompted by the desire "to protect the money that the [Troy] club's backers had placed in wagers on the [Troy] club."[7] Soon afterward, the National Association reversed the forfeit and declared the game a tie, the only stain on Cincinnati's 1869 consecutive-game-win-streak record.

The Haymakers' record of one close loss and one tie in two encounters with mighty Cincinnati gained them national notoriety and facilitated

The 1869 Lansingburg (North Troy, New York) Unions, who became the Troy Haymakers in 1870 and joined the National Association of Professional Base Ball Players in 1871. Esteban Enrique "Steve" Bellán, standing, second row, far right, played for Troy from 1870 to 1872. A Cuban native, Bellán graduated from St. John's College (later Fordham University), and was the first Hispanic player in the major leagues (courtesy Transcendental Graphics/theruckerarchive.com).

their formal entry into the ranks of the professionals. No longer advertising their Lansingburg roots, they joined the National Association in 1871 as the Troy Haymakers. Twenty-five hundred fans attended the team's first major league home game on May 9, a 9–5 loss to Boston. The club finished sixth in a nine-team league that year, despite the fine hitting of outfielders Lip Pike and Steve King. Pike hit .351 and tied for the league lead in home runs (four) in 28 games. King placed fifth in the league in hits and hit .396. Although early on the Haymakers were out of the pennant race, they still made history in 1871. Their third baseman, Esteban Enrique "Steve" Bellán, a native of Cuba, was the first Hispanic to play major league baseball. Bellán learned the game while studying at St. John's College (later Fordham University) and then started his baseball career with the Morrisania (Bronx, New York) Unions. After a year with the Lansingburg Unions he spent four years with the Troy Haymakers during their transition from an (allegedly) amateur club to a professional team. Afterward he returned to Cuba, "participating in the first organized game there in 1874."[8] In his homeland, Bellán player-managed the Havana team until 1886, winning the Cuban championship three times.

Troy's professional-league version of the Haymakers continued to be associated with some of the underhanded practices of its amateur predecessor, such as the use of locally-made "lively" baseballs. "The ball used by the Haymaker crew was reputedly the liveliest ball used among NA [National Association] teams. And it caused no end of controversy."[9] This practice was at least partially responsible for the team's dubious distinction of having participated in "the largest one-game scoring barrage in the history of professional baseball."[10] Playing at home in late June, the Haymakers lost to the Philadelphia Athletics, 49–33, in a game that featured 74 hits and 20 errors.

Although 12 teams started the 1872 National Association season, "only six played enough games to qualify for the championship."[11] Plagued by poor attendance and soaring travel expenses, Troy lasted until July 23, compiling a 15–10 record before folding. While slugger Lip Pike had moved on to Baltimore after the 1871 season, local star Steve King was still with the team, which was bolstered by the addition of 5' 4" "Wee Davy" Force at third base, who finished the season at Baltimore hitting .418. Veteran George Zettlein, abetted by a new rule that allowed pitchers to bend their elbow and snap their wrist when throwing, thus permitting a modified sidearm delivery, held opponents to two runs per game before transferring to Brooklyn in July. Halfway through a season they never completed, Troy had already captured one-third of its victories from the strong New York, Boston, and Philadelphia franchises.

Undaunted by its quick departure from the National Association in 1872, Troy returned to professional status in 1879 with an entry in the three-year-old National League. The League expanded to eight teams that year, dropping two of the 1878 franchises, Indianapolis and Milwaukee, and adding Buffalo, Syracuse, Cleveland and Troy. In this reincarnation, the squad's official name was Troy City or Troy Citys, and its occasional nickname was the Trojans.

As was the case with its original 1871 entry into the National Association, Troy's first National League team consisted largely of players with no prior major league experience. Predictably, they finished dead last at 19–56 in 1879, 35 games behind first-place Boston. The team's only league leader was pitcher George Bradley, who tied for the dubious honor of first place in number of losses (40). Rookie first baseman Dan Brouthers, who joined Troy in mid-season in 1879, led the team in hitting with an undistinguished .271 average. By the time Brouthers' major league career ended, however, his lifetime batting average would be 71 points higher, and he would be known as one of the most feared sluggers in the game.

Dennis Joseph "Big Dan" Brouthers was born in the tiny hamlet of Sylvan Lake, New York, and raised near Poughkeepsie. Although he was considered a physical giant in his era (6' 2", 207 pounds), early critics nevertheless felt "he did not have the build or dexterity to become a good player."[12] An on-field tragedy in which he was involved nearly ended his career in 1877. Brouthers collided with Harlem Clippers catcher John Quigley while trying to score. The blow killed Quigley, and the devastated Brouthers vowed he would never play again.

After sitting out the 1878 season, he was back in the game in 1879, pitching and playing first base for a Stottsville, New York, team when he was discovered and signed at mid-season by Troy manager Horace Phillips. Brouthers returned to the minors in 1880, playing most of the season for two financially floundering teams before returning to Troy for just the final three games of the campaign, thus briefly becoming Roger Connor's teammate. After signing with the National League's Buffalo Bisons in 1881, Brouthers' big bat finally awakened. In the ensuing 16 seasons he did not fall below the .300 mark and won five batting championships. Between 1889 and 1891, Brouthers had the unique opportunity to play for three different Boston teams in three different major leagues (National League, Players' League, American Association), hitting a blistering .351. During his prime, Big Dan annually vied with Roger Connor and Chicago's Adrian "Cap" Anson for the league's top offensive honors. Among all 19th-century players, he ranks second in slugging and walks, third in doubles, fourth in home runs and total bases, sixth in runs, and eighth in batting average.

Born less than a year apart in towns located just 50 miles apart, similar in physical size, power-hitting ability, and mild, sanguine temperament, Dan Brouthers and Roger Connor were active participants in the Brotherhood movement of the 1880s and the Players' League revolt of 1890. After retiring, the aging veterans frequently took in a game together at the Polo Grounds, where Brouthers held numerous positions. In 1945 Dan Brouthers was elected to the Hall of Fame.

Despite their grim first season in the National League in 1879, Troy's Trojans had reason to be positive looking ahead to their second National League campaign in 1880. Bob Ferguson, who had come over from Springfield, managed the team in the final month of the 1879 season and stayed on in that capacity through the 1882 season while covering second base. Born in the baseball hotbed of Brooklyn, Ferguson, major league baseball's first switch-hitter, had previously player-managed for three different teams during the National Association's five-year history. While some objected to his no-nonsense, authoritarian leadership style, his three-year association with Troy proved beyond a doubt his great skill at recognizing young talent. The crop of new faces that Ferguson recruited for Troy City's 1880 season included four future Hall of Famers: Roger Connor, Buck Ewing, Mickey Welch and Tim Keefe. Ferguson got a full first year of service from Connor and Welch; Ewing and Keefe signed on after mid-season.

William "Buck" Ewing was making deliveries for a Cincinnati distillery[13] when first discovered by officials from Rochester's minor league team. When Rochester folded in mid-season 1880, Bob Ferguson signed him to a Troy contract. Ewing's 13-game batting average of .180 for the team that year gave no indication of his future greatness. He could hit (.303 lifetime), steal a base (six 30-plus steal seasons), and play virtually any position well. Known today primarily as a catcher who could throw out advancing runners with a snap-toss from the squatting position, Ewing actually played more games at other positions over the course of his career, including all infield slots. Ewing was inducted into the Hall of Fame in 1939.

Like Troy manager Bob Ferguson, Michael Francis Welch, nicknamed "Smiling Mickey" for his affable, easy-going nature, honed his early baseball skills in his native Brooklyn. Ferguson plucked him from the same 1879 Holyoke team for which Roger Connor played. Standing 5'8" tall and weighing 160 pounds, the slender, right-handed Welch relied on mixing up his pitches rather than on overpowering speed. "I was a little fellow and I had to use my head. I studied the hitters and I knew how to pitch to all of them, and I worked hard to perfect my control. I had a pretty good fastball but I depended heavily on change of pace and an assortment of curve balls."[14] One of Welch's curves was an early version of the screwball, which two decades later was popularized by Christy Mathewson as the "fadeaway" pitch. "I had a fadeaway, although I didn't call it that. I didn't call it anything. It was just a slow curve ball that broke down and in on a right handed batter, and I got a lot of good results with it in the 10 years I pitched with the Giants."[15] Smiling Mickey also threw the spitball, whose use was not generally noted until

William "Buck" Ewing, New York Nationals and Giants, 1883–1889; 1891–1892; Players' League Giants, 1890 (courtesy Transcendental Graphics/theruckerarchive.com).

popularized by Jack Chesbro in the early twentieth century. In 1886, the *St. Louis Post-Dispatch* observed that Mickey, then hurling for the Giants, "expectorates on either hand" before preparing to pitch.[16] Smiling Mickey won 309 games over a 13-year span, including nine 20-game seasons, four 30-game campaigns, and one 40-win season. He was elected to the Hall of Fame in 1973.

Arriving in Troy in early August of the 1880 season after recovering from an illness, Tim Keefe pitched 12 games for the Trojans in his first season, posting a so-so 6–6 mark, but combining it with a major-league record 0.86 ERA, an average that speaks volumes about his team's poor defense (only 10 of his 27 runs allowed were earned) and lack of offense (though some timely offensive support did help him reach the .500 mark). Although he regularly used the brushback pitch to intimidate opposing hitters, Keefe, a tall, slender, sidearm (once that delivery was legalized) fireballer from Cambridge, Massachusetts, earned the gallant nickname "Sir Timothy" for his otherwise courteous demeanor. His catcher, Buck Ewing, cited Keefe's punishing speed as the reason for his own introduction of the padded catcher's mitt to baseball. After becoming the first pitcher to strike out 300 hitters in a season, Keefe twice repeated the feat during his career. Although Sir Timothy's three-year record at Troy was an uninspiring 41–59, this tally contrasts with the 301–166 mark he posted during his next 11 seasons. Like Roger Connor and Dan Brouthers, Keefe jumped to the Players' League in 1890, serving as its Secretary during its one-year existence. Ranked tenth all-time in career wins (342), Keefe was elected to the Hall of Fame in 1964.

By the end of the decade, Connor, Welch, Ewing and Keefe would all be teammates on two New York Giants pennant-winning teams.

Neither these four rookies and future Hall of Famers nor any other league player had any idea that their respective team's

"Smiling Mickey" Welch, New York Giants, 1883–1892 (courtesy Transcendental Graphics/theruckerarchive.com).

owners had taken steps well before the 1880 season to end their right to sell their services to another club. At the close of the 1879 season, the National League had enjoyed a major-league monopoly for four years and was ready to tighten its grip on the game even further. Looking to increase profits, team owners were determined to reduce their most expensive annual budget item — player salaries. The first step to achieve that aim would be to eliminate the annual bidding wars for quality players, a practice that inevitably led to higher salaries. Boston owner Arthur Soden

Tim Keefe, New York Giants, 1885–1889; 1891; Players' League Giants, 1890 (courtesy Transcendental Graphics/theruckerarchive.com).

offered a solution to the problem in the form of a deceptively simple contract clause. The clause stipulated that when a player signs with a team, "he is in reality signing for the duration of his career because he not only agrees to perform for the period specified (usually one season), but allows the club to 'reserve' him for the subsequent season. Since each succeeding contract which he signs contains the same provision, he cannot escape."[17]

The bitter pill of the reserve clause initially was made easier for the players to swallow due to a clever ruse. From 1880 to 1882, each team reserved just five players and no specific mention of the policy was made in individual contracts. All contracts, however, required adherence to the league's constitution, where the reserve clause was specified. From 1883–1886 the number of players reserved by each team rose to 12. In 1887, in addition to raising that number to 14 (in this era, virtually the whole team), the league dropped its earlier deceptive pretense and wrote the reserve clause directly into each player's contract. It would remain the most hated rule in baseball for nearly a century.

The 1880 National League season marked the ascendance of the Chicago White Stockings, who would win five pennants during the decade under the leadership of player-manager Adrian "Cap" Anson. Gruff, tough, and all business, Iowa-born Anson was a lifetime .334 hitter with occasional power who could steal a base and play virtually any position. An innovative manager, Anson required his fielders to back each other up, encouraged base-stealing, employed both offensive and defensive signals, and popularized the notion of a two-man pitching rotation.

The team he assembled in 1880 demonstrated all aspects of such strategies. Playing first base, Anson himself led the league in RBI (74 in 86 games); left fielder Abner Dalrymple did the same in the categories of hits (126) and runs (91). Centerfield speedster George Gore, one of only three men in the history of baseball to average more runs scored than games played, took the 1880 batting title with an average of .360. The White Stockings' team batting average of .279 topped their nearest competitor, Boston, by 26 points. Anson, third baseman Ned Williamson and catcher Silver Flint led the league in fielding their positions, and pitchers Larry Corcoran and Fred Goldsmith combined for a 64–17 record, with Corcoran leading the league in strikeouts. All told, Chicago's 1880 team delivered one of the most balanced and successful offensive and defensive performances in league history.

Bob Ferguson's five future Hall of Famers (including latecomer Dan Brouthers, though his and Ewing's contributions were minimal) helped

Troy turn in a respectable fourth-place 1880 finish. Although managing to win just two of the 12-game series against the league's seven other teams, Troy's finish was improved by an impressive ten-game win streak from late July to mid–August. Roger Connor had a banner offensive rookie season, playing in all 83 games and leading his team in hits (113), triples (8), home runs (3), RBI (47) and batting average (.332). On May 24, Connor hit his first major league home run off Boston's Tommy Bond, the Irish-born curve ball pitcher and three-time 40-game winner. While it proved to be an exceptional offensive afternoon for the Waterbury slugger, Troy's newspaper accounts differ slightly on the specifics of his outing. The *Troy Press* reported that the "heaviest batting was by Connor, who out of five times at bat scored a home run, a three-bagger, and two singles."[18] The *Troy Daily Times* published a game account on the same day that indicated that he had hit for the cycle. "Connor was the hero of the batting. In the third inning the ball sent thither by his longest and surprising hit cleared the south fence by many a foot and Connor made the circuit of the bases. In the second inning the same batsman reached the third base after a stroke which sent the ball full and fair against the fence, and a two-base hit and a single completed his unique record of strong and skillful willow-handling."[19] If the latter account is accurate, Connor was the first player in major league history to hit for the cycle. A decade later he accomplished the feat again while in the Players' League.

During the 1880 game against Boston in which Connor may have established the record, Boston's left fielder John O'Rourke, brother of future Hall of Famer and future Connor teammate Jim O'Rourke, was seriously injured trying to track down Connor's triple in the second inning. "In endeavoring to capture Connor's far hit in the second inning, John O'Rourke fell over a fence strut and was severely injured about the face and breast. He was led from the field bleeding from a long and gaping laceration of the cheek and throat. Dr. McClean, who was on the grounds, furnished the necessary surgical attention.... James O'Rourke took his brother's position."[20]

An equally impressive offensive performance by Connor occurred in a home game against league-leading Chicago on July 19, when he went 4-for-5, including two home runs, against league strikeout king Larry Corcoran. In the first inning, "as Connor stepped to the plate the cry was heard from the grandstand 'Knock it over the fence.' Six bad balls were pitched [eight were required for a walk in 1880] and then came a good one, which Connor struck squarely, sending it far over the centre field boundary, and he crossed the plate greeted by most enthusiastic applause."[21] In the ninth inning he again came to bat:

> Another home run was called for and Connor waited for a "good one." Six bad balls were pitched again, and then the "good one" came and Conner crossed the plate on the longest hit to left field ever made on the ground. The ball went far down into the extreme corner of the ground, giving [Chicago left-fielder] Dalrymple all he wanted to do to reach it before Connor had crossed the third bag. Such a shout went up from the excited throng in the grand stand as is seldom heard on a ball field.[22]

During a season in which the league lead in home runs, six, was shared by Worcester's Harry Stovey and Boston's Jim O'Rourke, two four-base blasts in one game, especially when accomplished by a rookie, was an exceptional feat.

At least one game account from the 1880 season suggests that at this point Connor had not made a complete transition to left-handed hitting. In September, the *Troy Daily Times* chided Troy's left-handed batters for hitting right-handed against Worcester's Lee Richmond, a left-handed curve ball specialist. "The left-handed batters of the home team played a child's game after the second inning and tried to bat right handed. Of course this was a failure, as they could not hit the side of a meeting house batting right handed. It is hoped that they will play ball in the last two league games here."[23] Nevertheless, it was common in the era for natural left-handed hitters to experiment hitting right-handed against left-handed pitching, particularly when the pitcher was Worcester's Richmond. In a July 1880 contest between Chicago and Worcester, for example, "[George] Gore and [Abner] Dalrymple, both left-handed, batted right-handed against [Lee] Richmond's pitching."[24]

The lefty-righty experimentation of hitters of the era is a reminder of the "trial-and-error" nature of professional baseball it its early years. Left-handed infielders and catchers were commonplace, and there was only one full-time switch-hitter in baseball — player-manager Bob Ferguson of Troy. This experimental aspect of the game even extended to its relationship to the new communications media that was benefiting financially by reporting game accounts to eager fans. As the following report indicates, Troy was fairly naive in this regard, but caught on quickly:

> The directors of the Troy City club learned recently that the telegraph company is compelled by nearly all the league's cities to pay for the privilege of placing an instrument on the grounds. Not to be behind in the matter of enterprise, the Troy directors notified the manager of the telegraph office here that operator and sounder could no longer work together on the club

grounds unless the privilege was paid for in money or by the extension of the franking privilege to official business. The telegraph company refused to comply, and when its representative reached the grounds yesterday he was not permitted to "work the little machine." Thereupon he climbed a pole, tapped the wires, and from his commanding position telegraphed to headquarters the result of each inning, thereby winning the first battle for the telegraph in its contest against the directors. It is rumored this morning that a platform is to be built near the top of a convenient pole, and that it will be occupied by the operator, who has been through the war, whenever a game takes place. This probably accounts for the fact that the Troy City directors purchased to day [sic] a quantity of canvas, which it is surmised will be stretched upon a framework in such a position as to shut out the operator.[25]

Playing third base in all 83 games in 1880, Roger Connor's defense still remained shaky. He twice committed four miscues in a game and ended the season with an error total of 60. Although he led the league at his position in chances, his fielding average of .821 was over 70 points below that of league leader Ned Williamson of Chicago. Nevertheless, there were occasions during the season, as in a June 4 game against Cincinnati, when Connor displayed flashes of his future defensive prowess:

Connors [sic] ... made a fine catch in the sixth inning and sent the ball to first base in time for a double play. The play of Connors [sic] shut out the best chance the visitors had of scoring. A man had reached third base and another first by errors of [second-baseman] Coggswell and [right-fielder] Cassidy. But one man was out and it seemed as though the visitors would score but [third-baseman] Connors' [sic] long arm reached the ball that was whizzing over his head and the hope of the visitors ... was gone."[26]

As has been made abundantly clear from the previous example, one persistent and ultimately humorous reminder of Connor's newcomer status in the National League was the press's continuing inability to spell his simple last name correctly with any regularity in their game accounts. Initially, for example, the *New York Clipper* referred to him as Connors. In early June that became Conners. On the same page of one *Clipper* number he was referred to as Connors in one game account and as Connor in another.[27] Through September the Connors/Conners versions continued to be used interchangeably. Perhaps one cannot be too hard on the press in this regard, for his last name was even printed incorrectly (O'Connor) on his Troy City player photo. Three decades later, reporters were still misspelling his name. In July 1910, the 53-year-old former Giant, now playing semi-pro ball, was again mistakenly listed in a box score as "Connors."[28] At the end of the 1880 season, however, the *Clipper* temporarily offered the correct spelling of the then-rookie's name when it published a brief biography of him accompanied by a line-drawing profile sketch. After providing some basic details about his prior amateur and minor league experience, the *Clipper* noted that:

> Manager Ferguson, seeing that he [Connor] promised to develop into a batsman and a baseman equal to any in the country, secured him for the Troy club during the present [1880] season. The wisdom of this choice has been amply attested on more than one occasion.... He is as fine a specimen of physical development as any in the profession, being a few [inches] over six feet in height and weighing over two hundred pounds, without an ounce of superfluous flesh, and being admirably proportioned. Notwithstanding his great size, he is endowed with more than the average amount of activity and evidently possesses extraordinary powers of endurance. Although he shines more as a batter than as a fielder, yet his expertise in handling the ball this season shows his average will rank among the best of third-basemen.[29]

The *New York Clipper* biography concluded by praising the Connor's honorable and affable nature, as illustrated in this chapter's epigraph.

　　　Whether referred to as O'Connor, Connor, Connors, or Conners, the Waterbury rookie's first biography served notice of the arrival of a rising

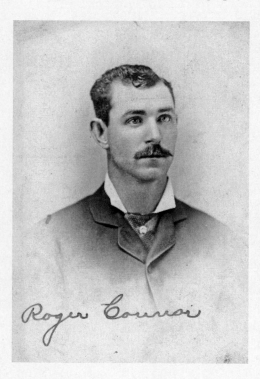

star in the National League. In the main, it would also prove to be remarkably accurate portrait. Connor confirmed his "powers of endurance" by missing only four games in his first five seasons, all occasioned by a dislocated shoulder in 1882. After moving permanently to first base in 1885, he led the league four times in fielding percentage and twice in total chances. His .993 average in 1887 was the highest of any first baseman in the first quarter-century of the professional game, and the second-highest of the 19th century, after Cleveland Spider Patsy Tebeau's .994 in 1897.

Street-clothes photograph of Roger Connor, Troy Trojans, circa 1880. (National Baseball Hall of Fame Library, Cooperstown, New York).

As for Connor's "above average activity," which was praised in the *Clipper* biography, he averaged nearly two dozen steals a year for a decade after stolen bases began being counted officially in 1887, and was still stealing bases into his fifties while playing in semi-pro leagues. Connor's noted sportsmanship and gentlemanly conduct remained a constant during his major league playing years, although such virtues were sorely tried when he later became a manager. Never ejected from a game in 17 major-league seasons, he was a perennial fan favorite who was hailed during his last full year as a player with the St. Louis Browns as the "Gentleman of the Diamond."[30]

The 1880 Troy team won more than twice the number of games (40) that they did in 1879, and moved from eighth place to fourth place in the standings. By early September, a city newspaper published a story originally reported by the *New York Star* that indicated the Troy owners had already renewed player-manager Bob Ferguson's contract:

> To the superior management of Bob Ferguson is credited the recent fine playing by the Troy league club. At a meeting of the Trojan baseball association it was voted to secure the very best players that money could procure if Ferguson would take charge for 1881. Although a man of independent financial circumstances, and not dependant on base ball for a living, he is such a devotee of the game that he consented. If Troy does not win the pennant next year it will not be for want of good and strong efforts.[31]

Near the end of September 1880, the *New York Times* reported an event that would soon become relevant to Roger Connor's baseball career: "The polo grounds [*sic*] of this city were opened to the public yesterday for the first time as a base-ball arena. Between 2,000 and 3,000 people were there for the largest assemblage that has gathered on a ball field in this vicinity in three years."[32] Prior to this date the only substantial venues in the area were in Brooklyn (then an independent city and not incorporated into New York until 1898) at the Union or Capitoline grounds. Until the completion of the Brooklyn Bridge in 1883, the only method of traveling to those grounds from Manhattan was by ferry.

At the conclusion of the 1880 season, the National League's Cincinnati franchise came under league scrutiny for trying to keep afloat financially by renting its ballpark to semi-pro teams on Sundays and allowing alcohol to be sold at such contests. For violating two of league President William Hulbert's commandments (no Sunday ball or alcohol sales), Cincinnati, the cradle of professional baseball, was summarily expelled from the league and a new Detroit franchise substituted in its place. This action would set into motion "a string of vengeful egos and clandestine events that would result, some 10 months later, in the birth of the League's most formidable nineteenth-century challenger,"[33] the American Association.

While his professional star was on the rise, there were also portents of change in 23-year-old Roger Connor's personal life. His giant-sized physical proportions (he was one of only a handful of men over six feet tall in the league in 1880), the presence of a multitude of shirt and collar factories in Troy, and a good measure of serendipity led to his first encounter with the woman with whom he would spend the rest of his life.

When Connor joined the Trojans for his rookie campaign, the largest team uniform size available proved too small for him, and he was sent to a local shirt manufacturer to be measured for a custom-made model. There, according to his granddaughter Margaret Colwell, Connor "struck up a conversation with a young girl with long blonde hair working on a [sewing] machine not far from where he was being fitted. Connor always remembered his conversation with this girl, [and] enjoyed her knowledge of baseball. He liked her looks very much."[34]

The young blonde seamstress who caught Connor's eye was named Angeline Meir. Part of the difficulty in discovering her personal history stems from the fact that she was also frequently known by a more "Americanized" first and last name. An 1896 history of Waterbury written by her contemporaries, for example, refers to her as Anna Mayer.[35] The 1870 U.S. Census, which likewise refers to her family name as Mayer, reveals that the then ten-year-old Angeline was one of five children born to German-born baker Jacob Mayer [Meir] and his wife, Apoline, in Unadilla, Otsego County, New York.[36] By 1880, Angeline, now 20, was living as a boarder in the Queensbury, New York, home of widow Pheba Harris, and described as working "in a collar shop."[37] Angeline "was an expert dressmaker [and] made all her own clothes. She wore her long blonde hair in pompadour style, the waves starting at her forehead clear up and down the back of her head."[38] The beautiful young seamstress subsequently moved with her sister Addie to the Troy collar-manufacturing district, where she would meet her husband-to-be.

Some amount of time after the couple's original encounter, Connor returned to Angeline's factory at six o'clock one morning as her shift began, "and waited at the door where the employees entered. He spotted her walking toward the factory door and he went up to her. Would she recognize him? Would she ignore him?"[39] When she stopped, smiled, called him by name, and held out her hand, "he knew he had his girl and she would be his wife."[40]

Accounts differ on the exact date of the couple's marriage, which occurred in the early 1880s. Granddaughter Margaret Colwell contends that it took place on June 15, 1883, while other sources identify September 21, 1881, as the wedding day. Neither date is verifiable historically. New York State vital statistics show no marriage between them from 1881 through 1884, and all Waterbury records prior to 1886 were destroyed in a fire. It is clear, however, that during their long, successful marriage, Angeline showed Connor "all her warmth and understanding. She was devoted to him."[41] The feeling was mutual. Connor customarily referred to her endearingly as his "Engle," her family nickname, which in German means "angel."[42] The couple, whose brief courtship reads like a page from a romance novel, shared life together for nearly a half-century until Angeline succumbed to a heart attack in 1928.

Events on the ball field in 1881 were completely overshadowed at mid-season by a tragic event that occurred in Washington, D.C. On a sweltering July morning at a capitol train depot, a deranged, disappointed office-seeker, Charles Guiteau, shot President James Garfield twice at point blank range. After a brief period during which the President's recovery appeared possible, his condition worsened. As he lingered between life and death for two months, the nation obsessively followed the daily reports of his condition, and was understandably distracted from the game that was being hailed as the "American Pastime." President James Garfield died on September 19.

There was hopeful news in 1881 for New York baseball fans, whose city had been excluded from the only professional league in the country since the National League's inception in 1876:

> New York will be represented on the ball field this season by two first-class nines, the Metropolitan and the New York, the latter being the name of a professional team recently organized by John Kelly, formerly catcher of the Flyaways of this city.... He will catch for the nine.... The ground has not been selected but will probably be the Union [Grounds], Brooklyn. Arrangements are also being made for this professional nine to play two days each week at Newark, New Jersey, provided a suitable inclosed [sic] ground can be obtained.[43]

The Metropolitan team manager was Jim Mutrie, who had briefly teamed with Roger Connor at New Bedford in 1878. In a few years, the New Yorks would gain admittance to the National League, Mutrie would leave the Metropolitans to manage the team, and Roger Connor would be his first baseman.

In order to combat 1880s anemic .244 league batting average and the negative effects of the ever-increasing number of still-illegal pitching deliveries that umpires either found difficult to distinguish or simply chose not to punish, the National League increased the pitching distance to 50 feet in 1881. While league batting averages surged 15 points to .259 as a result, Troy's average unaccountably fell from .252 to .248. Although the Trojans led the league in fielding (.914), offensively they ended the season seventh in hits and runs, and last in batting average, a performance that resulted in a fifth-place finish, 17 games behind pennant-winner Chicago.

In 1881, Troy's player-manager, Bob Ferguson, made three significant changes to his starting squad. Buck Ewing took over behind the plate for light-hitting Bill Holbert, Roger Connor replaced British-born Ed Cogswell at first, and Frank Hankinson, acquired from Cleveland, manned the hot corner in place of Connor. Mickey Welch and Tim Keefe shared the pitching duties. Keefe apparently became dissatisfied at mid-season and sought to be traded; "The management of the Troy club is under the impression that Keefe is pitching poorly purposely in order to obtain his release."[44] Clearly, "Sir Timothy" had yet to realize the implication of the league's reserve contract: he would play for Troy City or he would not play at all.

On April 19, Troy played an exhibition contest against the Metropolitans in New York. It was Connor's debut at first base and his first game at the Polo Grounds. Playing errorless ball, he went 3-for-4 in a 5–2 win. After two more victories on succeeding days against the same opponent, the press pronounced Connor "a tip-top first baseman."[45] As the season progressed, however, it was evident that Connor was experiencing a sophomore slump. He made 46 errors in 85 games at first base, including four in one game (of a team total of 11), and finished the campaign with a .950 fielding average, 25 points behind Cap Anson's league-leading .975 and eight points below the average of the league's remaining first basemen. While still leading his team in hitting, his .292 mark represented a significant decline, especially given the pitchers' new disadvantage of throwing from five feet further back. Connor's offensive heroics in one game late in the season, however, accomplished at the expense of Worcester's left-handed ace, Lee Richmond, would go into the record book as a baseball first.

Son of a Baptist preacher, Lee Richmond, the Ohio-born lad with the deep South-sounding name, was the *wunderkind* of the 1880 National League season. The major league's first full-time left-handed pitcher,[46] Richmond was a student at Brown University who had received a special dispensation from the American College Base Ball Association to play professional and

Troy National League Team, circa 1881, including Mickey Welch, first row, left; player-manager Bob Ferguson, second row, center; Roger Connor, second row, far right; Buck Ewing, third row, far right. Not shown: Tim Keefe (courtesy Transcendental Graphics/theruckerarchive.com).

college baseball simultaneously. A *Boston Herald* portrait of the young hurler that was published in the *Troy Press* in May offered high praise for the rookie's work habits. "Richmond of the Worcester team is a hard worker. He is actively engaged in his preparation to graduate from Brown university [*sic*] the coming week, in addition to fulfilling his engagement with the Worcesters. He studies every night till 12 or 1 o'clock, recites in the forenoon, takes the 11:30 train from Providence for Worcester, pitches his game in the afternoon, and returns to Providence on the 6:30 train the same evening and resumes his studies."[47] The young hurler pitched a sparkling 1–0 shutout against Cleveland on June 12, recording his third consecutive whitewash. This effort, however, was special — it was a perfect game; the first in major league history, made all the more noteworthy due to the fact that his infielders and outfielders played barehanded.

Although, as we have seen, Richmond's curves gave Troy fits in early-season games, even prompting their left-handed hitters to try batting from the opposite side, this was not the case when the two teams met on September 10. Richmond would participate in another baseball record that afternoon, but the glory in this instance would go to Roger Connor, and not to him:

> Troy won a game from the Worcesters on the Albany grounds Saturday. At the opening of the ninth inning the game stood 6 to 3 in favor of the Worcesters. The latter club scored one more in the ninth. When Troy went to the bat they needed four to tie and five to win. When the bases were full Keefe got his first on balls, which let one man in. When Connors [sic] came to bat there were two hands out; a home run would win as the bases were full. He hit it hard over the center fielder's head and made the home run. The game ended 8 to 7 in favor of Troy.[48]

A Troy newspaper reported that the jealous press corps from nearby Albany, whose city boasted no National League team and whose town team was regularly whipped in exhibition games by the Trojans, did their best to trivialize the Trojans' victory and Connor's accomplishment:

> The *Albany Argus* says that the 100 persons who attended Saturday's Troy-Worcester game at Riverside park [sic] saw the most "barbarous baseball" and "funny fumbling" ever seen on the diamond. The errors of the Troys, it says, were more numerous than their hits, and the play was only notable for its lack of life. The ruby legs [Worcester] scored five runs in the sixth chiefly on errors, and the Trojans in the last innings made five runs and won the game by the "funny fumbling" of Carpenter, the poor pitching of Richmond, and the accidental hit of the Megatherian Connor."[49] [*Megatheria* was a prehistoric, elephant-sized sloth that weighed five tons.]

Connor's record-breaking home run against Worcester thus also earned him the distinction of becoming the first (and perhaps the only) player to be nicknamed after a prehistoric beast.

Strictly speaking, Connor's September 10, 1881, blast off Lee Richmond needs to be classified as the first National League grand slam. Ten years earlier during the National Association of Professional Base Ball Players' era, another first baseman, Charley Gould of Boston, hit the first professional league grand slam off Chicago's George Zettlein. Today, however, Major League Baseball does not recognize the National Association as a major league. Connor's homer, nevertheless, is imbued with special significance, for it not only was the first National League grand slam — it was the first walk-off grand slam, and one of only 14 walk-offs hit with two outs in the ninth inning, a feat often categorized as an "ultimate" grand slam.[50]

When the American Association arrived on the scene in 1882, the

National League publicly ridiculed its rival but privately feared it. Occasionally the League went to great lengths to avoid being perceived as outdone by the Association. The best example of such behavior was the League's near-immediate agreement to follow the Association's startling innovation in team uniforms for 1882, perhaps the most outlandish change ever attempted in baseball. All teams wore white pants and belts, but each position player's shirt color, regardless of team, corresponded to a color selected to represent that position. Catchers' shirts, for example, were scarlet, while pitchers wore light blue, and first basemen sported scarlet and white stripes. The only team identifier was the sock color — Troy's hose, for example, were green.

The result was sheer chaos, and by mid–July teams had changed back to their original uniform colors. "The uniform experiment ended soon enough as field incidents made it apparent that fans and players alike could not tell who was a friend and who was a foe."[51] A tongue-in-cheek report in the *Albany Express* that was reprinted in the *Troy Daily Times* in May 1882, took delight in mocking the radical uniform color scheme on some of the Troy players, and also christened Roger Connor with another nickname. "The players looked very picturesque in the variegated uniforms, no two men being dressed alike. Connor, the Jumbo of the field, wore a suit of zebra stripe; Keefe the beloved of Albany enthusiasts [he had pitched there before joining the Troys] was decked in suggestive green; Ferguson looked angular and hollow-chested in dingy maroon, while Gillespie, robed in virgin white, indicated that purity of character which he undoubtedly possesses."[52]

In its final National League season, 1882, Troy dropped to seventh place in the standings, winning 35 games and losing 48, while Chicago, paced by Anson, Dalrymple, Gore, and Troy native Michael "King" Kelly, fought off the Providence Grays to win its third consecutive pennant.

The Trojans' financial troubles began to surface in 1881, when "the club complained of bad treatment by its financial backers and a possible transfer of the club to Pittsburgh."[53] Attendance was low for home games at Riverside Park, on Center Island, an islet in the Hudson River between Troy and West Troy, with crowds averaging in the hundreds. A mere 12 Troy City fans had braved the rainy weather to see the final home game of the 1881 season against the champion Chicago White Stockings. In hopes of increasing attendance, team owners spent $5,000 to develop new playing grounds in West Troy, but bad weather, construction delays, and prior conditions at the new site precluded its use early in the season.

It is improbable that the [new] Troy city base ball grounds [at West Troy] will be in such condition that a game can be played upon them tomorrow. Wheat was raised on the lot last year and it was seeded with clover. The diamond has been sodded, and many spots covered with water, and the catcher's position is soft and muddy. A drain has been made at the northeast corner and open ditches have been dug close to the east and south fences. The water is flowing rapidly from the grounds but the soil is saturated and outside of the diamond is soft. A thin growth of clover makes a slight matting over the mud.... [Troy owner] A.L. Hotchkin, while looking at the grounds this morning, said they would not be fit for use in five days. The grand stand is not completed and the seats are very dirty.[54]

To make matters worse, heavy rains had flooded the access area to the old park on Center Island. "The Greenbrush swamp outside the ball field was flooded yesterday, and in reaching that magnificent affair termed 'Riverside park [sic],' it was necessary to walk a single plank, underneath which was muddy water of unknown depth.... Troy and Providence will try it again today at the Greenbush swamps, the grounds at West Troy not having reached a condition for use."[55] Troy played well at its new grounds when they finally opened, but the team performed miserably on the road. Their previously commendable defense collapsed to seventh in the league and pitchers Keefe and Welch finished sixth in ERA. A mediocre .244 team batting average could not overcome such handicaps, and the team closed out the season in seventh place.

Roger Connor's defense continued to be problematic in 1882, and he was further hampered by an injury. He began the season at third base, but after dislocating his shoulder at mid-season, he spent the remainder of the campaign playing first base or center field under considerable duress. "The Troys appeared on the field with a team evidently out of form ... as Connor, who had a lame arm, could not throw from center-field."[56] Local news accounts provide no explanation or details of Connor's injury, and it is possible that at the time he was not aware of the nature or extent of the problem. Decades later, he noted that "the last season [at Troy] I dislocated my shoulder in sliding to one of the bases. In spite of the injury I played all the time and never lost a game on account of it."[57] Fortunately, the shoulder injury, from which he would not fully recuperate until well into the following year, did not affect his hitting, and he returned to his rookie-year form. His 18 triples led the league — his first such distinction — and he was third in hitting (.330, behind Dan Brouthers and Cap Anson), and second in slugging and total bases (behind Brouthers). Connor's four home runs, two of which were hit in the last two weeks of the season, doubled his

Troy Baseball Monument, North Troy (formerly Lansingburg), New York, located near the site of the Haymakers' original ball field. The front side of the monument contains an etching of the original Lansingburg Unions (courtesy Howard P. Ohlous).

previous year's total. One of the blasts, hit in a losing cause at Buffalo, gained the attention of that city's daily, the *Commercial.* "For the Trojans, Roger Connor distinguised [*sic*] himself by making a home run, hit over the right field fence, and a long high rap to the lower right field corner."[58]

Connor's heads-up base running was also drawing notice. In the eighth inning of an August contest against Chicago, his quick thinking on the base paths sparked a rally that won the game. "Ewing batted for three bases but was fielded out at home, Connor gaining first on the play. Suddenly Connor sped toward second, whither [catcher] Flint threw the ball. It went several feet over the baseman's head and dodged the center fielder, Connor coming to the plate amid wildest excitement."[59]

Rumors of the impending demise of the Worcester and Troy clubs, which had circulated all season, were compounded by the added threat of enticing offers to the teams' best players from American Association clubs. The new league, completing a successful first-year challenge to the National League's baseball monopoly, was capitalizing on player dissatisfaction over the reserve rule.

It is stated that the league is in danger of losing many of its best players, who are considering offers to attach themselves next season to clubs in the American association [*sic*]. The reason given for these anticipated changes is that the players interested are determined to rebel against the league rule allowing each club to reserve five men, which the aforesaid players claim prevents them from obtaining larger salaries with other teams.[60]

The Association was likewise offering other incentives.

One of the baits thrown out by the American association [*sic*] whereby to catch league players for next season, is to promise them a release from the obligation to purchase their own uniforms and to rescind the rule whereby fifty cents a day is deducted from a player's salary while the team is away from home. Promises are also made to deposit certain sums of money in the bank for the benefit of said players in advance of the season.[61]

The Philadelphia Athletics reportedly had made a lucrative offer to Roger Connor. "It is said Connor has been offered $1,500 and a house and lot to go to Philadelphia."[62] Ten years later, at a different stage in his career, Connor would recall Philadelphia's earlier offer when he finally did jump from the Giants to the Athletics. By the time he did so, however, the Association itself was on its last legs. Connor would play in Philadelphia, not with its defunct Association team, the Athletics, but with the National League Phillies.

In late September, Collar City residents were informed of the news of their team's demise:

Base ball admirers were surprised this morning by an associated press [*sic*] dispatch from Philadelphia stating that the executive committee of the league had accepted the resignation of the Troys and Worcesters, in accordance with the desire of the league that the membership should consist only of cities large enough to ensure paying patronage. None were more surprised that the directors of the Troys. President Hotchkin is in Philadelphia attending the meeting and had not informed his colleagues up to this morning of the resignation or withdrawal of the Troy club.... At noon to-day a prominent stockholder of the Troy club said he believed the club was given the choice between resigning or being summarily dropped from the roll, and that Mr. Hotchkin accepted the former alternative.[63]

Troy played its last major league game against Worcester on September 29. The team won the contest, 10–7, on the strength of a Roger Connor home run, the last ever hit by a Trojan batsman.

The Troy years served as a baseball apprenticeship for five future Hall of Famers who played for the Collar City team during the Trojans' brief four-season major league history. Pitchers Tim Keefe and Mickey Welch each compiled two losing seasons in their three years at Troy; each would experience only one other losing season during the remainder of their long and successful careers. Buck Ewing and Dan Brouthers, neither of whom hit close to .300 for Troy City, would only dip under that mark once again, in both cases during the twilight of their illustrious careers. On the field, Roger Connor would transform from the awkward fielder he was with Troy to a graceful four-time defensive league-leader. As a hitter, there would be no need for subsequent transformation. With the exception of increased home run production, which began in the mid–1880s, Roger Connor had already hit his major league stride in every other offensive category before taking leave of Troy. He remains today the Troy National League team's all-time single-season leader in runs, hits, doubles, triples and RBIs, and is tied for the lead in home runs.[64]

In June 1992, on land close to the playing fields of the original Haymakers in North Troy (originally Lansingburg), the Collar City dedicated

Partial rear view of the Troy Baseball Monument in North Troy, New York, featuring etchings of the five players from Troy's National League team (1879–1882) who were elected to the Hall of Fame: Roger Connor, Buck Ewing, Mickey Welch, Tim Keefe and Dan Brouthers (courtesy Howard P. Ohlous).

a monument to its baseball past. The 12-foot-wide granite structure stands four feet high and features commemorative bronze plaques and engravings on each side. Its front includes an etching of the original Unions of Lansingburg. Its rear contains plaques listing the names of all players of the Unions (1866–1870), the National Association Troy Haymakers (1871–1872) and the National League Troy Trojans (1879–1882). Accompanying the plaques is an etching of the seven Hall of Famers associated with Troy: two Troy-born players, Michael "King" Kelly and Johnny Evers (of the famed Tinker-Evers-Chance trio), and the five Troy City players who eventually were enshrined at Cooperstown: Keefe, Welch, Brouthers, Ewing, and Connor. More than a monument of granite and bronze, the Collar City's tribute to its past

Detail of the Troy Baseball Monument featuring Roger Connor. The 1967 induction date shown is incorrect; Connor was inducted into the Hall of Fame in 1976 (courtesy Howard P. Ohlous).

symbolizes history, pride, and the love of the game that has been labeled our National Pastime. It transfers forgotten memories into a permanent reminder of Troy's important role in professional baseball. The monument is a tribute to the players who have made it to the major leagues and it is a small way of saying "thank you" to these players for giving Troy a special place in baseball history.[65]

3

—◆—

The Veteran

"the giant of the Giants, Connor..."

—*New York Times*, August 1, 1885

As Troy's professional baseball star sputtered, dimmed and died in the early 1880s, down the Hudson River in New York City, the Big Apple's major league aspirations were rising from the ashes. Named after the New York Fire Department's Mutual Hook and Ladder Company, the Mutuals of Manhattan — known as the "Mutes" by their fans — were a founding member of the National Association in 1871, and managed decent finishes (fourth, third, or second place) in all but the organization's final year, 1875, when they finished seventh. After the National League supplanted the Association in 1876, the Mutes switched their affiliation to the new league, but were expelled near the end of their first season after failing to make their final western road trip in September due to financial problems. Despite being a Manhattan team, the Mutuals played their "home" contests both as an Association and League affiliate at the Union Grounds in Brooklyn — then an independent city — since at the time there were no suitable enclosed baseball grounds in Manhattan. As we have seen, this situation changed in 1880 when the Polo Grounds was converted to a baseball venue. Baseball came to the Polo Grounds through the efforts of two Massachusetts transplants: tobacco merchant John B. Day and a second-rate infielder for several New England teams named James Mutrie.

Mutrie, whose father was a Scottish immigrant, began his sports career as a cricket player but soon switched to baseball. He played professionally into his mid–20s, including a season at shortstop on Frank Bancroft's New Bedford squad, where he briefly teamed with Roger Connor. Moving to

49

New York City in 1880, Mutrie worked in a box factory and on the side played on local "picked nines," makeshift teams that took on all comers. At a game that summer, Mutrie met amateur pitcher John B. Day, who had made a fortune as a wholesaler of tobacco. "As the story goes, Mutrie convinced Day that he, Mutrie, could bring together a winning team if Day was interested in investing."[1] Day accepted the proposal. Through the latter's Tammany Hall political connections, the pair managed to lease a four-block-square parcel of land known as the Polo Grounds, between Fifth and Sixth Avenues and 110th and 112th streets. Mutrie quickly organized a new, independent professional team, the Metropolitans, who, as previously mentioned, played and won the first game at the original Polo Grounds on September 29, 1880.

The scope of Mutrie's and Day's accomplishment and the speed with which they completed the task were remarkable; "with the financial resources and connections of [John B. Day], he [Mutrie] had established a professional team in the nation's largest and wealthiest city."[2] In early

October, Metropolitans manager Mutrie rewarded team owner Day for his financial backing by allowing him to pitch a game for the home team against Manhattan College. Day went the distance and collected the win.

Over the next two seasons, 1881–1882, the Metropolitans took on all comers at the Polo Grounds, including National League teams, other independents and college squads, winning two-thirds of their games and the hearts of their

John B. Day, owner and founder of the New York Metropolitans (Independent, 1881–1882; American Association, 1883–1887) and the New York Nationals (1883–1884), later known as the New York Giants (1885–1957) and the San Francisco Giants (1958–present) (courtesy National Baseball Hall of Fame Library, Cooperstown, New York).

Manhattan fans while raking in substantial profits. Flush with the economic success of their venture, Day and Mutrie made two more bold moves at the end of the 1882 season. First, they enrolled the Metropolitans in the upstart, one-year-old American Association, which was challenging the National League's prior monopoly of professional baseball. Then, after securing most of the quality players from Troy's defunct squad, they placed a newly-formed second Manhattan team, the New Yorks, in the National League. Within a few years the Metropolitans were dropped from the American Association and disbanded. They would not be resurrected as the modern-day Mets for nearly three-quarters of a century. Thanks to the efforts of two baseball lovers from Massachusetts, however, the remaining city team, the New Yorks (or New-Yorks), initially known informally as the Gothams or the Maroons (owing to their magenta-colored stockings) would by mid-decade be renamed the New York Giants, and in the twentieth century become the progenitors of today's San Francisco Giants.

Roger Connor played 10 of his final 14 major league seasons in New York (nine with the National League Giants, one with the Players' League Giants), and consequently is customarily associated with both the city and the Giants team. During the New York years he matured into a veteran player and became a nationally-known athlete. Unlike many of his contemporaries, the laconic Connor left behind few oral or written statements about his own hitting, fielding and running strategies and techniques. Press commentary of the era, however, provides a clear, and for the modern fan at times perhaps a surprising, picture of his overall playing talents.

Describing Connor's left-handed hitting stance, a contemporary report observed that he "bends his body over the plate and watches the pitcher much closer [than does Dan Brouthers]; his hitting is to right field. He uses a very heavy bat."[3] While playing for Philadelphia in 1892, Connor's lumber was described as a "small telegraph pole."[4] He preferred low pitches and disliked change-ups, a fact noted by *Sporting Life* after a game between the Giants and Boston. "Pitchers of high degree generally 'work' Roger Connor on a fast high ball on the outside corner of the plate. Roger hates a slow ball of any kind. His strong point is a fast low ball and it was one of this description that he converted into a home run in the second game with the Bostons."[5] Although primarily a left-handed hitter, Connor could "turn around against a left-handed pitcher and hit successfully right-handed."[6]

In 1912, Sam Crane, a light-hitting second baseman from the Connor era who became a successful sportswriter, affirmed that Connor "detested the bunt or sacrifice," although "he always dropped his individuality for team work and was progressive enough to adopt up-to-date methods when [this] style of play was found to be best for emergencies."[7] Game reports, however, reveal that Connor was an adept sacrifice bunter, particularly in the latter stage of his career, and most notably during his year with Philadelphia, when he batted second in the lineup behind leadoff man Billy Hamilton. Hamilton, who still holds the all-time record for runs scored per game in a career, also led all 19th-century players in walks. Many 1892 game accounts note that Hamilton often would start an inning with a walk, be sacrificed to second by Connor, and then be brought home by the hitting of either Ed Delahanty or Sam Thompson.

The "sacrifice hit" first appeared officially in baseball box scores in 1889, and through the 1893 season "players received credit for advancing runners on bunts, ground outs and fly balls,"[8] but were not exempted from an official time at bat for such actions. Beginning in 1894, sacrifices were limited to bunts and the batter was not charged a time at bat. Connor's documented abilities as a sacrifice bunter during this period strongly suggest that he developed and employed this skill long before it was noted officially in game accounts. Needless to say, the batting averages of players skilled in the sacrifice during the years in which its practice represented an official time at bat (1889–1893) would have been higher, and in some cases significantly higher, had they not been penalized an official time at bat for their efforts.

Among 19th-century players, Roger Connor was second only to fellow Hall of Famer Billy Hamilton in walks. He studied pitchers, knew what they threw, and when they threw it. Phillies hurler Kid "Cannonball" Gleason remarked that as a hitter, "Roger was one of the most difficult men to deceive that he had ever faced."[9] Providence and Boston star Charley "Old Hoss" Radbourn, who served up the pitch that Connor famously hit out of the Polo Grounds on September 11, 1886, put it even more bluntly, stating that there was only one man he could not fool — Roger Connor."[10]

After being positioned at first base on a permanent basis in 1885, Connor developed into one of the 19th century's finest at the position. That year, John Ward, then the Giants' captain, declared Connor "as solid as a stone wall"[11] at first base, and the *New York Times* found him deserving of great praise for his efficient play, noting that "nothing thrown near him escapes his clutches."[12]A year later the *Times* elaborated on this assessment: "Rodger [*sic*] Connor saves [Joe] Gerhardt, [John] Ward and [Pete] Gillespie many errors by his wonderful one-handed catches of poorly thrown balls."[13] *Sporting Life*, citing Connor's steady, reliable play, wonderful reach and great ability to pick up grounders, pronounced him the most valuable at his position in 1890.[14] Tim Murnane, sportswriter for the *Boston Globe*, himself a former major league first baseman, supplied a knowledgeable addendum to this litany of praise, writing, "Roger Connor is the most graceful first baseman; his experience at third taught him how to handle difficult ground balls, and his throwing is good."[15]

Regarding Big Roger's running skills, John Ward "questioned whether there is a man his size in the profession who runs as well."[16] *Sporting Life* concurred with this evaluation: "He gets over the ground ... with a great deal of speed for a man of his bulk."[17] After Connor dislocated his shoulder during a slide while playing for Troy in 1882, he practiced and then popularized the "stand up" or "pop up" slide, an innovation that helped protect his upper body and at the same time struck fear in the heart of infielders covering the bag in question.

As the 1895 season approached, *The Sporting News* offered this at-times humorous description of the then 38-year-old Connor's well-known sliding/stealing technique:

> One of dear old Roger's slides is worth many times the price of admission to a league park. There is a disposition to class the giant first baseman among the ice wagons of the profession, but the truth is he is fast on his feet when his size is considered. It is certain that he always is willing to take a chance and he uses good judgment in getting a start and tops it off with a slide. He often steals a base at a critical stage of the game. The big fellow gets on quite a head of speed as he nears second base and within 10 feet of the bag he hurls himself into space feet foremost. His large frame is in the air only for a moment. He alights on that part of his anatomy which was often tanned at home and at school during his boyhood years. No sooner does he or it [Roger's posterior] strike the ground than he rebounds to his feet. It has never happened in the history of the game that any player has tried to block Roger Connor off a base. Everybody gives him a wide berth and no one is anxious to collide with his spiked feet, propelled by enough momentum to drive them through the side of a house. How the cranks [fans] yell with delight when Connor treats them to a slide. There is none of the awkwardness about him that characterizes big Dan Brouthers when he makes a burlesque of a slide. When Dan strikes the earth he is anchored, as he seems to be lacking the India rubber properties concealed about Connor's person.[18]

An 1893 *New York Times* article, "New York Runners," likewise noted the "fear-factor" component of Connor's sliding technique: "Connors [*sic*] ... is a good starter and a first class bogie man. He gets many bases because the basemen are scared off when they see Roger's irresistible one-eighth of a ton body coming at them on a feet first plunge."[19]

Smart, agile, graceful, fast and powerful, Roger Connor could steal a base, drop a sacrifice bunt, wait out a walk, or hit the long ball. Defensively he could stretch for an errant throw, dig balls out of the dirt and cover first base with the best of his era. "Home Run Connor,"[20] as contemporary evidence attests, was much more than the nickname implies. He was a complete player.

Press assessments of Connor's character and personality remained remarkably constant from his rookie year to his retirement from major league baseball. An early *New York Clipper* portrait praised his "honorable and straightforward conduct, and affable and courteous demeanor toward all."[21] Sixteen years later, at the start of Connor's last full year in the major leagues (1896), nothing in that description had changed:

> Connor is one of the most popular men in baseball. His popularity was not acquired by the antics of a clown [an oblique reference to Arlie Latham] or the pugnacity of a [John] McGraw or a [Mike] Kelly. Great ability as a ballplayer and an honest, strong personality were his recommendations to the people. They proved more enduring than the paroxysmal brilliance of a season's play. Every ball patron ... is Connor's friend, and they will not be slow to take their hats off to him.[22]

After resigning from the St. Louis Browns and heading home to Waterbury in May of 1897, Connor was sent off with a similar accolade. "But no matter what he does [after retiring] ... Roger Connor will have the best wishes of every baseball admirer in America, and he will always be remembered as much for his gentlemanly traits as for his conscientious work and terrific slugging qualities."[23]

By inclination if not by design, Connor himself did little to provide details to promote such a broadly-painted character portrayal. He rarely spoke to the press, a fact that at the height of the 1890 Players' League revolt led the pro–National League *Sporting News* to publish a scathing account suggesting that Connor was either tongue-tied, dim-witted, or both.

> Few people are aware that Roger Connor once attempted oratory.... It happened this way: the Adonis and Athletic Base Ball Clubs played for the championship of Harlem at a church picnic not a long while ago. The winner was to receive a silver ball and Roger was to make the presentation speech. In introducing Mr. Connor, the chairman told of his wonderful feats with the bat and ball and the crowd broke forth with cheers. When all was silent Roger stepped forward and made a pretty bow but unfortunately forgot what he had to say. He glanced at the floor, then at the ceiling, and then, spying the door, he beat a hasty retreat. Roger is more eloquent with the bat.[24]

This attempt at character assassination appears to have been a form of retaliation for Connor's unwavering support of the Players' League near the end of its first (and last) season. As we shall see, however, Connor, when so inclined, could be a convincing and articulate speaker.

Some members of the press asserted that Connor's "naturally retiring disposition" was the reason he lost his job with the Giants in 1894. "Roger could never be induced or driven to get up on the lines and coach. In fact it was his refusal to do so that was given as the cause of his release by the New York club."[25] Another press account of Connor's release provided different details while reaffirming that the rationale for the decision had more to do with the slugger's personality than his baseball skills. The Giants initially benched Connor in 1894 in favor of "Dirty Jack" Doyle, a converted catcher. Doyle, like Roger's father, was a County Kerry, Ireland native and one of the most aggressive players of the era. He frequently "engaged in brawls with umpires, fans, opposing players, and even his own teammates,"[26] and on several occasions "went into the stands to battle fans."[27] The Sporting News suggested that Connor's ultimate departure from New York was linked to his refusal to exhibit similar behavior on the diamond: "Roger ... decided that since the New York team needed an 'operatic' demonstration of first base playing and he was not an operatic artist, that he would go where he could play first base and keep an active trim."[28]

Connor's gentlemanly conduct is reflected in his respectful treatment of umpires, who in turn respected him. "Honest John" Gaffney, "arguably the greatest umpire of the nineteenth century,"[29] suggested that there was a connection between Connor's demeanor and his on-field production. "There is that conscientious player, Roger Connor, for instance. He is free of care and annoyance and is bound to play good ball."[30] Connor's most celebrated encounter with an umpire took place during his owner/manager/player years in the Connecticut League. During a 1902 league game, rookie umpire Bill Klem received continued abuse from Meriden's manager, but worried most after he made a close call at the plate on the towering old veteran Connor. "Connor astounded him by not saying a word.... After the ball game he [Connor] flabbergasted Bill by coming over to him, shaking his hand and saying, 'Young man, let me congratulate you for umpiring a fine ball game.'"[31] Klem subsequently would umpire for 35 years in the major leagues, and was hailed as the "dean of umpires." Until his death in 1951, he waged an unsuccessful one-man campaign to elect Roger Connor to the Baseball Hall of Fame. He himself would be chosen for that honor in 1953, 23 years before Connor's selection.

Connor may not have yelled, shouted, or harangued from the bench or while playing first base, but when the chips were down, the team looked to him for leadership. Nowhere is this more evident that in an 1886 Polo Grounds incident. Having just returned from a poor western road trip, the Giants team was afraid to take the field, fearing they would by physically assaulted by the home-town Manhattan fans. "All talk was cut short by Rodger [*sic*] Connor volunteering to lead against the enemy, and trembling, the Leaguers walked toward the crowd. But cheers, not jeers greeted them, and the welcome shouts infused new life in the team."[32]

Fellow Giants players chose Connor as their protector not only due to his physical size, but also for the pugilistic skills they knew he possessed. Connor was "one of the best boxers in base ball"[33]; "Roger Connor of the New Yorks is said to be the 'blizzard' of the baseball arena. When 'Rog' feels well, don't fool with him. They say a horse kick is nothing compared to his hitting power."[34] In 1896, Connor's St. Louis Browns teammate and fellow Waterbury native Frank "Red" Donohue suggested that Connor's boxing prowess exceeded that of an amateur:

> "Do you know," said Frank Donohue, "that Roger Connor is one of the best boxers and hardest hitters that ever put on a glove?" The baseball reporter was happy to say from personal experience he did not know about Mr. Connor's fistic prowess, but he admitted that he had heard much about Roger's ability to handle himself to advantage in a rough and tumble fight. "Well, 'tis a fact," continued the red-headed pitcher. "You know how strong Roger is and you can imagine what a blow he can hit. In addition he is a good swift man on his feet and can duck like a trained goose. Maybe you don't know that Roger was once matched to meet John L. Sullivan.... It was in 1887 when Roger was so popular in New York that he could have owned the town if he wanted it. Sullivan about owned the country, and when he and Roger were matched Madison Square was enlarged to hold the expected crowd. But if you remember, Sullivan was sick and the match was called off." "Good thing for Roger," said [second baseman] Tommy Dowd. "Oh, I don't know," said Donohue, as he dodged one of [center fielder] Tom Parrot's liners. "I think Roger would have whipped him."[35]

Perhaps no sports note of the era better epitomizes the Connor ethos than this 1889 *Sporting Life* report: "All New York players but one [Tim Keefe] have signed contracts, Connor being the last. I saw Roger put his name on paper Tuesday. As he did so he said, 'They want, thus I sign, but they don't need any contract to hold me and never did.' This remark was characteristic of the man. Once let them accept terms and his word is as good as his bond."[36]

While the image of the famously private Connor that emerges from such commentary presents more of a collage than a full personality portrait, it reveals a consistency of character that is much in accord with many of the era's Victorian norms. Having come from extremely modest circumstances, Roger Connor's self-betterment agenda was closely linked to the concepts of decorum, individual integrity, hard work, respectability, loyalty and courage. Although we shall see that in all these areas he was not always a perfect exemplar, his public persona routinely transmitted such values. On "the diamond green," his actions closely followed the pattern of manliness outlined by historian Mike Higgins in *The Victorians and Sport*: seriousness, robust masculine strength, skill, steady perseverance and stoic acceptance."[37] Giants fans of the era, drinking from the same fountain of cultural values, might have laughed at the antics of visiting-team scalawags like Mike Kelly, or roared themselves hoarse praising the remarkable skills of Mickey Welch or Buck Ewing, but it was the quiet dignity of "Dear Old Roger" that they loved.

As the 1883 season approached, John Day found himself the owner of two major league teams, but the holder of a lease on only one baseball venue — the Polo Grounds. He resolved this dilemma by remodeling the Grounds, squeezing in two fields at the park's opposite ends. The original southeast diamond was ceded to the National League New Yorks, whose fans would pay a premium 50-cent admission fee, while the American Association Metropolitans, whose followers could see a game for just 25 cents, were assigned the new southwest-west field, a decidedly inferior location, portions of which were reportedly leveled "with the use of raw garbage as a landfill."[38] A portable canvas-covered fence separated the diamonds, and the clumsy device led to unusual on-field developments when both teams played at home on the same date; "balls rolling under the fence remained in play, causing the bizarre scene of an outfielder emerging into the opposite field in pursuit of a ball."[39] Fortunately for both squads, their home schedules coincided for just three weeks during the season.

Owner John Day's new 1883 League team included a collection of has-beens, promising youngsters, and one authentic star. Roger Connor, Buck Ewing, Mickey Welch, and Pete Gillespie joined the club from the defunct Troy Trojans team. Pitcher Tim Keefe, the remaining quality Trojan player, was dealt to the Metropolitans, a move in all likelihood determined both by his three-year losing record with Troy and, as previously noted, his alleged intentionally poor pitching performances there in his final year. Several second-tier former Troy players, Mike Dorgan, Ed Caskin, and Frank Hankinson, all of whom had been out of the major leagues in 1882, were reinstated for New York's National League entry.

1883 New York Nationals, known informally as the New Yorks, the Maroons (for their magenta hose), or, less frequently, the Gothams. First row, left, Mickey Welch; second row, center, player-manager John Clapp; far right, Roger Connor; third row, far right, John Montgomery Ward; far left, Buck Ewing (courtesy National Baseball Hall of Fame Library, Cooperstown, New York).

Seeking a skipper with League experience, owner Day chose John Clapp over partner Jim Mutrie as manager of the New Yorks. A journeyman catcher, Clapp had played on National Association and National League teams since 1872. As a player-manager he led the Cincinnati club to a miserable 29–51 last-place finish in 1880, but at least had League experience both as a player and a manager. Jim Mutrie, who played some first base for the Metropolitans in their years as an independent team, became the manager of the American Association team in 1883.

To complete New York's roster, John Day acquired two players from Providence — diminutive, light-hitting infielder Dasher Troy, and star pitcher John Montgomery Ward. Dasher Troy would retire from baseball after the 1885 season. Ward's 47–19 record for Providence in 1879 had powered the Grays to the National League pennant. When he signed with New York in 1883, his pitching days were numbered due to an arm injury. Nevertheless he played another dozen years as an outfielder-infielder, captained and managed the New York and Brooklyn teams, organized and directed the Players' League rebellion of 1890, and ultimately was elected to the National Baseball Hall of Fame.

Born in rural Pennsylvania, Ward attended Penn State University (then known as the Pennsylvania State College) intermittently as a teenager until being dismissed — some say for fighting, others for stealing chickens. At 5' 8", the slender, 160-pound pitcher relied on curve balls, a change of pace, and a thorough knowledge of every hitter's weaknesses to win 164 major league games, including the second perfect game in major league history (just five days after the first, pitched by Worcester's Lee Richmond), in which Ward took down the Buffalo Bisons on June 17, 1880, 5–0. After injuring his right arm from overuse, Ward learned to throw left-handed and played in the outfield until the right arm recovered sufficiently to allow him to play the infield. Owing to such adaptability, Ward became the only player in history to win over 100 games and collect over 2,000 hits. On the field, he was scrappy, smart and speedy (he stole 111 bases in 1887). Off the diamond, he earned a law degree by taking courses at Columbia University in the off-season, learned to speak French, became a devotee of the theater and mingled easily with New York City's social elite. His notoriety increased after he married noted actress Helen Dauvray, who later divorced him in a scandalous trial in which he was charged with infidelity. In 1885 Ward founded the Brotherhood of Professional Base Ball Players in protest over the reserve rule, and in 1890 he organized the Players' National League of Baseball Clubs after National League owners established a salary cap. In retirement, he devoted his energies to his law practice, hunting, fishing and golf, at all of which he excelled. John Montgomery Ward was elected to the Hall of Fame in 1964.

Several unrelated 1883 baseball events would have a long-term impact on the national game. First, the National League's Rules Committee recognized the inevitable by legalizing sidearm pitching. Ever since the 1872 ruling permitting the pitcher to snap his wrist when releasing the ball, that is, to "throw" rather than "pitch," the pitcher's arm angle had been creeping up from the knees and waist to the shoulder. The new shoulder-high rule allowed for greater velocity on the fast ball and produced a more effective curve ball that would "break down instead of just away from the batter."[40]

Second, the challenge to the National League offered by the American Association in 1882 proved successful. The Association not only survived financially, but developed a working-class following that could afford its 25-cent admission on their only day off — Sunday — and enjoy a mug of beer while watching the action. All of these innovations were eventually accepted by the National League. The rivalry and competition that developed between the two organizations contributed to the marked rise in baseball's national popularity during the 1880s. The National League soon implicitly acknowledged the Association's success by hastily suing for peace. In February 1883, both parties signed the National Agreement, by which each league recognized the other as an equal and pledged to honor the other's contracts and blacklists.

John Montgomery Ward, New York Nationals, 1883–1884; New York Giants, 1885–1889; 1893–1894 (courtesy Transcendental Graphics/theruckerarchive.com).

Out in Saint Louis at the American Association St. Louis Browns' ballpark that season, a chance encounter between team manager Ted Sullivan and a rabid follower of the Browns was overheard by first baseman Charles Comiskey, giving rise to a new baseball term, one that is still with us today:

> Ted Sullivan and Charles Comiskey were meeting at team headquarters when an unknown man strolled into the office. Without warning he launched into a series of nonstop, unsolicited opinions about the Browns. Exhausting his comments of the locals, the stranger proceeded to critique the sport itself. After endless commentary, the man was finally called outside. Sullivan said to Comiskey, "What name can you possibly apply to a fellow like that?" Comiskey replied, "He's a fanatic." Ted Sullivan then said, "I will abbreviate that and call him a fan."[41]

Although already considered by some as the "National Pastime," baseball still vied with other sports for news coverage in 1883. The *New York Herald* that year regularly highlighted cricket results on its sports page, while baseball scores were relegated to below-the-fold coverage.[42] The *New York Tribune* followed suit, sandwiching the ball scores between college crew results and the activities of such organizations as the Providence Homing Pigeon Club.[43]

On the ball field, the ongoing reluctance to put a new ball in play when needed continued to cause consternation for players and teams alike, and occasionally allowed fans to dictate a game's outcome.

> The game of baseball at the Polo Grounds yesterday between the Chicago and New York League nines was brought to a close after one man was out in the fifth inning. In the fourth inning when the score stood at 3–2 in favor of the Chicago nine, the rain came and the players were drenched. The fifth inning began amid shouts to the umpire to call the game, but he could not be moved. At last a small boy picked up the ball and threw it to a companion who ran off as fast as he could with it. The umpire could have called for another ball, but he did not, and finally he called the game, much to the satisfaction of the spectators. In thirty minutes, "No Game" was declared.[44]

On May 1, 1883, National League baseball made its debut in Manhattan as John Clapp's New York squad, called the Gothams, played host to Boston, which had recently changed its classy nickname, the "Red Caps," to the more prosaic "Beaneaters."

> The largest number of persons that ever assembled on a ball ground in this city witnessed a game of base-ball played on the Polo Grounds between the New-York and Boston clubs. It was the first time in the history of baseball that a New-York club played for the League championship, and that fact seemed to have inspired new life in the patrons of the national game in the New York vicinity.[45]

At 3:55 in the afternoon, Boston won the coin toss and elected to field first (although home teams were not *required* to bat last until 1950, the tradition to do so became well-established only in the twentieth century). Buck Ewing led off for New York and struck out. Roger Connor "then went to the bat and after two strikes being called off him, he made a long hit to right field, the ball touching the fence. This hit yielded Connor three bases."[46] John Ward followed with a grounder to Boston shortstop Sam Wise, who fumbled the ball, allowing Connor to score. Within the space of five minutes, "the Squire of Waterbury" had recorded the New York franchise's first hit and scored its first run.

By the end of the afternoon, 15,000 jubilant fans had seen the New Yorks record their first victory, 7–5. To everyone's surprise, they went on to sweep the three-game series from the powerful Bostons, who would claim the pennant at season's end. New York's early season jubilation was quickly muted a few days later, however, when they hit a roadblock named Radbourn of the Providence Grays. Charles "Old Hoss" Radbourn began his major league career with Providence in 1881, and took over as the team ace when John Ward signed with the New Yorks in 1883. During his 11-year career he averaged 28 wins a season, retiring from the game with a total of 309 victories. His 1884 tally of 59 wins represents the most season wins by a pitcher in history and appears safe for posterity.

True to his "iron-arm" reputation, Old Hoss pitched and won all three contests in a span of four days at the Polo Grounds in early May. The New York press had praised the home team's defense during the Boston series; "Ewing's catching was excellent, as usual, while the first and second base play of Connor and Caskin was perfect."[47] However, the final game of the Providence series, a 14–2 loss in which the team made eight errors, began a pattern of poor fielding and light hitting that would be the team's downfall. They showed signs of life in mid–June by sweeping the woeful Phillies and then, aided by Roger Connor's two triples and a double, taking a July 4 doubleheader from powerful Boston.

Injuries then hit the team hard. Both catchers were hurt — player-manager Clapp with a broken finger and Buck Ewing with a sore hand — a common ailment now that pitchers were throwing harder from the sidearm position. Third baseman Hankinson had a dislocated thumb and utility outfielder Mike Dorgan was felled by sunstroke. The injuries prevented the team from making up any ground on fifth-place Buffalo over the last third of the season, and they ended the campaign in sixth place, 16 games behind the league-leader Boston.

Roger Connor started the 1883 campaign on an offensive tear and never let up. He followed up his opening-game triple with another in the second game of the Boston series, although he was thrown out at the plate trying to stretch the hit into a home run. In early June, he stroked 12 hits and scored eight runs in five games against Detroit and Chicago. By late July he was hitting .338, fifth in the league, but a blistering finish, including a four-hit, three-run effort against third-place Boston on August 22, brought his year-end average to .357, second only to Dan Brouthers' .360 mark, and more than a hundred points higher than the average of the rest of his team. On an off-day that month, New York played an exhibition game in Waterbury against the Monitors, an occasion that allowed the town to honor its most famous citizen.

> A game at Waterbury, Connecticut between the New-York and Waterbury clubs last Thursday resulted in favor of the New-Yorks by 11–6. Conner [*sic*] of the New-York club, formerly of the Monitors, was presented after the first inning with a diamond ring by his Waterbury friends. Mayor Kendrick made the presentation. Conner [*sic*] responded with a three-base-hit.[48]

The triple and double, not the home run, were Connor's signature hits at this stage of his career. He clubbed 15 three-baggers in 1883, two short of Dan Brouthers' league-leading 17, and hit 28 doubles. He also showed patience and a good eye at the plate, as evidenced by his team-leading 25 walks, a significant total given that seven balls were required for a walk in 1883. The 19th century's leading home run hitter hit only one four-bagger during his first season with New York, and he waited until October to hit it. The victim was another pitcher named Radbourn — George, a cousin of "Old Hoss" Radbourn, and whose brief major league career lasted just 22 innings for Detroit, during which he gave up 38 hits, including Connor's home run. The solo 1883 homer was the lowest total of his first four major league years. The long-ball phase of his career would not begin until 1887.

After two years spent in the outfield and at second base, Connor's fielding at first base was still shaky — he committed 44 errors in 98 games for a .958 average — fifth in the league. Connor and veteran outfielder Pete Gillespie were the iron men on the 1883 team, playing in every game of the season total of 98.

The two other bright spots on the 1883 team were Buck Ewing and Mickey Welch. Ewing had a breakout season, doing most of the catching, hitting over .300 for the first time (.303) and leading the team in runs scored (114). His 10 home runs led the league, and represented the highest total of his long career. Ewing began the year sharing the captaincy of the team with manager John Clapp, but eventually assumed the role full-time.

Mickey Welch was the workhorse of a pitching staff whose other members included rookie Tip O'Neill and tired-armed John Ward. Mickey accounted for more than half (25) of the team's 46 victories and posted a 2.73 earned run average. Ward started only 25 games, compared to Welch's 52. He won 16 contests, but would pitch only six games the following season, his last at that position. Canadian rookie O'Neill, like John Ward, abandoned pitching after the 1884 campaign, found success for another decade as an outfielder and retired with a lifetime batting average of .326.

The 1884–1887 seasons were years of trial and error, both for major league baseball and the New York nine. They were outstanding years for Roger Connor.

On the national level, the number of leagues and teams increased to three and 34 respectively, and then shrank back to two leagues and just 16 teams. Playing regulations changed yearly, often in wildly erratic fashion. Club owners imposed a $2,000 annual salary cap per player, and then cheated on their own regulation by paying their best veterans extra on the sly. Chicago White Stockings star Mike Kelly was sold to Boston for the then astounding sum of $10,000, yet Kelly did not receive a penny from the sale. First secretly, then openly, players began to unionize, an action that would culminate in the last great player revolt of the 19th century.

During these four years, the New York Nationals acquired a new nickname, the "Giants," and a new manager, Jim Mutrie, changed team captains, hired raw rookies and future Hall of Famers, and became an integral part of the city cultural scene. They did not, however, win a pennant.

On the diamond, Roger Connor became the Giants' star slugger, winning the batting title in 1885 and leading his team in multiple categories, including batting average, hits, doubles, triples, home runs, RBIs, and walks. A fixture at first base from this season on, the once erratic fielder would lead the league in chances and fielding percentage in 1887. Despite his performance on the field, his retiring nature continued to keep him in the background on New York and national sports pages, whose writers preferred to highlight the on-field and off-field exploits of Buck Ewing, the urbane John Ward, or the antics of the team's new manager, "Truthful" Jim Mutrie (the nickname, introduced by famed sports writer Henry Chadwick, was, as we shall see, deliberately ironic). Off the diamond, Connor, the quiet Giant, was methodically securing his family's financial future. He bought his widowed mother a house next to his own and assumed responsibility for her affairs. Turning 30, he and Angeline began thinking about starting a family. He passed a Civil Service test and spent a winter working in a New York customs office. Investing in real estate back in Waterbury, his endeavors were successful enough to allow him and Angeline to take a winter vacation to Europe. In the prime of life and of his career, he never forgot the humble circumstances from which he came.

The 1884 advent of the Union Association, a third major league, is arguably the most quixotic episode in the history of major league baseball. The Association was the brainchild of Henry Van Noye Lucas, a 27-year-old heir to a railroad fortune, whose life's obsession with the game ultimately became his downfall. He "loved baseball dearly, playing third base on a self-sponsored semi-pro team, building a private diamond on Normandy, his estate."[49] Frustrated in his attempts to acquire a National League franchise — St. Louis already had an American Association franchise, the Browns — and "convinced of the wrongness of the reserve rule,"[50] Lucas and a group of investors founded the Union Association, placing franchises in six cities that already had either League or Association teams, and a seventh in Washington, D.C. Both the seriousness of purpose and the sanity of the endeavor were compromised by the addition of tiny Altoona, Pennsylvania, as an eighth venue.

Lucas himself became the owner of the St. Louis entry, the Maroons, and spent $250,000 acquiring the best talent for the team, outfitting them "in silk stockings and lamb's wool sweaters"[51] and building them a lavish new grounds, the Palace Park of America, on a portion of his 3,000-acre estate. The Maroons' talent monopoly was too much for the Altoona Mountain Cities and for the remainder of the league — which briefly included such entries as the Wilmington Quicksteps and the St. Paul Apostles. The Maroons finished 94–19, killing interest in league competition by early May, and signaling the Union Association's demise at season's end. Unaccountably, Lucas was then granted a franchise by an organization he had challenged — the National League — for the 1885 season. The nine, bearing the Maroons' Union Association team name, could not compete for fans in St. Louis with the established American Association Browns; neither could the team compete in the National League, where it finished last in 1885 and sixth in 1886. Lucas lost the remainder of his fortune in this second baseball venture, and died in poverty in 1910 at the age of 53. At the time of his death he was earning $75 a month working for the St. Louis Department of Streets. As bizarre and quixotic as Lucas's venture may seem, it was a telling reminder of the simmering anger over baseball's reserve clause, an anger that would come to a boil in 1890.

Playing regulations in the National League changed at a dizzying pace from 1884 to 1887. The number of balls required for a walk was lowered from seven to six in 1884, increased to seven again in 1886, and then dropped to five in 1887. The height of such madness was reached in the latter year, when for a single season the three strike rule was increased to four strikes — the first (and last) such change in this regard since the Knickerbocker Rules were established in 1845. Walks were also counted as base hits that year. Baseball statisticians have corrected the latter excess by recalculating 1887 averages for modern record books.

After legalizing sidearm pitching in 1883, the League capitulated completely in 1884, removing all restrictions on pitching styles and ushering in the overhand era. While a few "workhorse" underhand pitchers such as Jim "Pud" Galvin and "Hoss" Radbourn remained successful (and, given their less strenuous delivery, avoided arm trouble) under the new rules, others benefited from the changes. Younger pitchers like Tim Keefe and John Clarkson came into their own as full sidearm hurlers. Late–1880s to early–1890s rookies such as Kid Nichols, Cy Young and Amos Rusie, armed with the extra speed and the sharper-breaking curve achieved through overhand throwing, were waiting in the wings to add a different dimension to the game. Pitchers gained yet greater leverage over hitters in 1887 with the abolition of the low/high strike zone options for the hitter. The new strike zone extended from the top of the shoulders to the bottom of the knees. To compensate for such largesse granted the pitcher, a final 1887 rule change moved the pitching distance back five feet and restricted pitchers' movements in the pitching box. Hurlers were now required to keep one foot on the back line of the box, a distance of 55'6" from home plate, until completing their delivery.

John Day's first order of business of the 1884 season was to replace New York's manager John Clapp with James L. Price, about whom little is known and even less has been written, other than the fact that "he was not a player, so his duties in the field were to be handled by the captain."[52] At this point in baseball's history the role of team manager was still evolving. The first professional league manager, Harry Wright, set a standard for the position so high that it became impossible to equal. The son of a British cricket professional at New York's St. George Cricket Club, Wright excelled both in baseball and cricket, playing both sports into his 20s before devoting all his time to baseball. Hired originally as a pitcher by the Cincinnati Base Ball team, he was subsequently directed to assemble there the best salaried team possible. The result was the 1869 Cincinnati Red Stockings squad, the first well-known professional team, whose famous 1869 Eastern tour has been discussed previously. In addition to serving as the Red Stockings' regular center fielder in 1869, Wright's team responsibilities included every conceivable administrative duty. He managed budgets, arranged travel and accommodations for the tour, and even designed the team uniform, all in splendid fashion. Wright was a hard act to follow.

In the 1880s and 1890s, most teams were managed and captained by full-time or former full-time players like Cap Anson of the White Stockings or Charlie Comiskey of the Browns, who, like Harry Wright, were also expected to handle the business aspect of the team. Many such men were good field generals but bad accountants. Accordingly, some franchises experimented with a different model in which a business man with little or no field experience assumed the title of manager but relegated the nuts and bolts of everyday play to a team captain. Occasionally, a hybrid version of these two models developed, as in the cases of Frank Bancroft or Boston's Frank Selee: business types with some minor league playing experience who kept the books, bench-managed in street clothes, but still made major on-field decisions. Each option had its strengths and weaknesses. The modern distribution of responsibilities among a general manager, business manager, and bench manager did not become the standard until well into the twentieth century.

In 1884 John Day chose the second of these options. As team manager, James L. Price handled the New York team's finances while John Ward replaced Buck Ewing as captain and directed the team on the field. Ward was a judicious choice. Price was not. In October the *New York Times* reported that

> James L. Price is no longer the manager of the New-York Base Ball Club. There has been a rumor that his accounts have been short, and several charges to that effect have been made against him. They were yesterday admitted by the President of the club.... It was said that Price was detected early in the season in stealing, but, promising to reform, he was allowed to retain his position. Other defalcations came to light while the club was on its last Western trip, and after the Buffalo trip the finances were handled by John M. Ward, second baseman and Captain. Price was discharged and remained in Detroit, fearing to come back to this city.[53]

Day's changes to the team roster had similarly ambiguous results. He added three rookies, all from New York: pitcher Ed Bagley, utility man Danny Richardson, and first baseman Alex McKinnon. The most puzzling of these moves was Day's decision to replace Roger Connor, a five-year major-league veteran and undisputed team offensive leader, with 27-year-old rookie McKinnon at first base. After three years with teams in Boston and Syracuse, McKinnon had signed on with Troy during its first National League season in 1879, but jumped his contract to play for Rochester of the International Association, a rival organization opposed to the reserve clause. McKinnon then became seriously ill at Rochester and was out for the season. Expelled and blacklisted by the National League for contract jumping, he was out of baseball until 1883, when he was reinstated by the League and signed with Philadelphia. Once again McKinnon became too sick to play, and was released.[54] Supplanting Connor at first base in 1884, McKinnon hit .272 and made 53 errors at his position, registering the lowest first-base fielding average in the league.

Shunted between third base, second base, and center field, Roger Connor's fielding suffered. Starting the season at second base, he committed 71 errors there in 67 games. After mid-season, he alternated between third base and center field, feeling equally ill-at-ease at both, committing more than two dozen errors at the two positions. It was the worst defensive season of his long career. Offensively, Connor again led the team in hitting, although his .317 average was 38 points below his 1883 mark.

While there is no record of how Roger Connor reacted to being displaced at first base by a rookie, the decision clearly had to be humiliating for him. As a reserved player, however, his options were few: he could protest and be fined, sit out the season without pay, or play the positions assigned. Should he be inclined to jump his contract in retaliation, he could be assured of the same fate that his replacement McKinnon had experienced: expulsion from the league, blacklisting, and a bleak future as a player. Connor played where he was assigned.

The fates were not kind to McKinnon. He played two years at St. Louis after being traded at the end of the 1884 season. Moving on to Pittsburgh in 1887, he developed typhoid pneumonia at mid-season and died. He was 30 years old.

John Day's second rookie, Ed Bagley, was expected to share the pitching load with Mickey Welch, but fared poorly, finishing 12–18 and not winning a game after mid–July. He would pitch 15 games for the Metropolitans the following season and then retire from baseball. Danny Richardson, Day's third rookie, filled in at shortstop and the outfield, hitting .253. A fan favorite, Richardson would move to the infield in 1887 and become the Giants' regular second baseman.

Despite a sixth-place finish in their first season, the New York Gothams "had become a distinct psychological success"[55] in the city. Returning team members were popular heroes whose exploits were celebrated, and their "pictures hung in the gaudier saloons."[56] The quaint amateur-era custom of entertaining the visiting team before or after a contest on the diamond was often practiced by the New York team, which took advantage of the city's many entertainment opportunities to invite rivals out for a night at the theater. In kind, theatrical performers soon took to whiling away their afternoons at the Polo Grounds prior to an evening on stage. Wall Street also caught baseball fever. "As early as 1884 large delegations started coming regularly to the games, which began at four o'clock, after the Exchange closed."[57] Two years after the club's creation, the New Yorks had become a fixture on the city's cultural scene.

With all restrictions on pitching eliminated in 1884, pitchers ruled the diamond, and among the rulers, Providence's Hoss Radbourn reigned supreme. He pitched 678 ⅔ innings, struck out nearly a hundred more batters (441) than he had the previous year, won 59 contests, completed all 73 starts, held opponents to 1.38 earned runs per nine innings, and almost single-handedly won the pennant for the Grays. For good measure, Radbourn pitched and won all three games of a hastily-organized post-season "World's Series" against Jim Mutrie's American Association Metropolitans, surrendering only three runs in 27 innings.

The New York Gothams started the 1884 season at home, pummeling the mighty Chicago White Stockings by a score of 15–3, with Roger Connor going 3-for-5, including a double and two runs scored. The victory began a 12-game win streak during which New York swept Chicago, Detroit and Cleveland, and took two games from Buffalo before finally falling to the Bisons, 4–1, on May 17. Offense led the way during the streak, with the New Yorks scoring 104 runs to their opponents' 28. When run production tapered off, so did the team's winning ways. New York scored nearly a hundred fewer runs in the second half of the 116-game campaign than in the first half. Roger Connor was dominant in May, hitting .361, scoring 23 runs, and going hitless in only two games. He connected for his first home run on July 1 in a 12–5 win against Detroit, and four days later hit two solo shots against Chicago's Larry Corcoran. Connor certainly had Corcoran's number; four of his first 12 major league home runs were hit off the Brooklyn native whose brief career included three no-hitters, and who died of kidney failure at the age of 32.

When Ewing and Gillespie went down with injuries in mid–July, Connor briefly moved into the clean-up spot in the lineup, stroking seven hits and scoring four runs in five games. In August, John Ward moved to second base from center field, and Connor began alternating between that outfield position and third base. Ward did no better at second than Connor had done — in an early–September contest with Chicago he made five errors at the position. Despite his defensive woes and a dip in his average in the second half of the season, Connor's offensive contributions were significant. He had 11 three-hit outings and five four-hit games, and his 98 runs scored tied with Ward for the team lead. His fourth and final home run of 1884 came in a 5–1 loss at Detroit in October. It was the only hit New York could muster against hard-luck Wolverine hurler Charlie Getzein, whose 5–12 won-loss record belied a 1.95 earned run average. Despite weak overall hitting — Connor was the only man who hit over .300 — and over-reliance on Mickey Welch in the pitcher's box, Manhattan's National League entry was tied for fourth place with the White Stockings with a 62–50 record when the season ended. In its last number of the year, *Sporting Life* noted that "Roger Connor, of the New York Club, is now in Europe on a pleasure trip."[58]

Several key personnel acquisitions made by New York prior to the start of the 1885 season established a foundation that would lead the team to two consecutive pennants. Three years transpired before the seeds sown by such moves bore fruit. John Day's first decision was to name Jim Mutrie manager of the team. Mutrie's fourth-place and first-place finishes as skipper of the Metropolitans during their first two American Association seasons gave clear indication of his leadership abilities. Such leadership in the main was limited to financial matters and seeking new talent, since on-field decisions were left to the team captain. Mickey Welch confirmed Mutrie's role in an interview decades later with sports writer John Kieran, saying, "Mutrie was what you would call today the business manager of the club. The real manager and leader on the field was Buck Ewing. Mutrie often sat up in the grandstand."[59]

Seventy years later, 82-year-old Fred Engle, who was the Giants' first batboy, described in detail how Mutrie played the role of team cheerleader while in the grandstand. "Mutrie rarely sat in the dugout. He would arrive at the park dressed formally — high-hat, tails and all — and parade around the park shouting, 'Who are the people?' Without waiting for a reply he would scream, 'The Giant fans are the people.' The fans cheered in the same way they did Leo Durocher."[60]

Once on board, Mutrie talked Day into picking up prominent batsman, "Orator" Jim O'Rourke from the Buffalo Bisons for $4,500, the highest salary offered any ballplayer in the era. O'Rourke, a burly 34-year-old from Bridgeport, Connecticut, was with the Middletown Mansfields in 1872 when the team joined the National Association. He subsequently played for Harry Wright's Association Red Stockings, who became the Red Caps when they joined the National League in 1876. Leaving Boston after the 1878 season, he spent the following year with the Providence Grays, where he helped John Ward win the pennant. After returning to Boston for a year, he signed on as player-manager at Buffalo before joining the Giants.

The son of Irish immigrant parents, the Orator was a hard-nosed player and disciplinarian manager who prided himself on his gentlemanly behavior off the diamond. While playing for New York, he completed a Yale law degree in the off-seasons and coached the university's baseball team. O'Rourke earned the nickname "Orator" for his booming voice and bombastic prose. His biographer cites his reply to a reporter regarding the reason his team lost a game as a typical example of an "O'Rourkism": "[An] unfortunate combination of heterogeneous circumstances compelled us to succumb to the simultaneous and united endeavors of our opponents."[61]

Bombast or not, O'Rourke could play ball. A fine outfielder and catcher, he hit over .300 in 13 seasons, and after 22 major league campaigns spent another 15 years as a minor league player/manager/ owner. The Orator holds the distinction of making the first hit in National League history. In the League's first game, played at Athletic Park in Philadelphia on April 22, 1876, he singled to right field off Philadelphia pitcher Alonzo Knight. Boston won the contest, 6–5. Orator O'Rourke was elected to the Hall of Fame in 1945.

Jim Mutrie's underhanded method of acquiring two other key players, Tim Keefe and Thomas Jefferson "Dude" Esterbrook of the Metropolitans, drew loud protests both from League and Association officials. A year after the legalization of sidearm pitching, side-

"Orator" Jim O'Rourke, New York Giants, 1885–1889; 1891–1892; 1904; Players' League Giants, 1890 (courtesy Transcendental Graphics/theruckerarchive.com).

winder Keefe had become an established star after winning 41 games for the Metropolitans in 1884. Esterbrook hit .314 for the team while guarding the hot corner. Rules established by the National Agreement of 1883 required a ten-day waiting period before clubs could begin negotiating with players who had been released by their teams. In order to evade the requirement, John Day sent Jim Mutrie, Keefe, and Esterbrook on a ten-day cruise to Bermuda, "ostensibly as a reward for winning the pennant."[62] After boarding ship, Mutrie, now technically the manager of both the Metropolitans and the New Yorks, released the pair from their Mets contracts, and upon return to shore, signed them to Gothams contracts at a higher salary. For this and other such devious exploits, Mutrie acquired his ironic nickname, "Truthful Jim" or Truthful Jeems."

With the signing of Jim O'Rourke and Tim Keefe, the New York Giants' list of future Hall of Fame players reached six: Connor, Ward, Ewing, O'Rourke, Welch and Keefe. Between 1885 and 1888, Keefe and

Welch occasionally played the outfield (Welch three times in 1886 and once in 1887; Keefe once each in 1885 and 1888). On the few days in which one of them pitched and the other played a different position, perhaps the rarest of baseball events occurred: six future Hall of Fame stars on the same team, playing on the field at the same time.

In early spring, 1885, New York acquired the nickname that is still applied to the franchise. In a report of an April 13 exhibition game between New York and the Eastern Association Jersey City team, the *New York World* referred to the National League team as the "Giants."[63] Thirty years later, however, "Truthful Jim" Mutrie claimed he himself had coined the term during an 1888 game. In truth, the 1885 Giants roster did contain a number of players who, for the era, were very tall men. Roger Connor at 6'3" led the list, followed by Pete Gillespie and Joe Gerhardt at 6'1" and 6' respectively. Dude Esterbrook, Buck Ewing, and Tim Keefe all were in the 5'10"–5'11" range. Other local and national news outlets, however, did not immediately take to the new epithet suggested by the *World* in April. The *New York Times* continued to refer to the team as the New Yorks or New Yorkers through May, using "New York Giants" for the first time on June 11. Prior to their adoption of "Giants" as a team descriptor, the *Times* and *Sporting Life* (in 1885 still the only national baseball magazine), both seemed to suggest that their decision to employ the new team nickname was due to a prior association of the term with its tallest player — Roger Connor. The May 30 edition of the *Times*, for example, commenting on Connor's slugging in a 10–9 win over St. Louis, noted that "The feature of this contest was the heavy batting by Connor, the *giant* of the team" [emphasis added]. The same wording was repeated in *Sporting Life*'s later review of this game.[64] Two weeks earlier, similar terminology was employed by the Philadelphia publication in its coverage of New York's 12–7 win over Detroit: "The *giant* of the team [emphasis added], Connor, led the work at the bat. He made one three-base hit, two doubles and a single, a total of eight bases."[65]

Thanks to Day's and Mutrie's roster changes, the newly-nicknamed Giants missed winning the 1885 pennant by just two games. The team's batting (.269), fielding (.928) and pitching (1.72 ERA) were the best in the League. Keefe and Welch accounted for 76 of the squad's 85 wins as they battled Cap Anson's White Stockings down to the wire until a late September four-game showdown in Chicago. Entering the series on a seven-game winning streak, the Giants lost the first three games, securing the pennant for their rivals.

Toward the end of June 1885, *Sporting Life* re-published an innocuous item from the *New York Sun* that within a few years would assume great importance in the baseball world. "The ball playing profession is gradually swelling in dignity and importance. A protective union has been proposed, and more than 200 players have signified their willingness to join this organization. Each player will be assessed $5 a month."[66] The "protective union" mentioned was the Brotherhood of Professional Base Ball Players, the brainchild of John Ward, and its formation was the first shot fired over the bow of the National League in a war that would break out in 1890.

Along with New York's disappointment over not winning the 1885 pennant came the realization that the Giants were now, "for the first time, a really good team."[67] Leading the way was Roger Connor, fresh from his European vacation, reinstated at first base, and enjoying his best season yet. Batting second behind Jim O'Rourke and before Buck Ewing, both of whom hit above .300, Connor led the League in average (.371), hits (169), and total bases (225) while playing in 110 of the season's 112 games. He also figured in the League's top five in walks, RBIs, runs, and slugging. Facing overhand pitching from a distance of 50 feet, Connor was the hard-est man in the League to strike out — once every 56.9 at-bats. Despite such numbers, the century's home run king had not yet found his long-ball stroke. An inside-the-park pre-season exhibition game clout against Wash-ington in April seemed to be a good omen: "Connor made the circuit of the bases by a tremendous hit to the extreme right corner of the field, it being the first home run ever made on the grounds when the ball did not go over the fence."[68] Only one home run followed during the regular sea-son, however, a three-run shot off St. Louis Maroons rookie pitcher Billy Palmer on May 30. Connor's batting heroics did prompt the press to chris-ten him with a new nickname, one of more than three dozen that would appear in the press during his long career. After a contest at Boston in mid–June, the *Times* reported that "Connor's batting was the feature of the game. The Hercules of the New York team went to the bat five times. He made four safe hits and received his base on called balls once."[69] Connor also recorded his best defensive season to date in 1885, improving his field-ing average by nearly 20 points to .975.

At the conclusion of the 1885 season, the Giants played a series of exhi-bition games against League and Association teams, including one trip to New Orleans for a four-game set with the St. Louis Browns. Major league baseball first came to New Orleans in 1870, when the Cincinnati Red Stock-ings and the Chicago White Stockings came to town to play local amateur clubs.[70] White Stockings manager Tom Foley liked the location so much that he kept his team in town for the remainder of spring training. In 1884 the National League Boston Beaneaters also held their spring training there. Apparently distracted by the attractions of the Crescent City, the Giants did not fare well. "Financially the trip has paid the New Yorks well, but in a playing sense they did very poorly; indeed, they could not well have done worse, as they failed to win a single game out of the four games they played. The best they could do was to tie one of them."[71]After playing third base in the first two contests, Roger Connor packed his bags and went home. New Orleans' horse-racing and casino-gambling lifestyle, which had attracted (and bedeviled) other ballplayers, held no allure for Big Roger. Having passed a "very creditable Civil Service examination,"[72] he spent the remainder of the off-season in a new line of work. "Roger Connor of the New Yorks is filling a position for the winter in the United States public store [U.S. Customs House] in New York. Roger does not fancy New Orleans much for a winter resort and was very glad to return home."[73]

The 1885 season marked the beginning of a six-year period that was the most productive in Connor's career. Over that span he would hit .328 with a slugging percentage of .522. In seasons that were 20 percent shorter than modern campaigns, he would average 157 hits, 111 runs, 25 doubles, 18 triples, 11 home runs, 91 RBIs and 70 walks. In the five years of this six-year period in which stolen bases were counted (1886–1890), he averaged 26 thefts per season.

Roger Connor's journey from obscure minor leaguer to the batting champion of the National League finds a parallel in his life journey from shanty–Irish immigrant child to Waterbury's favorite son. The physical route he took on both these journeys is revealed in the public record of his numerous Waterbury residences during the era. As a child, Connor lived on Stone Street in the "Abrigador," the "Irish Town" section of the Brass City, which was cloistered on the west end, across the river from the finer parts of town. Waterbury City Directories indicate that in 1880, the year he became a major leaguer and started earning a better salary, he had moved to 29 Pleasant Street, just north and west of the Abrigador, and had installed his mother and younger siblings next door at number 27 on the same street.

In the period 1882–1885, during which Connor married Angeline, he took another step out of "Irish Town" by moving a bit further north to Elm Street. At the height of his baseball career, the end of the 1880s, he moved to 302 South Main Street, in the heart of downtown Waterbury. At this point, his personal journey from Shanty Town to Main Street had, both figuratively and literally, been completed. Roger and Angeline then moved seven blocks south, to a spacious three-story home with a rear barn and carriage house at 1014 South Main Street. In its day it was located in an elegant neighborhood, dotted with stately Victorian houses carved into the granite hills that overlook the river. The third story of the Connor home was capped with a unique cupola that sported a handmade weathervane on its crown that consisted of two brass bats and a ball — a gift from Angeline to her husband. In his journey from the "wrong side" of town to Main Street, Connor had not forgotten his family. Records from the 1892 Waterbury Directory reveal that his widowed mother, Catherine, and his sisters, Nellie [Nettie] and Mary, lived a block away, at 915 Main Street. That same year, younger brothers Daniel and Dennis were listed as saloon keepers, the former back on Pleasant Street near the Irish District, and the

Present-day photograph of Roger Connor's South Main Street home in Waterbury, Connecticut. The Connors lived here from 1894 to approximately 1903. A brass weather vane in the shape of two baseball bats crossed over a baseball originally adorned the cupola. The ornament was a gift from Angeline to Roger (courtesy Gary Laios).

latter on East Main Street. In all probability, their benefactor in these endeavors was their oldest brother, Roger.

During this period Roger Connor spent less time in home-town Waterbury, having taken an apartment in Manhattan. During the season most Giants ballplayers lived in the Harlem House hotel at Third Avenue and 115th Street.[74] Thanks to the recollections of an old-time Harlem resident, Alexander Henschel, which were published in the *Times* in 1938, we know that Connor and Angeline, along with Giants team captain John Ward, lived further north in the neighborhood:

> I lived on 120th Street, and as a boy, it was often my privilege to carry Johnny Ward's bat-bag. He and Roger Connor were practically next-door neighbors of mine, living on that street also.... Connor was the only player to hit a ball over any fence in the old Polo Grounds. I remember this distinctly, as you had to go to Clapp and Lynch's saloon on 109th Street and Third Avenue to get scores, and on the way there, would pass several saloons which displayed balls, claiming them to be the "one" that Connor belted out of the park.[75]

The Giants again disappointed in 1886 and 1887, finishing third and fourth respectively. Both the League and the Association agreed to begin adding stolen bases to the official game accounts in 1886. Apparently, the original legislation suggested the regular calculation of each player's stolen base per at-bat average, an idea that was never instituted, but one that gave *Sporting Life* the opportunity to expound on the idea at Roger Connor's expense.

> The averages will be made up from times at bat as compared to bases stolen, and here will be an incentive to a good base runner to "hump it" for first base and get a base on balls when he can, for every time he gets to first he has a chance to make one or two stolen bases. Thus a man like Connor, who leads the league batters, but is a slow base runner, may have a batting average of .380 percent, and yet a base running average of not more than .110 percent, while a moderate batter like [Hugh] Nicol may have a batting record of only .220 percent but a base stealing record of .370 or even higher....[76]

Connor was by no means as slow as reported. He stole 17 bases in the first year they were officially counted, and 43 in 1887. For the remainder of his career he would average more than 20 per season.

The Detroit Wolverines, who had finished last and sixth in the two previous seasons, acquired four players from the disbanded Buffalo club, including Big Dan Brouthers and veteran Deacon White, and shocked the league by finishing second to Chicago in 1886. The Giants still led the circuit in fielding, and they equaled the previous year's batting average, but their pitchers' ERA jumped by more than a run per game, even though

Tim Keefe won 42 contests and Mickey Welch added 33 wins. The team's downfall was the fact that although they loved the confines of the Polo Grounds, where they won 47 games and lost just 12, they fared poorly on the road, winning only 28 of 60 games. Their disappointing third-place finish, 12½ games behind the champion White Stockings, prompted a "poetic" complaint in *The Sporting News*:

> The New Yorks are called the "Giants"
> At the playing of Base-ball
> But the only reason for it
> Is: They cannot play a tall![77]

While Roger Connor's batting average dipped slightly to a still-hefty .355, in nearly every other offensive category except walks (hits, runs, extra-base hits and RBI) his 1886 numbers improved. The most significant increase was in home runs, with his historic September 11 blast out of the

Boston Beaneaters and New York Giants, Opening Day at Polo Grounds I, April 1886. First row, Mickey Welch, center; second row: Giants manager Jim Mutrie in top hat and frock coat, center; John Montgomery Ward, fifth right; Tim Keefe, third right; third row: Roger Connor, center; Jim O'Rourke, second right; Buck Ewing, in black sweater, fourth left. Boston's incorrigible Hoss Radbourn, third row, far left, extends his middle finger to the camera man in an obscene gesture (courtesy Transcendental Graphics/theruckerarchive.com).

Polo Grounds being the most note-worthy. His total of seven four-baggers, tallied over a 92-day period, represents nearly half the total he had hit during the five previous seasons. Some controversy arose in the New York press over conflicting reports of the distance of Connor's September 11 home run The *New York Sun* suggested that it only traveled 305 feet (a physical impossibility, given the trajectory and details outlined previously), while the *New York World* put the distance at 450 feet. Delighting in the New York press's "unreliability," *The Sporting News*, in its first year of publication and eager to establish its reputation for accurate reporting, asserted a definitive distance — 435 feet — for the blast, and humorously blamed Manager Jim Mutrie for the problem. "The difficulty all arose

Roger Connor, 1886, detail from a wood engraving of the Giants team published in Frank Leslie's *Illustrated Newspaper* (courtesy National Baseball Hall of Fame Library, Cooperstown, New York).

through Mutrie's neglect to tie a string to the ball when he saw the ball going over the fence. We could then have measured the string and got the exact distance, and thus avoided the dispute of a distance of 150 feet between the Sun and the World."[78]

In an interview given shortly before his death, Roger Connor spoke gratefully of a memento given him by admiring Giants fans of the era to commemorate the epic September 11 blast: a gold watch, watch case and chain, valued at $250, which the old slugger still carried with him four decades later. The watch case inscription read: "Presented to Roger Conner, First Base, of the New York Base Ball Club, for the unprecedented feat of batting the ball over the 112th Street fence, by the members of the club box." Connor's pithy comment on the gift — "I think a great deal of this watch"[79] — was a typical example of Connor understatement.

Manager Mutrie had made no changes to the 1886 squad from the previous year, but after the team's lackluster showing the Giants skipper cleaned house in 1887. He moved Pete Gillespie from left field to right field and brought Danny Richardson in from center to cover second base.

Composite photograph of the New York Giants, 1886, illustrating well that this was the era of the handlebar moustache (courtesy National Baseball Hall of Fame Library, Cooperstown, New York).

After releasing Mike Dorgan, Dude Esterbrook and Joe Gerhardt, he acquired rookie outfielder "Silent Mike" Tiernan and veteran White Stockings center fielder George Gore.

Born in Saccarappa, Maine (now the town of Westbrook), George "Piano Legs" Gore cut his baseball teeth in New England, where he first met Jim Mutrie. Signing with the White Stockings in 1879, Gore won the national league batting crown (.360) in his sophomore year. A patient leadoff hitter, he led the league three times in walks in an era when as many as nine balls were needed for a free pass to first base. Blessed with great speed, Gore stole seven bases in an 1881 contest, a record that has been equaled only once, by Billy Hamilton in 1894. Hamilton, Gore, and Harry Stovey are the only players in history to score more runs than games played in a career. Gore's great on-field talents were often compromised by his penchant for drinking and carousing, and his old friend Mutrie's gamble on his declining skills proved only marginally successful.

To relieve the tired arms of pitchers Keefe and Welch, Jim Mutrie picked up rookie hurler Bill George and second-year man Ledell "Cannonball" Titcomb. Neither pitcher proved effective, combining for seven wins and 12 losses, and giving up nearly five earned runs per nine innings pitched.

While Roger Connor's batting average dropped dramatically to .285, his power numbers and slugging average remained constant, and his home run production soared to 17, the highest single-season count of his career. He roared out of the gate in 1887, hitting six of his year's total of four-baggers in a span of two weeks, from May 4 to May 19. It was also Connor's best year for triples (22), RBI (104), and stolen bases (43). The notoriety received the previous September after propelling the ball out of the Polo Grounds clearly had a negative effect on Connor's approach at the plate in 1887; he struck out 50 times, the highest count in his career. There was nothing negative about his defense, however. In his third consecutive year at first base, he led the league in chances (1,379) and in fielding average, registering a .993 mark, the best for a first baseman in the gloveless era.

The 1887 Giants were neither a bad team nor a good one. They played .500 baseball or better the entire season, and their longest losing streak was four games. Their offense let them down in the second half of the season, however, when they scored 155 fewer runs than in the first half. With the team floundering in mid–July, Buck Ewing replaced John Ward as team captain. Relieved of his administrative duties, Ward was the one Giant who had a banner year offensively, hitting .338 and stealing 111 bases, both career highs. Ewing's team leadership failed to improve on Ward's, and the Giants finished in fourth place, 10½ games behind Detroit.

Although occasionally praised in the press, Connor's power hitting and new-found home run range, which had made him briefly famous the previous September, went largely unnoticed in 1887. Overshadowed by John Ward's and Buck Ewing's popularity, Ward's mid-season 24-game hitting streak, and Ewing's assumption of the team captaincy, Connor's long-ball efforts were largely ignored by the national press. In a *Sporting Life* report on a 14–3 win against Indianapolis, for example, much was made of the fact that Ewing was still out with a "lame hand,"[80] but nothing was said about Connor's 4-for-5 performance, including his fourth home run in five games. In June, *Sporting Life* reported that "[Chicago's] Mike Kelly already made six home runs,"[81] neglecting to mention that Connor already had slugged eight. A 4-for 5-effort against Washington in September, including a double, triple, walk, two stolen bases and two runs scored, likewise drew no press attention; the same was true of a mid–September

Posed studio photograph of Giants Roger Connor at first base, 1887. As a bare-handed first baseman, Connor led the National League this year at his position, both in total chances (1,379) and fielding average (.993) (courtesy National Base-ball Hall of Fame Library, Cooperstown, New York).

tear during which he collected eight hits, including three home runs and two doubles, in four days. The retiring Connor was not blind to such press treatment, as revealed three decades later in an interview with the *Hartford Courant*'s sports editor, Albert W. Keane. When the *New York World* unearthed the fact that Connor had once hit three home runs in a game against Indianapolis (in 1889), Keane reported that "Roger says he had to hit the three in order to make sure his name appeared in the story of that game."[82]

In November, several League teams made the long train trek to California to play a series of exhibition contests with California League teams. There, Connor's long blasts began again to garner press attention. In a late November matchup with a Los Angeles team, "Connor lost the ball over the roof of a house on Pearle Street.... Perhaps the longest [hit] ever seen."[83] Against San Francisco in December, "Roger Connor drove the ball over the right field fence, a distance of over 460 feet, when he scored his first home run in 'Frisco."[84] Soon afterward, however, the slugger made an unexpected departure from the tour. "Much to the regret of many friends and his comrades, Roger Connor, in response to an urgent telegraphic message from his sick wife, has departed from these shores and Dan Brouthers telegraphed for. He will have to be immense, in more than the physical sense, to fill the 'aching void' caused by Connor's withdrawal."[85]

While Roger's long-ball hitting had not captured the attention of the eastern press during the season, his departure from California in December did. *Sporting Life*, in an article entitled "Why Roger Connor Left San Francisco Early," noted that

> It is rumored that Roger Connor had other reasons than the illness of his wife for his abrupt departure home. It seems that he had an altercation with Charley Sweeney in which the latter, to offset the shoulder hitting of Connor, produced a little hole puncher [pistol] which frightened Roger — as though a band of Apaches were on his trail, and he departed for home the next day without even bidding his companions good-by.[86]

Sweeney's history suggests that there may have been some truth to the report. A native San Franciscan, Charley Sweeney debuted with Providence as the second man of a two-man rotation whose other member was Hoss Radbourn. Although possessing a blazing fastball, Sweeney's drunkenness and open disputes with manager Frank Bancroft resulted in his expulsion from the National League in 1884. Reinstated the following year, arm trouble, drinking bouts, and his frequent assault of other players ended his major league career in 1887. Seven years later, he shot and killed an acquaintance in a San Francisco bar, and was sentenced to 10 years imprisonment. He did not live to complete the sentence, dying of tuberculosis in 1902.[87]

Despite Sweeney's character and history, Roger Connor denied "that he was chased out of California by Sweeney and his pistol. He says that he simply was homesick and came home."[88] Perhaps there is a bit of truth in each of these reports. Given his early departure from New Orleans the previous year, it is clear that Roger eschewed the rowdy lifestyle that many players followed on such junkets. He may have just wanted to go home, and used that fact or the fiction of a sick relative as an excuse. Charley Sweeney's history clearly suggests that some threats by him also may have helped in Connor's decision-making.

The last two years of the 1880s would bring the Giants success in the quest for a pennant, but would see the team evicted from the original Polo Grounds and forced to play a portion of their schedule at the St. George's Cricket Grounds on Staten Island. These years would mark the height of Roger Connor's career, as the big slugger crossed into his early 30s. They were also years of personal joy and tragedy for him and Angeline. This era was the calm before the storm for major league baseball, which would soon be engaged in the last interleague struggle of the century.

After spring training and barnstorming sessions in Florida, during which they played exhibition contests in St. Augustine, Gainesville, and Jacksonville, the Giants returned home to start the 1888 season amid rumors that the city planned to extend 111th Street through the existing Polo Grounds site. As the season progressed, the press regularly reported on John Day's efforts to find a new location for the team. Speculation focused on a site at "about One Hundred Thirty-Eighth Street and Tenth Avenue,"[89] where the proposed new grandstand would "cast the Philadelphia and Boston structures in the shade."[90]

John Ward and Tim Keefe were holdouts, each demanding $5,000 salaries. Ward also sought release from his reserve clause. He signed on Opening Day for $1000 less, with his reserved status unchanged. Keefe held out for a week longer and then signed for the same amount as Ward. Roger Connor was reported as looking "as fine as silk,"[91] and regularly using his familiar "pop-up" slide to good advantage.

> Connor is beginning to find the ball with that powerful stick he wields, and his friends rejoice with him. He slides to the bases on the bosom of his pants in his old peculiar way. The slide may not seem to be the most graceful thing in the world, but he seems to "get there all the same." The club does not object at the style, and I am sure the tailor does not, so that if big Roger will continue his stern wheel slides, he will gain friends every day. He gets over the ground this year with a great deal of speed for a man of his bulk.[92]

By 1888, pitchers had adjusted to the previous year's rule requiring them to keep one foot planted on the back line of the pitcher's box, and were

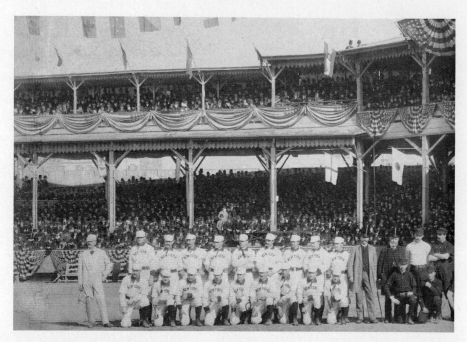

Opening Day at Polo Grounds I, 1888, New York versus Philadelphia. This is the left half of a panoramic shot that originally included the Phillies team (dressed in black). The two men in top hats on the right are Harry Wright (white beard), manager of the Phillies, and Jim Mutrie, manager of the Giants. The magnificent wooden grandstand in the background was demolished at the end of the season after New York City evicted the Giants from the original Polo Grounds to make way for the construction of 111th Street (courtesy National Baseball Hall of Fame Library, Cooperstown, New York).

taking advantage of the enlarged strike zone (top of the shoulders to bottom of the knees) and their new freedom to throw overhand. As a result, the League batting average dropped 30 points[93] and pitchers issued 640 fewer walks than the prior season.

The Giants spent the first two months experimenting with lineup changes until they acquired light-hitting, slick-fielding infielder Art Whitney from Pittsburgh in June. Outfielder George Gore was benched and Jim O'Rourke took over his position in left field. Union Association veteran Mike Slattery moved into center, with Mike Tiernan covering right. Newcomer Whitney took up residence at the hot corner, John Ward played shortstop, Danny Richardson and Roger Connor secured the right side of the infield, and Captain Buck Ewing did the catching. Keefe and Welch did most of the pitching, and were assisted by two "Cannonballs"—Ledell "Cannonball"

Titcomb and newcomer Ed "Cannonball" Crane.

In late July the Giants introduced their new, form-fitting, all-black uniforms, which John Day had purchased from Tim Keefe's new Manhattan sporting goods firm. "The New York men wore their new 'Nadjy' uniforms for the first time and made a fine appearance in tight fitting black jersey suits with white belts and white letters on the shirts."[94] *Nadjy* was the title of a popular operetta that debuted on May14 on Broadway, in which actress Fanny Rice (not to be confused with actress Fanny Brice) created a sensation by appearing in an all-black ballerina costume. The new uniforms apparently worked their magic. Tim Keefe won 19 consecutive games from June 23 to August 10, and the Giants maintained a comfortable lead over Chicago during the final months of the campaign. In the sixth season of the franchise's existence, New York won its first pennant.

A few days after Keefe's winning streak ended in August, the Giants and the rival Chicago

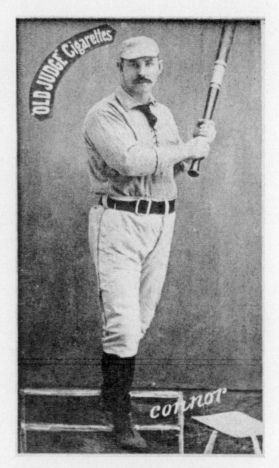

A stout Roger Connor wielding his big bat, late 1880s. The *Philadelphia Inquirer* described Connor's lumber as a "small telegraph pole" (courtesy National Baseball Hall of Fame Library, Cooperstown, New York).

White Stockings team attended a Broadway show together, after a game in which Anson's squad defeated Jim Mutrie's nine. A brief portion of the performance they witnessed at Wallack's Theater that evening is now a part of baseball history. In order to explain how that came about, we must travel back a few years and change location to the campus of Harvard University.

Ernest Lawrence Thayer, the frail, sickly heir to his father's wool mill and banking fortunes, matriculated at Harvard in the early 1880s. Despite

New York Giants Base Ball Club, 1888, winner of the National League pennant and the World's Series against the American Association St. Louis Browns (courtesy National Baseball Hall of Fame Library, Cooperstown, New York).

his weak physical constitution, Thayer possessed a fine sense of humor, so much so that in his senior year he became editor of the *Harvard Lampoon*. At the *Lampoon*, he befriended the publication's business manager, William Randolph Hearst. A few years later, Hearst assumed directorship of his father's newspaper, the *San Francisco Examiner*, and invited Harvard school-mate Thayer to contribute regular humorous pieces for the newspaper. On June 3, 1888, Thayer's poem, "Casey at the Bat, A Ballad of the Republic," appeared in the *Examiner*. He was paid five dollars for the entry, which was soon forgotten. Or so it was thought.

Two months later, the cast of Johann Strauss's operetta, *Prince Methusalem*, attended a ballgame between the Giants and the White Stockings at the Polo Grounds that the Giants lost, 4–2. One of the actors in the cast, DeWitt Hopper, a rabid baseball fan, convinced his company director to invite both teams to that evening's performance of the play. Hopper then began a frantic search to find a special theatrical piece to present to the baseball guests that evening. Author Archibald Clavering Gunter, a friend of Hopper's who was visiting him at the time, remembered Thayer's poem, which he had read while in San Francisco, clipped out of the newspaper, and placed in his wallet. During an intermission or after the performance that evening (accounts differ), Hopper walked on stage with his friend's newspaper clipping in hand and recited the poem that we know today simply as "Casey at the Bat." The audience, and in particular the ballplayers, went wild, clapping and cheering until they were hoarse.

The *San Francisco Examiner* subsequently syndicated the poem and it became a sensation across the country. Hopper recited it more than 10,000 times over the course of his long stage career.

Roger Connor's overall 1888 offensive numbers slipped slightly from the previous year, but his .291 batting average, accomplished in a season in which league averages dropped precipitously and only seven men reached the .300 mark, was tenth-best in the circuit. He hit eight of his year's total of 11 home runs in the month of May, including two over the right field fence off Indianapolis's "Handsome Henry" Boyle on May 5. These were followed by three in one game on May 9, again against the Hoosiers. Lanky, 6'2" John "Egyptian" Healy gave up the first two in successive innings, and 5'8" Jack McGeachy surrendered the final blow in the seventh inning. With the trio of blasts against Indianapolis, Connor became only the sixth man to perform such a feat. After cooling off in June, when he hit only one four-bagger, Connor stroked five more between mid–July and mid–August, ending the season with a total of 14. His homer off Hoss Radbourn at Boston on August 2 prompted an admiring observation from the *Boston Daily Globe*: "With two men on base in the first inning, Roger caught a rising ball about shoulder high, he knocked the curve out of it, away it sailed over the houses in [beyond] right field. The Connecticut boy went around the bases in much the same style as a six day pedestrian on the last day. The match was settled on that one hit."[95]

Although the National League had significantly increased the size of the strike zone the previous year — from a low or high zone from which a hitter could choose, to a full-body zone from the top of the shoulders to the bottom of the knees — paradoxically, the number of Roger Connor's walks continued to increase, a clear indication of his good eye at the plate. He led the league in 1888 with 73 walks, a factor that contributed to his on-base-plus-slugging (OPS) percentage of .869, third-best in the League. Defensively, Connor finished the season second to Cap Anson among League first basemen, with a .982 average.

Despite such significant offensive and defensive contributions to the team, Connor's accomplishments were rarely touted by the press, which credited the success of the Giants to the "Big Three"— Ewing, Keefe, and Welch: "Giants Doing Great Work—All Well as Long as The Big Three Hold Out."[96] Several city newspapers "carried a cartoon showing Mutrie for Governor, Ewing for Mayor, and Orator Jim O'Rourke for District Attorney."[97] Connor didn't figure among the imagined dignitaries. His three-home-run game in May was treated as a routine event by the *New York Times*: "Denny of the home team batted out a home run, while Connor made three of them for New York."[98] Four days earlier, his three-hit, two-run performance against the Hoosiers, including two home runs, wasn't even mentioned by the *Times*. *Sporting Life's* May 16 accounts of these two games, in which Connor hit a total of five home runs, contained no mention of them. In October, *The Sporting News* printed an article in which several Giants explained "How They Won the League Pennant This Year."[99] Participants included O'Rourke, Whitney, Crane, Gore, Ward, and others, but, either by accident or design, the account included no comments by Roger Connor.

Despite such continued slights by the press, there was joyous news for Connor from home in 1888. At midseason, Angeline had given birth to the couple's first child, a daughter, whom they named Lulu. In 1976, Connor's granddaughter, Margaret Colwell, asserted that the child's unusual name was chosen because it was "a fashionable name at that time."[100] The history of a young Georgia adolescent named Lulu Hurst provides a possible explanation for Angeline and Roger's decision to name their daughter Lulu, and offers us a brief but fascinating glimpse of Victorian-era popular culture.

In rural Georgia in the early 1880s, a slender 14-year-old girl of "an extremely nervous temperament"[101] began exhibiting strange powers that enabled her to move objects such as chairs without touching them. She also demonstrated enormous strength. " Lulu had three men sit stacked in a chair. She grasped the legs and lifted the whole configuration several inches off the floor."[102] At Alexander Graham Bell's laboratory in Washington, she lifted a 200-pound man off the floor. "The inexplicable aspect of that exercise was that Lulu was perched on a pair of scales, while the man was seated on a chair beside them. Yet, while she lifted the man, only *his* weight registered on the scales. The scientists double checked, weighing the two individuals separately."[103]

For several years Lulu Hurst gave demonstrations of her abilities across the country, and in the summer of 1884 she brought her act to Wallack's Theater on Broadway, the same theater at which Roger Connor and his teammates heard DeWitt Hopper give the first recitation of "Casey at the

Bat." After a few years on the road, Lulu Hurst retired, living the rest of her life in relative seclusion and dismissing her unusual abilities as nothing more than "unrecognized mechanical principles."[104] During and after her heyday, however, soap and cigar manufacturers paid Lulu well for the use of her name in their print advertisements, and for years, farmers plowed with implements touted to be "strong as Lulu Hurst."[105]

Lulu's brief period of national popularity and recognition coincides with Roger Connor's years with the Giants. Her appearance at Wallack's Theater, an establishment frequented by the Giants after their games, her exhibition of apparent superhuman strength, reminiscent of that of the "Hercules" of the Giants, and her press popularity both in articles and advertisements, plausibly suggests that the Connors found her name appropriate for their infant daughter.

At the conclusion of the 1888 season, John Day and Chris Von der Ahe, owner of the American Association pennant-winning St. Louis Browns, agreed to a ten-game "World's Series" to determine the champion of major league baseball. Although a winner would be declared after one team won six games, all 10 were to be played for obvious financial considerations. After splitting the first two contests at the Polo Grounds, the Giants won the third game there, a fourth played in Brooklyn, and a fifth played again back at the Polo Grounds. The opponents then went on the road, with the Giants winning the sixth game in Philadelphia, and finishing the series in St. Louis, where they won the deciding game and lost three others. No one imagined at the time that the final game of the series held at the Polo Grounds on October 20 would be the last game the team would ever play at that venue.

Big Roger Connor played in the first seven games of series, hitting .333, but then retired due to an injury. "Connor's leg was so badly sprained that he could play no more."[106] The Browns were more than happy to see him out of the lineup, since he already had collected a double, two triples, four walks, and four stolen bases.

According to an initial report in *Sporting Life*, the injury did not prevent Big Roger from saving a damsel in distress.

Just before the departure of the ball train from Pittsburgh, Mrs. Helen Duvray [*sic*] Ward [John Ward's actress wife] had a narrow escape from death on the Union Depot platform. She was walking up and down when suddenly an iron girder from the shed above on which several men were working fell, and would have crushed her but not for Roger Conner [*sic*] who caught it by one end and swung it to one side to save the lady's life.[107]

In its next number, however, the red-faced publication issued a retraction of the story, declaring that it "turns out to have been a blooming fake."[108] *Sporting Life*'s eagerness to print the unsubstantiated report of Connor's dramatic rescue effort after failing to provide any coverage or comment on the slugger's earlier three home run game at Indianapolis was a telling reminder of the fickleness of the press.

During the final months of the 1888 season, White Stockings owner and sporting goods magnate Al Spalding had been organizing a world tour of American baseball that would feature his own team and a "picked nine," dubbed the "All Americans," captained by John Ward. Spalding's aim was twofold: to spread interest in baseball around the globe, and to create a world market for his sporting goods products. This was the White Stockings owner's second participation in such a venture. As a star pitcher in 1874, he had toured Britain on a Boston and Philadelphia National Association exhibition trip organized by Harry Wright.

Spalding's 1888–1889 international tour left Chicago in late October, barnstormed in the western U.S. for a month and then sailed the Pacific, playing contests in Hawaii, New Zealand, Australia, Ceylon, Egypt, Italy, France, and the British Isles, and returning to the United States on April 7, 1889. For his squads, Spalding chose "men of clean living and attractive personality, men who would reflect credit upon the country and the game."[109] Roger Connor fit this description perfectly, but given his penchant during the two previous winters for abandoning off-season play before completing the schedule, it is doubtful he was considered for participation by Spalding.

Four days after the tour set sail for Hawaii from San Francisco, with Brotherhood President John Ward safely on board, the National League passed legislation that capped player salaries at $2,500 and grouped all players into five salary categories ranging from a low of $1,500 to a high of $2,500. Spalding, of course, was in on the deceit. This action would precipitate the Players' League revolt against the League and the Association at the end of the following season.

Where would the Giants play in 1889? The question was on the minds of John Day, Jim Mutrie, players and fans as the season approached. *Sporting Life*, remarking on "The Trials of the Homeless Giants," criticized owner Day for "not looking further ahead."[110] Since the previous summer, however, Day had made every possible legal effort to stop the city from cutting a new street through the heart of the Polo Grounds, all to no avail. In March, desperate to find a temporary playing field, he settled on two locations:

Oakland Park in Jersey City, and the St. George's Cricket Grounds on Staten Island, which had served as the home of the now disbanded Metropolitans during their last two seasons in the American Association.

After two games in cramped Oakland Park, Day scheduled all remaining games at the Staten Island location. Each of the 23 contests played there was an adventure. "The previous year the outfield area had been used for a theatrical production, leaving it bereft of grass. Scaffolding for the backdrop of the stage was still up, in some parts infringing on the playing field."[111] Even Mother Nature seemed to conspire against the Giants. Persistent heavy spring rains regularly flooded the outfield, forcing fielders to maneuver around wooden planks that had been placed over the soggiest areas. Attendance dropped precipitously at St. George's, located 20 miles south of the Polo Grounds: "Many New Yorkers prefer going to the Brooklyn games to taking the long [train and ferry] ride to Staten Island."[112]

On the first day of summer, a home for the Giants was found when John Day signed a contract with real estate entrepreneur James J. Coogan to lease the southern portion of a plot of land at 155th Street and Eighth Avenue. The site sloped down to the Harlem River from a steep embankment that eventually became known as Coogan's Bluff. Dubbed the "New Polo Grounds" by Day, the field was conveniently located just a few yards from the Eighth Avenue elevated station. The decision to locate the ballpark beneath Coogan's Bluff had an unanticipated downside, as the *Chicago Daily Tribune* noted: "The bluffs overlooking the grounds were black with people. Fully 2,000 spectators witnessed the game free of charge."[113] Two years later, the Giants would move their field a few yards north to a site at Coogan's Hollow not originally leased by John Day. This would be the team's home for the next 67 seasons.

Personnel matters were as unsettled as the issue of playing fields for the 1889 Giants. John Ward and Tim Keefe were again holdouts. Rumors about Ward's desire to leave the Giants had circulated even before he left on Al Spalding's World Tour, with Washington and Boston listed as potential destinations. The *Chicago Tribune* suggested that the Giants' former captain didn't get along with some of his teammates. "Ward is not liked by the members of the champions. Ewing, O'Rourke, Keefe, and others never speak to him."[114] Still smarting from the salary policy that the League conveniently had instituted while he, the President of the Brotherhood Union, was out of the country, Ward was now actively developing plans for Players' League competition during the following season. He ended speculation by signing again with the Giants on Opening Day. In June, however, he left the team for nearly three weeks, complaining of a sore arm, and did not return until the opener at the New Polo Grounds on July 8. It would soon become apparent that during his recuperation he was doing more than just resting his shoulder.

Tim Keefe held out for the first two weeks of the season. Retuning out of shape, he hurt his arm and pitched in only four games before June. Ledell "Cannonball" Titcomb, who had won 14 games for the team in 1888, performed so poorly in his first three starts — giving up 26 runs in his first 26 innings — that he was released in early May. Such early pitching woes forced Jim Mutrie to be creative, enlisting Buck Ewing and utility infielder Gil Hatfield as pitchers. A month into the season, besides Keefe's sore arm, Mickey Welch was complaining of a strained back, Cannonball Crane was disabled by a strained knee, and outfielders George Gore and Mike Slattery had leg injuries.

The 1889 pennant race would be the closest and most exciting thus far in National League history. The Boston Beaneaters, featuring former White Stockings star and Troy, New York, native Mike Kelly and pitchers Hoss Radbourn and John Clarkson, were fortified by the acquisition of Big Dan Brouthers from Detroit. Brouthers would lead the league in hitting (.373) and the temperamental Clarkson would win "everything but the pennant,"[115] taking league honors in wins (49), strikeouts (284) and ERA (2.73). The formerly itinerant Giants settled in nicely at the New Polo Grounds, winning nine of their first ten games there, and moving into second place behind the Beaneaters. By mid–September, a 12-game win streak left them a half-game ahead of Boston. After the games of October 4, with both teams down to their last game, the Giants' record was 82–43; the Beaneaters were 83–44. Boston then lost to Pittsburgh while the Giants defeated Cleveland to win the pennant by a won-lost percentage margin of .659 to .648.

While Tim Keefe and Mickey Welch's combined 55 wins brought the Giants the pennant, the pitching stars of the World's Series against the Association's Brooklyn Bridegrooms were little-known backups, Ed "Cannonball" Crane and Hank O'Day. Crane pitched four games in the nine-game series, winning three. O'Day, who was 2–10 when acquired from Washington at mid-season, went 9–1 with the Giants down the stretch, won a masterfully-pitched 11-inning decision over Brooklyn's Adonis Terry in the sixth game of the series, and won the deciding game, 3–1. After retiring as a player, O'Day spent 32 years as an umpire, officiating in more than 4,000 major league games. Crane's fame was short-lived. A powerfully built fireballer who once won a contest by throwing a baseball a distance of 406 feet, he pitched for eight major league seasons in four leagues: the Union and the American Associations, and the National and Players' Leagues. Plagued by alcohol abuse, Crane committed suicide by drinking chloric acid in 1896. He was 34 years old.

The Giants lost the Polo Grounds in 1889; Angeline and Roger Connor lost their infant daughter. In 1976, the couple's granddaughter, Margaret Colwell, recounted the sad event and the subsequent guilt that plagued Roger:

> On their fifth wedding anniversary a baby was born. They called her Lulu, a fashionable name at that time. The happiest man in the world was Grandpa [Roger].... Their happiness was short lived. Nana [Angeline] and Lulu had been travelling with Grandpa and the baby contracted dysentery, a fatal attack, her death coming just before her first birthday. Grandpa thought he was being punished by the Lord above for neglecting to have his daughter baptized.[116]

Despite the trauma of his daughter's death and the unsettling lack of a permanent home playing field for the first half of the season, Connor had an outstanding year in 1889. He hit 13 home runs, raised his batting average 26 points to .317, and led the league in slugging (.528), RBI (130), and extra-base hits (62). The press seemed to take greater interest in Connor this year, in part due to the "tape-measure" status of some of his home runs, and in part because some of their more regular attractions, John Ward and Tim Keefe, were either preoccupied with Brotherhood business or sidelined with sore arms. Connor drew high praise in the *Times* for his fourth home run of the year, hit off of Charley Geitzen, at Indianapolis. "He set [*sic*] a ball out of the grounds like a rifle shot in the sixth inning, making the longest hit ever seen in this city.... Connor succeeded in losing the ball. He hit the buckskin with all his might and to the intense joy of his club mates it sailed far over the fence and landed about a block away from the grounds."[117] On July 10 against Pittsburgh, Connor christened the New Polo Grounds, hitting the first home run in the new park over the center field fence, 360 feet away. "Connor made the first home run over the fence and will get the gold medal."[118] Two other notable home runs were the June 26 blast over the right field wall at West Side Park and onto Harrison Street in Chicago, and a July 23 drive over the 25-foot-high fence in right field at Philadelphia that bounced onto Broad Street.

Connor's offensive displays increasingly were not limited to four-baggers. The stolen base, the walk and the sacrifice, alone or in combinations, were weapons that he used as frequently as the long ball. In one May win against Chicago, he recorded only one hit, but also walked, stole two bases, and scored two runs. The next day he hit two doubles, scored a run, and stole a base. In August against Indianapolis, he went 2-for-4, with a double, a stolen base and a sacrifice, scoring two runs. Having reached his highest home run total (17) in 1887, Roger, now entering his mid–30s, had become a more patient hitter. Consequently, while still considered a long-ball threat, he was also adept at beating opponents by means of multiple strategies. The fans and the press seemed to sense this new direction, as evidenced by the account of a game-winning, walk-off hit against Philadelphia in June. With the score tied 2–2 in the bottom of the ninth, John Ward doubled and then stole third base. "An air of confidence seemed to pervade the atmosphere when the biggest of the Giants, Roger Connor, grabbed his bat and walked to the plate. In the vernacular of the profession he hit the ball 'square in the nose' sent in Ward, won the game, [and] caused a feeling of joy to reign in the hearts of the spectators."[119]

Connor's fine overall play continued through the World Series. He "did brilliant work in the field"[120] and hit .343, including a 3-for-4 performance in the eighth game, in which he tripled, sacrificed, stole a base and scored two runs.

The enthusiastic festivities that were organized to celebrate the Giants' 1889 World's Series victory were overshadowed by the revelation a few weeks earlier of the Brotherhood's intent to challenge the American Association and National League's monopoly of major league baseball by fielding a new league The Sunday, October 20, World's Series victory dinner for the Giants was held at a Broadway theater, and the long and varied program that followed, a wild hodge-podge of theatrical tributes, included songs, recitations, an aria, a banjo duet, and a concertina solo. The tuxedo-clad ballplayers divided more than $3,000 in proceeds from the event. There were "cheers for Buck Ewing, Tim Keefe, Mickey Welch, and John Ward,"[121] and general accolades for the remaining players. Unlike his future Hall of Fame teammates, however, Roger Connor, the quiet Giant, was not singled out for special praise.

The celebration ended in the wee hours of the morning, and the team then split up and headed for their home towns. Having full knowledge of the coming year's confrontation between the players and the leagues, there must have been a moment of realization among the six men who had made the entire seven-year journey of the Giants from first-year franchise to World Champion — Day, Mutrie, Connor, Ewing, Ward, and Welch — that they were witnessing the end of an era.

4

—*w*—

The Brotherhood Rebel

"There isn't enough money in New York to buy me to jump my contract with the Brotherhood."
— Roger Connor, *Sporting Life*, January 8, 1890

A league of their own. In 1890, for the first time in 15 years, professional ballplayers were able to ply their trade — although with considerable risk to their futures — in a league they had helped organize and over which they had some control. True to his character and personality, Roger Connor was never a general in the Brotherhood battle against the League and the Association, but he was always a loyal soldier.

The seeds of player discontent that led to the Players' League war were first planted in 1879, when the National League established the reserve clause. Players' frustrations grew when they subsequently realized that they were prevented from selling their services to other teams and leagues without being blacklisted. The 1883 National Agreement between the League and the Association, by which each pledged to honor the other's player contracts, and the failure of the Union Association in 1884, added a sense of desperation to the players' plight.

By 1885, the National League felt confident enough to expand the reserve clause from 5 to 12 players per team, to make it, "perpetual, simply rolling over year after year,"[1] and to impose the "Limit Agreement," a salary cap of $2,000. These moves proved to be the breaking point for John Ward, who was completing his law studies at Columbia University. Four days after the announcement of the Limit Agreement, Ward, Roger Connor, and seven other Giants players formed the Brotherhood of Professional Base Ball Players, whose stated aims were:

95

To protect and benefit ourselves both collectively and individually.
To promote high standards of professional conduct.
To foster and encourage the interests of the game of base ball.[2]

While the Brotherhood's goals seemed innocuous, the timing of their formulation and the fact that their organization's existence was kept secret for nearly a year suggests that there were ulterior motives for its founding. On their road trips and at home during the 1886 season, the Brotherhood's charter members met clandestinely off the playing field with their league opponents from other cities and enlisted most of them in the cause. Players from Detroit, Chicago, Kansas City and St. Louis teams joined in May. Philadelphia, Washington, and Pittsburgh players signed on in July and August. At the close of the 1886 season the Brotherhood made its existence known to the public. John Ward was named President and Dan Brouthers was selected as Vice President. Tim Keefe, who had "practiced short hand at night in his hotel room rather than carouse with his teammates,"[3] was elected Secretary.

In August 1887, Ward heightened his publicity campaign by publishing the essay "Is the Base Ball Player a Chattel?" in *Lippincott's Magazine of Popular Science and Literature*, a widely-read monthly journal. The magazine gained fame three years later for introducing American readers to Sherlock Holmes (Arthur Conan Doyle's "The Sign of Four") and Oscar Wilde ("The Picture of Dorian Gray"). Ward's elegantly written 4,000-word article provided a history of the conflicts between baseball owners and players and a blistering critique of the reserve clause.

> Like a fugitive-slave law, the reserve rule denies him [a player who seeks to evade the reserve rule] a harbor or a livelihood, and carries him back, bound and shackled, to the club from which he attempted to escape. We have then, the curious result of a contract which on its face is for seven months being binding for life, and when the player's name is attached thereto his personal liberty is gone forever.[4]

Ward's conclusion left no doubt about the Brotherhood's resolve to address its complaints against the League. "Whence shall the remedy proceed?... Shall it come from the clubs or from the players.... If the clubs cannot find a way out of these difficulties the players will try to do it for them."[5] As previously noted, the League's November 1888, response to such rhetoric was punitive; it established a salary classification system known as the "Brush Plan," so named for its creator, John T. Brush, then owner of the Indianapolis Hoosiers. The Plan was doubly offensive to the players, since it not only sought to pay them according to a League evaluation of their performance on the diamond, but also included in the mix an assessment of each man's personal conduct both on and off the field.

All attempts by the Brotherhood to meet with owners over these issues during the first months of the 1889 season were rebuffed. On July 14, as Brotherhood representatives met in New York, John Ward revealed to them a plan to form a new league. By September, word of the plan had leaked out, and Ward called a press conference with the editors of *Sporting Life* and *The Sporting News* to clarify the Brotherhood's intentions. Players, however, "did not entirely trust the press to deliver their stories to the public,"[6] so they endeavored on their own to shore up support for the coming conflict. They sought and received backing from Samuel Gompers' American Federation of Labor and other smaller unions, from several universities, including Princeton and Yale, and from the Benevolent and Protective Order of Elks, which passed a resolution in support of the new league.[7] After retiring from the game, Roger Connor, a loyal member of the Elks, worked tirelessly for the Waterbury chapter by organizing baseball leagues and participating in fundraisers.

Four months after their "Bastille Day" secret meeting on July 14, the Brotherhood formally went public with its "Brotherhood Manifesto," concluding: "We began organizing for ourselves and are in shape to go ahead next year under new management and new auspices."[8] *Sporting Life* reported that Roger Connor was among the 34 players who attended and "assisted in forming a new league."[9]

Months of intense planning and organization had resulted in the creation of an eight-team league, with clubs placed in six cities with existing National League teams, as well as in Brooklyn and Buffalo. The League was governed by a 16-man Senate made up of two players from each team. The Senate elected two from its ranks as President and Vice President. An eight-man board consisting of four players and four financial backers governed each club. Each player was asked to invest a minimum of $500 in his club by purchasing stock shares valued at $100 per share. Roger Connor purchased $1,000 of stock shares "in hard cash."[10] Teams would divide attendance receipts equally; concession stand earnings were reserved for the home team. The classification system and the blacklist were abolished. The reserve system was eliminated and replaced with one-year contracts that were renewable for two years.

Despite the Players' League's symbolic association with and appeals to the working man, and the moral support that it received from many unions, it declined to condone Sunday baseball or liquor sales at its games, and charged a 50-cent admission. In siding with the National League's position on these issues, the new league missed an opportunity to attract and gain the loyalty of large numbers of working-class fans to their ballparks.

The National League responded to the news of the birth of the rival league by seeking an injunction from the New York State Supreme Court to prevent John Ward from playing on any team but the League's Giants. In late January the injunction was denied. Further legal maneuvers against other players, including a U.S. Circuit Court request for an injunction against Buck Ewing, also failed. In lieu of the threat of legal action, Giants owner John Day sought to entice Roger Connor and others to desert the Brotherhood by means of personal persuasion or bribery. His efforts succeeded in some cases, but fell on deaf ears with Connor.

> Mr. Day came up to Waterbury from New York yesterday to convert Mr. Connor to a more favorable impression of the League, but he did not get an opportunity as the New York's first baseman was as immovable as a mountain. Connor told Mr. Day that he cared not what [Silent Mike] Tiernan or any other player did, that he had signed with the Brotherhood and was going to stay with that organization to the last.... Connor has abundant faith in the Brotherhood and very little faith in such backsliders as he termed Tiernan and [Smiling Mickey] Welch, if the story that Welch is weakening, which is current here now and was endorsed by Mr. Day is true. Mr. Day ... left for New York this morning looking somewhat discouraged.[11]

The Waterbury star's unwavering position earned him a new nickname from *Sporting Life*: "Connor — The Oak."[12]

In early January, while Day and other National League owners continued to pressure players who had jumped from their teams to join the new league, word came of "a great coup," the defection of St. Louis Browns player-manager Charlie Comiskey.[13] "The Old Roman," as the Chicago native was known, had signed on with Chris Von der Ahe's American Association St. Louis Browns for the first season of Association play in 1882. A fine first baseman and average hitter, he was known for his aggressive play. He captained and player-managed Von der Ahe's team for five years, leading them to four successive Association pennants (1885–1888) and an 1886 World's Series win against the Chicago White Stockings. Along the way he earned the unsavory reputation of being one of the most vicious umpire baiters in baseball. Ultimately frustrated by Von der Ahe's day-to-day meddling in team matters and penchant for selling star players in order to pay debts, Comiskey jumped to the Players' League Chicago Pirates in 1890. He later owned and managed the Western League's St. Paul franchise for five years until the advent of a new League, the American, in 1901, allowed him to return home to Chicago as owner of their American League entry. His American League White Stockings, rechristened the White Sox subsequently won three pennants during his life-time.

The ironic counterpoise between Comiskey's avowed player-rights position in 1890 and his later career as a dictatorial owner who underpaid players finds a parallel in the figure of a tall, gangly catcher, an early and fervent convert to the Players' League, who later managed and owned a major league team for a half-century. A light-hitting, good-fielding backstop from East Brookfield, Massachusetts, Cornelius Alexander McGillicuddy (Connie Mack) was a fan favorite who was not above chatting with batters to distract them or even tipping their bats as they swung. He began his career with Washington, invested and lost his life savings in the Players' League Buffalo franchise, and then moved on to Pittsburgh. Mack found his true calling when given a chance by Western League President Byron "Ban" Johnson to player-manage Milwaukee in 1897. When Johnson formed the American League in 1901, Mack joined him as owner-manager of the Philadelphia Athletics. He retired from that position in 1950 at age 88, having managed for more than 50 years. Frustrated by the salary cap and the reserve clause while with Washington, Mack became an early supporter of the Players' League, but later he became notorious for his tight-fistedness as an owner-manager. As a baseball magnate, he likewise found the reserve clause to his liking.

The rebel league's elation over the enlistment of the likes of Comiskey and Mack was muted by the defection of star pitcher John Clarkson. The Cambridge, Massachusetts, native shared laurels with Hoss Radbourn as the best pitching duo in baseball during the 1880s. Trained in the family watchmaking and jewelry trade, Clarkson's approach was the antithesis of fireballer Radbourn's. The slender right-hander possessed a fine curve ball, a rising fastball, and a change-up. He had excellent control and a thorough knowledge of the weaknesses of each hitter. Pitching around the best of them, he coaxed the rest into putting "the ball in play for his infielders to do their job."[14]

In his first full season in the major leagues, 1885, Clarkson won 53 games and lost 16 for the White Stockings, led the league in strikeouts (308) and posted a 1.85 ERA. For the next seven seasons he averaged 34 wins a year, reaching a high of 49 in 1889 and never falling below 25. Traded to Boston in 1888, he won 82 games in two years before defecting to the Players' League. His initial enthusiasm for the movement, however, was short-lived. "I am with the boys, and if it is in my best interests to go with them I shall do so. But I am not bound."[15]

Soon after the November 1889, Brotherhood Manifesto became public, Clarkson secretly began backtracking. He eventually signed a three-year contract with the National League Bostons for $25,000, an unprecedented sum in the era, and then added insult to injury by actively encouraging other Players' League rebels to return to the National League fold. His efforts in this regard brought second baseman Charles "Pop" Smith and catchers Charlie Ganzel and Charlie Bennett back to Boston's National League Beaneaters. Clarkson's treachery earned him the perpetual enmity of his former Players' League comrades. He was reviled and shunned by his Cleveland teammates, where he ended his career in 1894, and where it was reported that his infielders "refused to field balls behind him in an attempt to drive him off the team"[16] A decade after retiring from the major leagues, the quiet, methodical Clarkson was institutionalized for a nervous breakdown. He died in a Massachusetts psychiatric hospital in 1909, at age 47.

In mid–January 1890, the Players' League Giants leased a plot of land adjacent to the New Polo Grounds at Eighth Avenue and 157th Street in Manhattan. A year earlier, Jim Mutrie had the option of leasing this parcel along with the one he chose for the New Polo Grounds. He demurred. Other Players' League teams would play in the same cities as their National League rivals. New York's team would play next door to their National League rival. Other teams would adopt new nicknames: Boston Reds, Chicago Pirates, Philadelphia Quakers, Pittsburgh Burghers, and Cleveland Infants. New York's Players' League team added insult to injury by adopting the same nickname, the "Giants," as their National League counterparts. When league schedules were released in mid–April, it was noted that in New York, whose parks were "side by side ... nearly every one of their home games conflict."[17]

Of the 123 players on Players' League team rosters in April 1890,[18] more than 100 had previous major league experience. In the year that the Brotherhood had been secretly signing players, however, some of them — Clarkson, Mickey Welch and Mike Tiernan — jumped back to the National League before the start of the season. Another, Indianapolis's Jack Glassock, a hard-hitting, West Virginia-born shortstop who had already played in two leagues and for four teams before he signed with the Brotherhood, deserted the rebel league and jumped back with the National League Giants. He compounded his offense by persuading two of his teammates, Henry Boyle and Jerry Denny, to do the same, though Boyle wound up not playing at all. Such conduct was considered intolerable by Brotherhood members, including Roger Connor, who, as we have seen, regarded a man's word as his bond. Connor's normally decorous behavior and mild temperament took a violent turn during a chance encounter with turncoat Glassock just before the 1890 season began: "Connor and Glassock met in an elevated railroad station the other day and Connor gave Glassock the cut direct."[19] As we shall see, this was not the last time Connor took matters into his own hands over issues that he considered sacrosanct.

The National League plans to disrupt the new league did not cease. Special attempts were made to bribe former New York Giants who had had started the Brotherhood, in the hope that one deserter from their ranks might demoralize many others. After his court action against Buck Ewing failed, John Day and another Giants stockholder, Joseph Gordon, visited Ewing at his home in Cincinnati in February, just as he had done in the case of Roger Connor in January, in the hope of bribing the Players' League manager-captain.

> These two pretty fellows came here [Cincinnati] for no other reason but to bribe Buck Ewing to go back on the Brotherhood. They offered Ewing $8,000 a year and a contract for three years if he would ... desert his comrades. Ewing stated that he told them, "It is ten to one that I stay in the Brotherhood. I haven't given him [Day] a decided answer yet."[20]

Although Ewing stayed the course, the lack of complete certainty expressed in his statement to the press ["*ten to one that I stay*"] was disconcerting to many in the Brotherhood. In a few months Ewing would come under suspicion of treason. When contacted by the press in late February, Roger Connor's succinct statement to them contrasted sharply with Ewing's indecisiveness: "Have declared myself from the first. Nothing can tempt me."[21]

The Giants Brotherhood Grounds opened unofficially on April 8 for exhibition games, with its $15,000 dollar grandstand still incomplete. Manager Ewing selected new team uniforms. "The home colors will be pure white, trimmed in black, and the traveling suits will be of a light cream color, similarly trimmed."[22] Tim Keefe's fledgling sporting goods company supplied the League ball, reputedly livelier than the National League's. In compensation, the back line of the pitcher's box was extended to 57 feet. Two umpires, rather than the older league's one, oversaw every game.

The Players' League Giants opened the season at home on April 19 against Philadelphia, outdrawing their National League counterparts next door, "over two to one [12,013 to 4, 464]."[23] This attendance pattern remained constant throughout the season. As all three leagues waged a war for fans and for at least the appearance of success, attendance figures were

Center fielder Mike Slattery of the Players' League Giants makes an over-the-shoulder catch in an 1890 game at Brotherhood Field, 157th Street and 8th Avenue, New York. Coogan's Bluff is in the background. During the Brotherhood revolt, the National League Giants played on an adjacent diamond, Manhattan Field (also known as Polo Grounds II). After the Players' League collapsed, the National League Giants relocated to Brotherhood Field, renamed it the Polo Grounds (III), and occupied it until the franchise moved to San Francisco in 1958 (courtesy Transcendental Graphics/theruckerarchive.com).

regularly and wildly exaggerated. After splitting a four-game series with the Quakers, Roger Connor's Players' League Giants went on the road for two weeks, visiting Boston, Brooklyn, and Philadelphia. Connor's first of 13 1890 home runs came against rookie lefthander Matt Kilroy at Boston, a line drive "over the fence for a solo homer."[24] Three days later his towering opposite-field drive off Bill Daley evoked wonder from the *Boston Daily Globe*. "Connor hit one that disappeared in the direction of Bangor [Maine]. It had all sails set, and nothing but a huge chimney or a church steeple could stop it this side of Providence [Rhode Island]."[25] The direction of the blow was as significant as the distance it traveled. Of the 13 four-baggers that the normally dead pull-hitter Connor registered in 1890, five were to left, left-center, or dead-center field. Of the 67 home runs that preceded

Connor's blast off Daley in Boston and whose trajectories can be determined by game accounts, only a handful were placed in the same direction. The fact that the left-field fence at Boston's Congress Street Grounds was only 250 feet from home plate[26] was a good rationale for going to the opposite field. On June 2, Connor again touched lefty Matt Killroy for a homer, this time at the Polo Grounds. "Roger Connor with his Othello stride and big bat came up in the eighth and gave the ball such a crack that Richardson [Boston's left-fielder] lost three pounds chasing it. It was a home run."[27] However, over the course of the season, he also continued to pound four-baggers into unusual (for him) areas of the field at other parks. In July at Buffalo, he hit for the cycle, including a ball knocked "over the center field fence for a home run."[28] Five days later in Cleveland, he "made the longest hit ever made upon [owner] Al Johnson's ground and the first that went over any fence surrounding the park."[29] In August in Chicago, "Connor came up and lined out a four-bagger to left center ... one of the prettiest ever seen at the grounds."[30]

In addition to hitting the ball for great distances or to the opposite field in 1890, Connor continued experimenting with swinging from the opposite side of the plate, sometimes with insignificant results. "Roger Connor took chances batting right-handed off [Chicago's Mark] Baldwin. He did no heavy batting here."[31] A dozen years after being dropped by Frank Bancroft's New Bedford team for not being able to hit right-handed, the veteran had not kicked the right-handed offensive habit. More success in this regard would come his way in the future.

Perhaps it was the circumstance of being on a new team in a new league, or perhaps, at age 32, Roger felt he needed to make some adjustments to his hitting style. In any case, offensively he was doing things differently in 1890. Defensively, his now customary play sparkled, and for the second time in his career he led his league both in fielding percentage (.985) and total chances (1,436). In March, *Sporting Life* had chided him for his apparent weight gain; "Roger Connor seems to be very stout, but he says his weight is the same as in former seasons."[32] Three months later the journal praised his agility and nimbleness on the base paths. "Roger Connor is the most graceful runner on the New York team. This is remarkable when one considers he is the heaviest player in the New York Club."[33]

In early July, Buck Ewing met secretly in Cincinnati with John Day, who offered the Players' League Giants manager "a contract of $8,000 a year and an interest in the [National League] Cincinnati club if he would jump his contract and sign with Mr. [Aaron] Stern's team [Cincinnati].

This he refused to do."[34] At a second meeting, Day "asked Buck to put the question of consolidating the two New York clubs before the players. Buck promised to do so and when he arrived at Cleveland kept his promise. The players promptly sat down upon the scheme. They think they have all the best of the fight and are willing to see it out. Day denies the story but Ewing firmly holds to it and there must be some truth in it."[35]

At the end of July, John Day developed an elaborate scheme with Al Spalding to attempt again to get Buck Ewing to defect. The two National League owners began by asking Mike "King" Kelly, player-manager of the Boston Reds and the most popular baseball player in America, to meet with their representative, Cap Anson, in Youngstown, Ohio, explaining to him that Buck Ewing would also be attending the meeting. Ewing had no knowledge of the proposed meeting. Kelly saw through the ruse, and then "invited the magnates collectively to confer among themselves in a warmer climate."[36] Undaunted, Day and Spalding, through Cap Anson, then invited Ewing to a meeting, affirming that Kelly would also attend. Ewing attended the meeting, remaining after he discovered that Kelly would not attend. *Sporting Life* reported that "Just what occurred at the conference has not yet developed."[37]

In August, amid rumors that three former National League Giants wanted to defect — Ewing, Keefe, Richardson, Whitney, and Hatfield were among those suspected — Roger Connor went on the offensive: "Weaken! Well I guess not. What would we weaken for? We have nothing to fear. Every man on the team is as firm as a rock."[38] At this juncture even the leader of the Players' revolt himself, John Ward, fell back on stalwart Connor for support. "Well, what's the use of the League people trying to win over any of our men? I would like to see any person approach Roger Connor and make him a proposition."[39]

Late in November, a retrospective article on the League Wars that appeared in *The Sporting News* corroborated the meeting that Ewing had with his teammates, and clarified that the leader of the opposition was Roger Connor: "Buck kept on the path he had chosen. In July Roger Connor and he quarreled in Buffalo over some discouraging talk Buck had made to the New York players, and from that time he was under suspicion."[40]

Despite the attempts to undermined the viability of the rebel league through press propaganda, lawsuits, bribery and intimidation, the Players' League Giants played good, but not great baseball in 1890. They led the league in fielding (.921), aided by Roger Connor's .985 mark at first base, and came in second in batting average to Cleveland, whose Pete Browning led the league at .373. Their 1,018 runs scored also led the league for the year. Browning's teammate, a strapping young player named Ed "Del" Delahanty, who had been a substitute in Philadelphia the two previous years, played shortstop for the Infants and hit a respectable .298. In a few years he would blossom into one of baseball's most feared hitters, whose lifetime average of .346 ranks fifth all-time. Like Roger Connor, Del struggled before finding a comfortable defensive spot on the diamond. Unlike Connor, Del preferred the high life off the field, gambling and drinking heavily. His career came to an abrupt end on July 2, 1903. Thrown off a train in New York State for drunkenness and abusive behavior, Delahanty walked out onto a trestle bridge over the Niagara River, tumbled in and drowned. His body went over Niagara Falls and was recovered days later, horribly mutilated. He was 38 years old, and left behind a penniless young wife and child. Batting champion Browning's end was equally tragic. Afflicted his entire adult life with mastoiditis and alcoholism, he died at age 44 in 1905.

The Giants loved to play at home in 1890, going 47–19 at Brotherhood Park, but dropping to 27–38 on the road. Scheduling played a large part in their downfall. The team played 19 of their last 20 games on the road losing 12. Four pitchers, including Buck Ewing's younger brother Long John Ewing, combined for 73 wins, but star Tim Keefe, nearing the end of his fine career, slipped to 17–11 after having averaged 35 wins a year for the previous seven seasons. In his last great season, Connor hit .349, led the league in slugging (.548), and finished in the top five in on-base-percentage (.450) total bases (265) and runs (133), in addition to leading the league in home runs and in fielding percentage for his position. After a slow start offensively, he warmed up in mid–July. In four games at home against Chicago and Cleveland between July 12 and 16, he had eight hits, scored six runs, hit two doubles, two triples, and a home run. On the road from July 21 to August 4, he banged out 17 hits in 13 games, including five home runs, four doubles, and three triples. He finished the season with 21 stolen bases. In May *The Sporting News* declared him "a model player in his position and a deservedly [*sic*] favorite on the diamond."[41]

The Boston Reds, thanks to Hoss Radbourn's pitching and Dan Brouthers' hitting, took the only Players' League pennant with an 81–48 mark. John Ward's Brooklyn Wonders really were wonderful, finishing a surprising second, thanks in large part to veteran Gus Weyhing's 30–16 mark and the hitting of Ward (.335), and Dave Orr, who finished second in the batting championship to Pete Browning. Orr, who stood 5'10" was one of the very few major leaguers who outweighed Roger Connor (Orr weighed 240 while Connor, five inches taller, weighed 230). However, 1890 would be the Brooklyn slugger's last season. During an exhibition game a few weeks after his 31st birthday in September, he suffered a stroke that paralyzed his left side permanently.

With its legal efforts thwarted and bribery incentives only partially successful, the National League opted for another tactic against the upstart league, one that ultimately proved successful. "As the 1890 season opened, a pattern of economic war emerged with the league putting pressure on the players' financial backers, hoping to scare away faint hearts."[42] Through this move the league discovered the weakness of the rebel movement. None of the new league's backers had any prior baseball ownership experience. Cleveland's Albert Johnson owned a streetcar company; Philadelphia's major investors were in the wholesale meat business. E.A. McAlpin of the Players' League Giants was a tobacconist; his partner Edward Talcott was a stockbroker. Buffalo's "financiers" consisted of lawyer Moses Shire and three players, Connie Mack, Deacon White and Ellsworth "Dummy" Hoy, a deaf-mute. None of these men had a fraction of the baseball administrative experience or the deep financial pockets of Al Spalding, who by default had become the National League's field general and propaganda minister in the league wars.

After having signed players to high salary contracts, invested more than $250,000 in fields, facilities, equipment and legal fees, and issued thousands of free game passes to maintain the impression of success, these rookie baseball investors found their revenues from game attendance woefully inadequate to cover their costs. By August, the Philadelphia Quakers were reported near collapse, and Buffalo and New York defaulted on their final salary payments. National League teams were also in trouble. Spalding himself put up $80,000 to enable John Day's Giants to finish the season.[43] There were no such financial rescuers to be had for investors in the Players' League. In November a meeting was held between owners from both the National League and Players' League. Brotherhood members, who were stockholders of their own teams, were excluded. At the meeting, Pittsburgh and New York rebel-league backers offered to sell out to their counterparts in the Senior Circuit. John Ward "wearily admitted that the Players' League was dead."[44] The grand experiment had failed. The player once again was "a hireling," his salary once again "geared to his muscles and skills."[45]

Although Ward was magnanimous in defeat, hard feelings among players persisted. In New York this animus was directed at Buck Ewing.

His mid-season talks with Spalding, Day, or their representative, Cap Anson, earned him the enmity of his colleagues. "The Players' [League members] feel rather bitter over Ewing's readiness to attend league conferences at the old magnates' beck and call, and are outspoken in their condemnation of the secrecy with which he invested these talks."[46] Early in September, *The Sporting News* reported that Ewing had already signed a National League contract for 1891.[47] By November, his actions had been deemed partially responsible for the rebel league's demise: "Buck Ewing and Day: Their Old Friendship Threw Down the Player [*sic*] League."[48]

In stark contrast to the behavior of his team's captain and manager, Roger Connor stayed the course. "Roger Connor ... recently admitted that he had drawn scarcely $1,000 in salary for this summer's work, and then added, 'and I would be willing to get along with half of the amount before I'd give in to the League people.'"[49] During the last week of September, although he probably knew the die was cast, Connor still maintained a brave front, insisting, "By next season we will have our playing talent equally divided, and then we will give you the prettiest race for the pennant you ever saw."[50]

At the end of the baseball wars of 1890, the National League, grievously but not mortally wounded financially, reigned supreme. Its only remaining rival, the American Association, was in its death throes. In 1892, four of the Association's eight teams were disbanded and the remaining four were added to the rival National League, forming a cumbersome 12-team behemoth known briefly by the amalgam title "League Association." As soon as its last rival had been absorbed, the National League flexed its muscles by reducing team rosters to 13 players and imposing a salary limit of $2,400. It would be almost a decade before a new league, the American, would challenge the Senior Circuit's baseball monopoly.

Jim Mutrie stayed on as the titular manager of the post–Players' League 1891 Giants, but had no say in the day-to-day matters of the team, which were handled by Captain Buck Ewing. Mutrie was released at the end of the 1891 season. Nearly bankrupt, Giants owner John B. Day was forced to concede majority control of his team to E.B. Talcott, former owner of the rival Players' League Giants. By late 1892, Day was out of baseball, returning to his tobacco business, which subsequently failed.

Two years after the Players' League's demise, all of the original Giants of 1883 — Connor, Welch, Ward and Ewing, were gone from the team, as were the later acquisitions — Keefe, O'Rourke, and Richardson — all of whom had led the club to its two championships. John Ward, after first stating that he would play no more upon the demise of his league, received a concession from the enemy that had defeated him. He was named manager of the new National League Brooklyn team. The League's motives in this regard were purely mercenary, for it knew that Ward's popularity would assure the financial success of the franchise.

Nearing the twilight of his career, Roger Connor spent the next six years as a journeyman player with three different teams. Returning to the Giants in 1891, he suffered the ignominy of sharing the bench with Brotherhood deserters Mickey Welch and Mike Tiernan, of taking throws at first base from defector shortstop Jack Glassock, and of receiving playing orders from Captain Buck Ewing, who was viewed by all Brotherhood members as a traitor to the cause. Stoic in defeat, Connor played on.

What was the effect of the 1890 League wars on baseball? In the words of historian Ed Koszarek, "It was as if the PL [Players League] didn't happen."[51]

5

The Journeyman

"Roger's name is known throughout the length and breadth of the land."
—*Saint Louis Post-Dispatch*, June 10, 1894

No National League team was wounded by the Players' League revolt more than the New York Giants. While Mickey Welch and Mike Tiernan had jumped back to the Gothams in 1890, 12 players who wore the Giants' colors in 1889 deserted the team for the Players' League: Connor, Ward, O'Rourke, Gore, Richardson, Keefe, Crane, Whitney, Slattery, Brown, Hatfield and O'Day. Jim Mutrie's 1890 "Giant-less" Giants finished sixth in the National League, a position that would have been even lower without the presence of young fireballer Amos Rusie, who had been acquired from Indianapolis after the Hoosiers team folded at the end of the 1889 season. Armed with a fastball "so swift that it could not be seen, along with a curveball that whipped by quicker than many other pitchers' fastballs,"[1] Rusie, the aptly nicknamed "Hoosier Thunderbolt," hailed from Mooresville, Indiana, and carried 200 solid pounds on a 6'1" frame. Rusie won 245 games in nine big league seasons, leading the league in strikeouts five times and winning more than 30 games on four separate occasions. Had he not lost three seasons as a holdout, his win total would have exceeded 300. After being fined twice for a total of $200 during the 1895 season by then–Giants owner Andrew Freedman, Rusie refused to sign his 1896 contract unless the amount was returned to him. Subsequently, he was laid off by Freedman. With John Ward serving as his legal counsel, Rusie succeeded in winning $5000 in damages from the Giants, becoming one of the few players to challenge League rules and win. A combination of a sore arm and continuing contractual feuds prompted Rusie to hold out again for the 1899 and 1900 seasons, by which time, his career was over. In his later years Rusie returned to the Polo Grounds to work as a superintendent for nearly a decade before his death in 1942. The Hoosier Thunderbolt was elected to the Hall of Fame in 1977.

On Opening Day, April 22, 1891, a banner proclaiming "United, Greater, Stronger than Ever"[2] was draped over the Giants' clubhouse door at the Polo Grounds. In pre-game ceremonies, "Giants who had remained in the National League lined up on one side of the field with those who had gone to the Players' League standing on the other. The two sides came together to indicate that past differences were settled and that they were one team again."[3] Despite such outward displays, bitterness and distrust on both sides remained. Boston's John Clarkson bested Amos Rusie in the opener, and soon afterward the Giants went on the road, posting a 3–5 record through April. In May, they won successive series against Cincinnati, Chicago, and Cleveland, and lost only six games in June. By July 4, the Giants, with a 35–22 record, were in first place, and held a slim lead over second-place Chicago when their long slide began. Rusie and Long John Ewing were pitching effectively, but Welch and Keefe were on their last legs. Both Smiling Mickey and Sir Timothy started the season out of shape, and they never recovered. Keefe was released on August 1, and was picked up by the Phillies. Shortstop Jack Glasscock wrenched a knee, and Buck Ewing's arm and shoulder were so sore he could barely throw, causing the press to complain, "Ewing and Glasscock ... are drawing about 10,000 [dollars] for being useless and needless."[4] By late September the Giants had fallen to third place, and Boston had slipped ahead of Chicago on the strength of Harry Stovey's bat and the arms of John Clarkson and second-year man Kid Nichols. The teams remained in those positions until season's end, and Boston's Beaneaters won their first pennant under manager Frank Selee.

Offensively, Roger Connor started off slowly and was batting just .272 in mid–September when a late surge raised his average to .290. His home run production declined to seven, but he finished second in the league in on-base percentage (.399), fourth in slugging (.449), and fifth in RBI (94). While his four-baggers were fewer in number, some were memorable. His two-run blast off Boston's Charlie Getzein at the Polo Grounds in April was described by the *Boston Daily Globe* as "one of the cleanest line drives seen on a ball park."[5] The *Globe* described Connor's seventh-inning home run off Billy Hutchison at Chicago in July as "the longest hit seen on the home grounds in years."[6] The *Chicago Daily Tribune* agreed, noting that Connor "put the ball out of the lot onto Harrison Street" and that the drive "cleared the club house corner [by] at least fifty feet."[7] Connor's total of three home runs off Hutchinson during the season prompted an unusual request from the Windy City's baseball fans: "of all the hard hitting in the league, none can approach Connor in the regularity with which he pounds Hutchinson.... It has reached the point in the Chicago crowd, when Connor faces Hutchinson, that all the spectators wish for is a single hit that does not do anything more than break an out-fielder's leg."[8] Near the end of the season, *The Sporting News* observed that "Roger Connor once more is the idol of home-run loving New Yorkers."[9] The journal also offered high praise for his work at first base. "Roger Connor has put out 978 men at first base and made 86 assists and only made 20 errors in 93 games. This is a marvelous record, and it shows that he only made one error in every 50 chances to put out an opposing player."[10] Connor finished the year in second place among first basemen with a defensive average of .985.

Discontent over the Giants' play that was manifested in the press spilled over into the clubhouse, where reports of divisions among team members focused on Captain Ewing; "the way [Ewing] talks about some of his fellow players is not conducive to the best interests of the team."[11] Given his disputes with Ewing during the Players' League revolt and the dissention on the 1891 Giants attributed to Ewing, Connor, noting the serious trouble the Giants' captain was having with his throwing arm, suspected that Ewing would replace him at first base the following year, and informed the press of his intentions. "Big Roger Connor the New York first baseman will ask for a release if Captain Ewing is tried on the bag."[12] New York denied contemplating Ewing's move to first base, but Connor, release or no release, had made up his mind to move on, and the timing appeared propitious for such a decision.

Emboldened by its victory over the Players' League, the National League took advantage of a paperwork error by the American Association's Philadelphia Athletics in 1891 to allow two of the team's players, Harry Stovey and Lou Bierbauer, to sign National League contracts. As part of the Players' League war settlement "the peace terms provided that all players were to return to their old clubs, the ones which had reserved them in 1889."[13] Each club was required to send the League a list of reserved players, but Philadelphia, through a clerical error, omitted Stovey and Bierbauer from their list. The Association argued that "the general decision allocating all players to their 1889 clubs should have been sufficient to protect the Athletics, even though the Wagners [the team's owners] had neglected to observe the formalities of listing the players in question."[14] The National

Board (the oversight committee for both leagues) sided with the National League, and the Association responded by withdrawing from the National Agreement of 1883, by which both leagues pledged to honor the other's reserve contracts. With the reserve clause temporarily suspended, each league began courting players from its rival. "Both leagues were about equally proficient in stealing one another's players. Once more jumpers were threatened with 'no mercy' and blacklisting 'forever.' Yet counter-raiding went on, and jumpers who returned were accepted."[15]

In April of 1892, Roger Connor revealed that he was one of the players courted by the American Association when it suspended the reserve clause:

> Last Fall [1891] Manager Billie Barnie of the [American Association] Athletics came to my house in Waterbury, Conn, and asked me to join his [Philadelphia] club. I realized that I had played in New York long enough and felt convinced that Capt. Ewing wanted my place on first base. Under the circumstances I took the offer made by Barnie under consideration. He offered me a fair salary and a three years' contract. I came to New York to learn what the Directors of the [New York] club were going to do with me, but could come to no satisfactory arrangement. The salary offered suited me, but I wanted the officials of the club to take off my hands $1,000 worth of Brotherhood stock that I had in my possession and give me a three years' contract. This was the offer made me by Manager Barnie. The New York officials would not agree to my proposition, and accordingly I decided to join the Athletics."[16]

While under no obligation to do so, Connor, true to his character, had given his old team the opportunity to match the Athletics' offer before signing with an American Association franchise. The logic that he employed in deciding to jump his contract seemed impeccable. He knew that minority owner John Day and manager Jim Mutrie's days were numbered with the Giants, and that at age 35, he could not count on old loyalties to guarantee his place at first base with the team. Furthermore, baseball's (temporary) abrogation of the reserve clause as a result of the Stovey/Bierbauer affair provided him the freedom to sell his services without fear of legal retaliation. Connor's miscalculation, however, was the presumption that the American Association would still be in existence in 1892. It would not be. Connor would indeed play in Philadelphia that year — not for the Association Athletics, however, but for the National League's Phillies.

The unsettling nature of Connor's professional career during these years of transition and change was balanced on the home front by his stable, contented marriage to Angeline, financial security achieved by his prudent real estate investments in Waterbury, and by the arrival of a second child to fill the void left by infant daughter Lulu's death. Lulu's passing sparked a religious crisis in Roger, who believed the tragedy was God's punishment for "marrying outside the Catholic Church and neglecting to have his daughter baptized."[17] After her daughter's birth, Angeline secretly began taking instruction in the Catholic faith and planned to surprise her husband by being baptized on Lulu's first birthday. The child's death prompted both parents to turn to the Church for spiritual support, and Angeline eventually become a prominent figure in "different undertakings of the several Roman Catholic parishes of the city [Waterbury]."[18]

A few years after Lulu's death, Roger and Angeline adopted a young orphan, Cecelia, from a New York City Catholic orphanage. He had specified that he was seeking a blonde-haired girl, that is, a child in the image of the deceased Lulu. While at the orphanage, however, he spotted a dark-haired child sitting in a rocking chair and singing to her doll. His granddaughter recounts that "Grandpa sat down and called to her. She and her dolly ran to him, climbed up on his knee, [she] snuggled her little head on his shoulder, and he never let her go."[19]

Legends about Connor's physical strength and boxing abilities that had began to circulate in the press in the 1880s continued in the 1890s. Journeyman pitcher Frank "Red" Donahue, a native of Waterbury whose father, a lawyer, represented Connor in his home town business dealings, spun the yarn about Connor's putative exhibition bout in the boxing ring with John L. Sullivan. Donohue also offered an attentive press a story about Connor's alleged encounter with a town bully:

> "Big Roger Connor had a hand clasp that makes the grip of a vice seem like a child's caress," says Frank Donohue. "Down in Waterbury one day Roger came up to a big bully who was always looking to fight and who had several times threatened to give the big first baseman a licking. Going straight up to the fellow Connors [*sic*] grasped him by the hand. 'Wow! Ouch! Let go!' yelled the man. Roger closed his hand a little tighter. 'Stop! Stop!' howled the bully. 'You're crushing my hand.' 'Going to stop this cheap talk about licking me?' asked Roger, and you could almost hear the sound of cracking bones as he spoke. 'Yes, Yes.' 'You can't lick anybody, can you?' Connor asked. 'No, no! Let go.' 'And you are a big coward in the bargain?' 'Yes, yes, Oh my hand, my hand!' 'All right then, goodbye,' said Roger, giving the chap's paw one terrible squeeze. 'Goodbye and keep out of my sight.' And as Connor settled back against a telegraph pole and laughed, the other fellow started on a run for the surgeon's office."[20]

Connor's prodigious home runs had also given rise to some tall tales. Box scores of official games offer no factual basis for the following reminiscence of former Cincinnati first baseman "Long John" Reilly on the occasion of the death of his former teammate, pitcher Will White, although portions of the tale find an echo in Connor's actual accomplishments. Reilly also may have been referring to an exhibition game for which there remains no press account or box score.

> I'll never forget one game in which we both [Reilly and White] played way back in 1880, when Troy was in the National League we were playing out on the banks of the Hudson at Lansingburg — the home of the famous old Haymakers. White was pitching. Cincinnati was two runs to the good when we reached the stage of the game in the ninth with two on base and two out. Roger Connor came to bat. Big Roger got within one ball of first by the balls route, and I suggested that it might be well to pass him and take a chance on Caskins, the next batter. Will White was a pitcher who didn't like to give anything to a batsman that he didn't earn. He simply tossed one across and Roger responded by knocking the ball into the River. It was a foul drive but one of the hardest I ever saw made. I still hoped that White would pass Roger up but he didn't. The big fellow landed on the new white leather and the last I saw of the ball it was going over the fence and traveling in the direction of Troy. I think it must be going yet![21]

In November 1891, a month after Roger Connor signed with the Athletics of the American Association, the Association itself dissolved, and four of its clubs were taken into an expanded National League. The Athletics franchise in Philadelphia was disbanded, and Connor was assigned to play for the Phillies. Before he could put on his new team's uniform, however, he was accused by his former Giants teammate, Danny Richardson, of having pressured him to jump his contract with the Giants and sign along with Connor with the Athletics. Richardson further suggested that Connor had gotten him drunk and bribed him to make him more amenable to the project.

Few circumstances could entice laconic Connor to be open with the press. Impugning his character, however, was one of them. In early April he met with a *Times* reporter to tell his side of the story, which began in the fall of 1891 when Connor encountered Richardson in New York while the big first baseman was visiting the Giants' owners in order to give them the opportunity to counter the offer he had received from the Athletics:

> While in New York ... I met Richardson and learned that [Athletics manager] Barnie too, was after him. He [Richardson] even went so far as to tell me what he was offered, and asked me to go to the office of the New-York club [*sic*] with him. This I did. We had a row there with J.W. Spalding [a Giants owner], and left to go to Philadelphia to sign my contract. Without any solicitation whatsoever on my part Richardson decided to accompany

me. We remained in Philadelphia four days before we signed a contract, and during that time neither of us touched a drop of liquor. This I can prove by witnesses, and when I say that Richardson was perfectly sober when he had his business transaction with the Philadelphia officials, I say it without fear of contradiction. As regards being under the influence of liquor, the only reason I can assign for the story is that he was too weak-kneed to shoulder the responsibility and he was anxious to shove it onto me so that he could retain his standing among the New York patrons of the game. As regards my offering Danny an inducement to join the Athletics, he simply wants to make capital out of a piece of generosity on my part. Richardson wanted $1,000 advance money and the Wagners [owners of the Athletics] only offered us $500 apiece. In order to settle matters I gave Richardson my $500 so as to make up the amount that he asked for. This is the plain truth and I defy Richardson to deny any of the statements that I have made. Until to-day [*sic*] I have remained quiet, but I think it is my duty to expose the workings of a two-faced player.[22]

When the Philadelphia Athletics disbanded, the team's owners bought a controlling interest in the Washington club, a team that had finished in the basement during the American Association's last year, and which then had been transferred to the National League. Danny Richardson, told to report there and not wishing to play for a former cellar-dweller, apparently concocted the Connor story to gain sympathy with the New York management, for whom he wished to continue playing. The National League's board of governors sided with Washington's owners, and Richardson, with his reputation in tatters, finished the 1892 season there. The brief remainder of his career was compromised by alcohol abuse, and he retired from the game in 1894.

In mid–February 1892, Roger Connor signed his Philadelphia Phillies contract, which, unlike the one he signed with the Athletics, did not contain a stipulation that management absorb Connor's $1,000 loss from his purchase of Players' League stock.

Roger Conner came to town and signed last Thursday, after a satisfactory interview with Colonel Rogers [principal Philadelphia owner] and [manager] Harry Wright. He signed a new contract at the salary he was to have received from the Athletic club, but without the special conditions contained in the Athletic contract. He was very reasonable in not insisting in those special conditions of his new contract. He recognized the import of the great change that has come over baseball and has enough confidence in himself to feel that he will be able to hold his own and earn his big salary under any conditions.[23]

Before leaving to join his new team at spring training in Gainesville, Florida, Connor accepted a memento from supporters in his home town.

"Roger Connor, the Phillies' great first baseman, received a diamond pin last Tuesday from his friends in Waterbury, Connecticut. Roger will join his club in Florida next week."[24] Connor found the Florida climate to his liking. As we shall see, in his retirement he and Angeline would spend several months there each year to escape Waterbury's frigid winters.

Philadelphia's baseball roots are as venerable as New York's. By 1831, amateur teams such as the Olympics were playing an early version of the game in the City of Brotherly Love. Four decades later, in 1871, the Philadelphia Athletics made their debut in the National Association, the first professional league. British-born Al Reach, who began his career with the Brooklyn Eckfords in 1861, played second base for the Athletics, and in his team's initial year in the Association, he was named by the *New York Clipper* to baseball's first All-Star team. Reach later started a lucrative sporting goods business, and by 1892, when Roger Connor joined the Philadelphia Phillies, he was part-owner of the team

A second Philadelphia nine, the White Stockings, joined the Association in 1873, making Philadelphia the only Association city represented by two teams. The Athletics transferred to the National League in 1876, but their stay was brief. After losing 45 of their first 59 games, they opted not to make their final road trip west for financial reasons, and were subsequently expelled by the League.

Half a dozen years later, baseball-hungry Philadelphians organized a new team for the upstart American Association, and chose to name it in honor of its previous decade's predecessor, the National Association Athletics. By 1884 there were three professional teams in the city competing for fan support: the Athletics, the Quakers, a new National League team, and the Keystones of the Union Association, whose first season would also be its last. When the National League and the American Association merged in 1892, the Association Athletics were disbanded and the National League Quakers, who had changed their name to the Phillies, hired Harry Wright as their manager and became the only team in town.

Although Harry Wright won six pennants in seven years for Providence and Boston, during his tenure at Philadelphia he only managed to finish second once, and otherwise no higher than third. Along with Roger Connor, the 1892 Phillies had acquired the core of the disbanded Athletics team: steady second baseman Bill Hallman, utility man Lave Cross, and pitcher Gus Weyhing. Weyhing won 32 games in 1892, thus becoming the only pitcher in history to win 30 games in three different leagues (American Association; Players' League; National League). Cross proved his value by

1892 Philadelphia Phillies team photograph, featuring six future Hall of Famers: Roger Connor, standing, third right; Sam Thompson, standing, second left; Billy Hamilton, seated, first right; Tim Keefe, seated, third right; Ed Delahanty, seated, second left; manager Harry Wright, center, in street clothes. Due to financial difficulties caused by the Players' League revolt and the merger with the American Association, the National League limited team rosters to 12 players in 1892 (courtesy National Baseball Hall of Fame Library, Cooperstown, New York).

playing at second base, shortstop, third base, and behind the plate. The Phillies' outfield included Sam Thompson, Ed Delahanty, and speedster Billy Hamilton. In 1894, the three would make history as the only outfield trio to hit over .400 for a season (Thompson and Delahanty .407, Hamilton .404). In Roger Connor and Sam Thompson, Philadelphia boasted a duo that would become the greatest home run hitters of the 19th century (Connor with 138, Thompson 127).

"Big Sam" Thompson, a Danville, Indiana, native who earned his living as a roofer/carpenter before joining the Detroit Wolverines in 1885, stood 6'2" and weighed over 200 pounds. In 1889 he transferred to Philadelphia, where he roamed the outfield for a decade, perfecting a one-bounce throw to home plate, smashing four-baggers, and stealing more than 20 bases six times. Retired from the major leagues for eight years in 1906, he took a big league curtain call, playing for Detroit at age 46, banging out seven hits in eight games.[25] Big Sam was elected to the Hall of Fame in 1974.

Despite good pitching, a speedy, powerful lineup, and a 16-game win streak in June, the 1892 Phillies finished fourth in the expanded 12-team National League, behind Boston, Cleveland, and John Ward's Brooklyn Bridegrooms. Roger Connor's one year with the Phillies arguably represents the most balanced performance of his career, highlighting every aspect of his playing abilities. In a year in which only two players hit above .320, Connor's .294 mark was tenth-best in the circuit. He led the league in games played (155) and doubles (37), placed second in home runs (12), third in slugging (.454), and fourth in runs (123), total bases (261) and on-base percentage (.420). Connor achieved a career high in walks (116), stole 22 bases, and as previously mentioned, regularly added the sacrifice bunt to his repertoire to advance lead-off man Billy Hamilton, whose life-time on-base percentage of .455 ranks third all-time behind Ted Williams and Babe Ruth. In a July contest against Chicago, for example, with Hamilton on first, "Connor bunted one down the first base line, which [pitcher] Hutchinson gathered in and threw to first, but Anson muffed the ball and Roger was safe."[26]

As fate would have it, the Phillies opened against the Giants, losing 5–4. In his first at-bat against his old teammates, however, Connor tripled, scoring Bill Hallman, and later added a double, prompting the *Philadelphia Inquirer* to remark that "Roger Connor worked manfully against his old colleagues."[27] Later that month, his offensive assault on the Giants continued. In an April 27 contest, he garnered four hits and a walk, clouting two home runs and a double off fireballer Amos Rusie in a 15–1 rout. "Roger Connor knocked out two home runs, a double and a single. He also got a base on balls. Roger made four runs himself and knocked in three more. The crowd thought Roger a hero, and he was cheered every time he came to the plate."[28]

Ten of Connor's 12 1892 home runs were hit at the Phillies' home park, the Huntingdon Street Grounds, and two of them traveled so far that they reached the tracks of the Reading Railroad beyond the right field wall. These blasts are the likely source for the tallest of tall tales told about Connor's epic home runs. In 1908 the *Dallas Morning News* published a column, "Conversations with an Old Sport," by "Jim Nasium" (pun intended) on long-ball hitters.

> But I think the long-hitting record that has them all skinned is the one made by Old Roger Connor. Now, don't laugh, but that big guy actually knocked a ball from Philadelphia to New York, and that's no nature fake. It was at a game in the old Phillies grounds and Roger caught one fair on the nose and slammed it over the fence and across Broad Street and down to the railroad

tracks at Huntingdon Street Station, where a train was pulling out for New York. John I. Rogers [Philadelphia's principle owner] was on the train, and when the ball Roger hit came smashing through the window of the coach in which he [Rogers] sat, he picked it up and took it to New York and the ball never stopped from the time it left 'til it landed in Jersey City. Can you beat it?[29]

By 1892, the debts incurred during the Players' League war and by the buyout of weaker American Association teams had left the National League and all its franchises in dire financial straits. Consequently, prior to the start of the season, each team was assessed a levy of 10 percent of their profits by the League office. In June the levy was increased to 12½ percent, and in September it was raised to 16 percent. These draconian measures left the near-bankrupt clubs with no recourse but to curtail expenditures through roster reductions, player salary cuts, and the elimination of multi-year contracts. The latter was accomplished at the end of the season by releasing all players after all clubs had agreed in advance not to engage in bidding wars. Earlier in the campaign, team rosters were reduced to 13 players, and in June, previously contracted players' salaries were reduced 10 to 20 percent. Outraged team members were simply informed that "outright release was the alternative to acceptance."[30]

Philadelphia's 1893 contracts, which purposely were not mailed to players until mid–February, capped salaries at $1,800. Roger Connor refused to sign, and was traded back to the Giants for two low-paid players: light-hitting catcher Jack Boyle and pitcher George Sharrot, who was 16–15 for the Giants from 1890 through 1892. Connor's return to the Giants was predicated on recent events in New York. Jim Mutrie was released after the 1891 season and replaced by Pat Powers, whose prior major league experience was a year with the Association's Rochester Hop Bitters, who placed fifth in that league in 1890. Powers released George Gore, Mickey Welch and Jim O'Rourke, and imported a series of marginal players from the defunct Association, whose salaries were a pittance compared to those of the team's old stars.

The consolidated League, now known by the amalgam term "League-Association," devised a split season in 1892 in order to deal with its new, cumbersome 12-team organization. New York finished tenth in the first half at 31–43, and sixth in the second half at 40–37. The Giants' combined record, 71–80, placed them eighth at season's end, more than 30 games behind league leader Boston. By October, fans had abandoned the team, with attendance numbering in the hundreds instead of the customary thousands. Seeking to bring a little of the old magic back to the Giants, principal owner E.B. Talcott fired Pat Powers and brought back John Ward as manager in 1893, although this required him to "give Brooklyn a percentage of the [Giants'] gate in payment for Ward's services."[31]

Upon his return, Ward's first act was to trade Buck Ewing, whom he had accused of treason during the Players' League war, to Cleveland for third baseman George Davis. The exchange proved to be a trade-off, with Davis hitting .355 for the Giants and Ewing posting a .344 mark for the Spiders. Such high batting marks were at least partially occasioned by the last significant rule change of the 19th century. "Tracing poor attendance in 1892 to too many low-scoring games, the League-Association's rules committee initiated the greatest change in the geometry of the playing field since 1881, when the pitching distance had been lengthened by five feet. For the 1893 season the pitching distance was lengthened ... to 60 feet 6 inches."[32]

Of equal significance, however, was the new requirement limiting the pitcher's boundary within the pitcher's box to a 12-inch-long, four-inch-wide, white rubber plate: "The pitcher plate was as much an added impediment as the extra distance, for a pitcher was required to take his position facing the batter with both feet on the ground and keep one foot in contact with the plate at all times in the act of delivering the ball."[33] In compensation, the pitching rubber was allowed to be implanted in an elevated area — the modern-day pitcher's mound. As a consequence of the new rule, League batting averages rose 35 points, and attendance rose in almost every city.

New Giants manager John Ward's last act of the 1893 pre-season was to add experience and maturity to the team, while harkening back to the team's glory days of the previous decade. In March he brought Players' League loyalist and fan favorite Roger Connor back to the Polo Grounds.

> As soon as [National League] President Young was notified of the agreement, Ward at once sent a telegram to Connor, who was at his home in Waterbury, Ct., to come in and sign a contract. It did not take the first baseman very long to respond to Ward's message, for at five o'clock last Saturday he strolled into the corridor of the St. James Hotel, where he met Ward, and after a short talk went to another part of the building and affixed his signature to a contract.[34]

Connor's nostalgic return to the Giants was quickly overshadowed in the press by the electrifying news that John Ward was seeking to sign Mike "King" Kelly to a contract. Although Connor and Kelly both possessed enormous athletic talent, their similarities ended there. A native of Troy, New York, Kelly, baseball's first superstar, arrived in Chicago in 1880 after two years with the Cincinnati club. With the White Stockings he formed part of Cap Anson's pennant winning teams of the early and mid–1880s. After leading the league in hitting in 1886, Chicago's management, exasperated by Kelly's on- and off-field antics, sold him to Boston for the then-unheard-of sum of $10,000.

Garrulous, gregarious, and often outlandish, Kelly loved the limelight as much as he loved liquor and gambling. Although primarily a catcher, he played all nine field positions in his 12-year major league career. He was a league-leading hitter whose base-stealing prowess became the subject of a popular song, "Slide, Kelly, Slide!" and was also known for playing loose with field regulations in the era of the single umpire. "He once ran from second base to home [not bothering to stop at third] to win a close game from Boston."[35] Kelly was the first player to write and publish an autobiography, and in the off-season played the vaudeville circuit, singing, appearing in skits, and reciting "Casey at the Bat." Late in his career, he observed, "I like to play baseball, but really ... I think I'm a born actor."[36]

By 1893, Kelly's drinking and boisterous lifestyle had eroded his baseball skills. This fact mattered little to Giants fans and the press, whose preoccupation with Kelly dominated the spring sports news:

> About the middle of the present month, he [Kelly] will bid adieu to the footlights and take to the ball field[37];
> "Mike" Kelly may shortly don a New York uniform[38];
> "Mike" Kelly says he will not play with New York until June 5, if at all. His theatrical engagement expires then, and he is making more now, he says, than Ward offers[39];
> "Mike" Kelly will wrestle a Greco-Roman match there [Cincinnati] with a local celebrity[40];
> Kelly is now a full-fledged Giant. He is practicing and will start to play n the latter part of the week. The sooner the better.[41]

At the height of this "Kelly mania," even exceptional on-field accomplishments by players already wearing the Giants colors didn't matter to the press. After the Giants beat the Phillies, 16–3, on May 25, for example, in a game in which Roger Connor collected four hits, scored three runs, and stole three bases, it was Kelly's name that garnered the headline: "Kelly in Harness Again: the great catcher is now a member of the New Yorks."[42] When the "King" finally got back into action, he was too out of shape to be effective; "Kelly is sore and stiff and cannot do himself justice."[43]

After all the hullabaloo, Kelly saw little action, playing in only 20 games, and he was released at season's end. A year later he died of pneumonia at age 37, leaving behind a penniless young wife and child.

There was other news of the decline of the great stars of the 1880s.

In April, New Yorkers received word that "'Smiling Mickey' Welch will retire from the diamond. Next month he will open a saloon in Holyoke, Massachusetts."[44] In August, the *Times* reported that "Our Tim,"[45] Tim Keefe, had been released by the Phillies.

Roger Connor, in contrast, played on, enjoying a good, if not spectacular year, and for the ninth consecutive season ranked in the League's top five in an offensive or defensive category — he was fifth in home runs (11), and first in total chances among first baseman (1,546). Big Roger raised his previous year's batting average from .294 to .305, stole 24 bases and drove in 105 runs. "Old Waterbury" garnered three hits in a game seven times in 1893, including two doubles and a triple in an August contest against Brooklyn. In the Giants' first series of the year with Philadelphia, he exacted his revenge on the Phillies, stroking four hits and stealing three bases in the first contest, getting two hits, including a home run, in the second game, and laying down two sacrifices in the third.

Of Connor's 11 1893 home runs, two hit in a game at Brooklyn in August, and one each hit against Washington and Pittsburgh at the Polo Grounds, are historically significant.

Referring to the pair hit in August, the *Times* noted, "Big Roger Connor did his share in shaking the confidence of the Brooklyn pitcher. He made two home runs credited to his team, and another occasion just tapped the ball gently for a single."[46] The true significance of these home runs, however, was noted only by the *New York Press*. Facing left-handed rookie George Sharrot, "Roger Connor just turned around and batted right handed and plunked out two home runs."[47] The *Press's* accounts of one game in May and another in June likewise highlighted Connor's switch from left-handed to right-handed. "Esper, the [Washington] southpaw, was substituted in the 5th but he could not stop the fuselage of hits. Roger Connor slammed out a home

Studio portrait of Giant Roger Connor, circa 1893 (courtesy Gary Laios).

run batting right-handed"[48]; "The New Yorks took kindly to Killen's left handed delivery in the first inning. Connor bats as well right handed as left, and corked out a home run, the ball going clear to the clubhouse."[49]

As noted previously, it was commonplace in Connor's era for left-handed hitters to experiment by hitting right-handed against left-handed pitchers. Apparently in Connor's case, it was so common that most game accounts don't even mention the switch. After 14 successful years hitting left-handed, his ability at age 35 to hit at least four home runs in a season from the right side is one of the most remarkable feats in baseball. It is also one of the best-kept secrets in the game's history.

The Giants, clearly in a rebuilding mode, struggled to stay above .500 in 1893. In sixth place at 27–30 in early July, John Ward, seeking a winning combination, brought in five rookies from the Southern League to little avail. Ultimately, 28 men wore the Giants' colors before the season ended. Thanks to Amos Rusie's strong right arm (33 wins, 21 losses), the Giants managed a fifth-place finish of 68–65, 19½ games behind Boston, the repeating champions.

On July 26, in a game against Baltimore, Roger Connor's home run off Tony Mullane took a back seat in the sports column to another game incident. "[John]McGraw, the Baltimore shortstop, distinguished himself by having a couple of tilts with umpire Snyder. On one occasion he was fined $5, and roundly abused the official, who added $25 to the fine already imposed, and ordered the player out of the game."[50] Adopting McGraw's "rowdy" style of baseball, the Orioles would add an aggressive new tone to the game that would be openly criticized, but which would help the team win three consecutive National League pennants.

As the 1894 season approached, rumors that New York was planning to trade Roger met with general disapproval.

> Roger Connor has missed but two games in two seasons, and his batting average is over .300. He has always been a good batter and a fine first baseman, yet he is not considered good enough for New York[51]; New York is trying to trade Roger Connor for Tommy Tucker of Boston. If the managers of the "Giants" possess the business acumen for which they are given credit, they will keep Connor.[52]

The Giants lost their first four games of the 1894 season, and by May 16 they were in seventh place with a record of 10–11. *The Sporting News* reported "a big row on the New York base ball club and a 'shake up' is looked for within the next few days. The directors are dissatisfied with the showing of the team since the beginning of the season."[53]

1894 team portraits of the New York Giants and the St. Louis Browns, both including Roger Connor. In the Giants photograph (*top*), Connor stands behind the seated John Ward, Giants manager, second row, center. Ward traded him to St. Louis in late May (courtesy National Baseball Hall of Fame Library, Cooperstown, New York). The "composite" format of the St. Louis team photograph (*bottom*) was useful to Browns owner Chris Von der Ahe, who changed rosters frequently, selling off players whenever he found himself in financial difficulty. In the Browns photograph, Connor is pictured in the top row, far right (courtesy Transcendental Graphics/theruckerarchive.com).

Roger Connor was playing excellent baseball, hitting .303 with 23 hits in 20 games, and in the field averaging .985. In early May he collected four hits and scored a run in a 19–7 rout of Boston. A week later he homered over the right field fence in Philadelphia off the Phillies' Jack Taylor. On May 17, however, at the start of a series with Brooklyn, he was benched by Manager Ward in favor of Jack Doyle. A week later *The Sporting News* reported that "Roger Connor, the celebrated first baseman of the New York Giants was signed for the St. Louis Browns."[54] Ward's decision drew immediate fire from fans and the press.

> Ward was widely criticized for his release of the popular Connor. The criticism, coupled with New York's sputtering start ... made him testy. He accused those who criticized the Connor move of suffering from "an attack of the big head." He followed with a labored analysis of his preference for Jack Doyle on first instead of Connor. His reasoning boiled down to this: Doyle hustled more, even though Connor was hitting well.[55]

After signing with St. Louis, Connor broke his silence on the matter, praising New York's principal owner, E.B. Talcott, and taking a parting shot at Ward:

> When Ward laid me off in Brooklyn, Talcott told me not to worry, that I was to look to him alone for anything, and that I could remain with the New York club for the balance of the season, drawing my salary [even] if I didn't play another game. Mr. Talcott also assured me that if any club wanted my service and was willing to pay me as much or more money than I have been getting from the New York club, I could have my release. He told me that the New York club would put no obstacle in my way, and he kept his word. I shall never forget his kindness to me.[56]

In St. Louis, Roger Connor would play for Christian Frederick William Von der Ahe, one of the most idiosyncratic team owners in the history of baseball. Born in the Westphalia district of Germany, as a young teenager he made the long sea voyage to America alone. Arriving in St. Louis in the mid–1860s, he found quick success as a partner in a saloon/food market. Married and a father at 18, Von der Ahe soon bought out his business partner, invested heavily in real estate, added a beer garden to his enlarged business on the west end of town, and became the chairman of the city's Eighth Congressional District Committee.

A St. Louis baseball team of the era, the Red Stockings, had a short-lived stay in the National Association, lasting from April to July of 1875. A rival local club, the Browns, joined the National League in 1876, finished in second place that year and in fourth place in 1877, but the team folded soon afterward when its financial backers pulled out after a game-fixing scandal. The Browns nevertheless played on as a semi-pro team in St. Louis.

Although Chris Von der Ahe knew nothing about baseball, his business sense convinced him to join another saloon owner, a brewer, a newspaper editor and a congressman to form the Sportsman's Park and Association in 1880. The corporation refurbished an old ball park, reorganized the Browns, and announced they would take on all comers. Fifty percent of the gate receipts would be shared by the teams, 40 percent spent on advertising, and 10 percent reserved for expenses and profits.

The experiment was an immediate success. Teams from as far away as Philadelphia rode the rails to St. Louis to collect a handsome profit, and in 1881 the Association cleared $25,000. Besides taking in the action on the field, fans could enjoy fireworks, lawn bowling, and concerts at the games while quenching their thirst at a beer garden down the right field line — all planned by the enterprising Von der Ahe, who had the concession rights at the ballpark. Balls hit into the beer garden were in play, and needed to be returned to the pitcher before making a play on an advancing runner. Impressed by the character and playing ability of a young first baseman, Charlie Comiskey, from the visiting Dubuque, Iowa, team, Von der Ahe immediately offered him a contract with the Browns. Comiskey would be the key to the Browns' future success.

At the end of the 1881 season, Chris Von der Ahe bought out the other company stockholders and enrolled the Browns in the newly-formed American Association, the National League's first serious rival. Comiskey assumed the managerial position in 1884, and beginning the following year led the team to four consecutive Association pennants. During these years Chris Von der Ahe's genius for marketing was compromised by his recurrent public exhibitions of outrageous behavior. One of the first owners to recognize the financial possibilities of marketing team memorabilia, Von der Ahe successfully hawked towels, lithographs, pennants and mugs bearing the Browns logo at Sportsman's Park. A loud and boisterous regular at the games, sporting a bowler hat, wide-striped suits and spats, Von der Ahe's rotund figure, bulbous nose, and heavy German accent made him easy prey for the press, who portrayed the self-proclaimed "*der* boss President" as half-financial wizard and half-country bumpkin. Von der Ahe's biographer, J. Thomas Hetrick, describes a ballpark incident years later involving Roger Connor that aptly and humorously summarizes the Browns owner's unusual antics during a game against Baltimore.

"Acting managerial, Von der Ahe grabbed his binoculars and surveyed the diamond. Raising his voice higher, Von der Ahe spoke to Roger Connor: "Vut t'ell is der madder [What the hell is the matter]? Your outfield is blaying [playing] about three blocks too deep and so is your infield. It's no vunter [wonder] dey are hitting Donohue. Pull in der whole field!' Noting Von der Ahe's less-than-scientific spyglass methods, Connor rolled his eyes.... The big first baseman said, 'Just switch and try the other end [of the binoculars] and see how they look, Chris.' Von der Ahe rearranged the ocular so that his men didn't resemble ants. 'Say old boy, der drinks are on me! I will buy after tis game, even if ve lose.'"[57]

As his team's success increased, Von der Ahe's behavior became increasingly strident and erratic. He fined or fired players for making errors, regularly blowing a whistle from the stands to notify them of his displeasure, and hired detectives to follow players after hours, fining them if they were caught drinking — a hypocritical stance given the fact that he himself was a heavy drinker. When experiencing financial difficulty due to bad investments, he thought nothing of selling off his best players to clear his debts. In 1892, Von der Ahe built a new Sportsman's Park in a lot adjacent to the St. Louis fairgrounds, and then proceeded to bring as many events associated with the Fair into or just outside the ballpark itself. His new 14,500-seat venue became home to regular Civil War re-enactments and a Wild West Show, both of which played havoc with the diamond's turf. A bicycle race track originally encircled the field; in 1895 it was converted to a 3/8-mile horse race track. In 1896 *der* boss President" spent $25,000 to build a shoot-the-chutes water ride behind the right field fence — customers were hauled to the top of the structure in a row boat and then swiftly descended a slide into an artificial lake. The Silver Cornets, an all-girl band, gave daily day and night concerts, and in winter the shoot-the-chutes' lake was used for ice skating. With considerable accuracy, the Browns owner proudly referred to his ball field/amusement park as the "Coney Island of the West."[58]

The Browns took a downturn in 1890, when an exasperated Charlie Comiskey left to skipper Chicago's Players' League entry, the Pirates. Von der Ahe, whose financial empire was unraveling, soon scandalized St. Louis society by divorcing his wife Emma, promising to marry his 22-year-old German immigrant housemaid, and then marrying another woman. Leadership on the Browns became a game of revolving doors between 1895 and 1897, when 10 different men, including Roger Connor, held the position of manager. "*Der* Boss" assumed that role himself three different times during the period.

Von der Ahe's reign came to an end when his team was put in receivership and then sold in 1899. Bankrupt and out of baseball, Chris ended his days working as a bartender, dying of cirrhosis of the liver at age 62. Despite his spectacular failures, one cannot hear Von der Ahe's story without realizing that his marketing and promotional techniques — for better or worse — foreshadowed many of those in use at today's ballparks. Boisterous, obnoxious, and gregarious, half-buffoon and half enterprising genius, "*der* Boss President" was one of the most colorful and controversial team owners in the history of baseball.

A decade earlier, Roger Connor had been part of the transformative years in New York that led to two pennants and two World's Series championships. With the St. Louis Browns, Connor, now in the twilight of his major league career, had the misfortune to play for a disintegrating franchise whose past successes in the American Association in the 1880s had rivaled those of the National League Giants. The 1894 Browns were player-managed by light-hitting, hard-drinking George "Doggie" Miller, who succeeded Bill Watkins as skipper. It would be Miller's first and last year as a manager.

Other than Roger Connor, the Browns starters were, at best, run-of-the-mill players with no national reputation. Manager Miller played third base, Bill "Bones" Ely covered shortstop, veteran Australian-born Joe Quinn played second, and Roger Connor completed the infield at first. Frank Shugart, Holyoke's Tommy Dowd, and Charlie Frank were the outfield starters. The Browns' all–St. Louis, all-ethnic–German battery included catcher Henry "Heine" Peitz and left-handed pitcher Ted Breitenstein, who featured a rising fast ball and a drop-curve. Emerson "Pink" Hawley was the second pitcher. This roster, however, changed daily, thanks to player injuries and owner Von der Ahe's penchant for fining, benching, hiring, and firing team members. Eleven substitutes played infield and outfield positions, and six other pitchers combined for a 10–25 mark during the season.

Connor's offensive presence was immediately felt on the 1894 Browns. Fittingly, his first game was against the Giants at the Polo Grounds. Although the contest was called due to rain with the score tied 2–2, Connor's hit drove in the run that tied the score.

Connor's first game with the St. Louis team was played last Saturday. He was the star of the Polo Grounds in New York on that occasion. A steady, drizzling rain which prevailed through the six innings played took lots of enthusiasm out of the spectators, but could not dampen the kind feelings towards the player who had left the New York club after years of service. No player ever received the ovation which marked Roger's first turn at bat, and in fact, every play he made was followed by the most indiscriminate applause. When he made the hit which virtually saved the game for St. Louis, the assemblage went wild. It was a Connor day and no mistake."[59]

A few days later against his other former team, Philadelphia, Connor's ninth-inning home run, once again off the Phillies' Jack Taylor, won the game for St. Louis. The following day, Connor stroked three hits, including two doubles, and scored two runs against the same team.

When the Browns opened their first series of the year at Boston, the *St. Louis Post Dispatch* waxed eloquent on Connor's acquisition. "It is impossible to say how delighted the Browns are to have Roger Connor with them. He strengthens the team in a place that has not been first class in every respect. He played great ball in the game [against Boston], and he made one of the longest hits in the series, driving the ball clear out to the seats in center field for three bases."[60]

By mid–July Connor was hitting .316, fielding .983, and the St. Louis fans had discovered another aspect of his game: "Roger Connor is looming up as a base stealer."[61] At age 37, he would steal 19 before year's end. His home run off Philadelphia's Gus Weyhing on July 11 at St. Louis (complemented by a triple) was "the third ball ever knocked over the right field fence at Sportsman's Park."[62] In a three-game series at Brooklyn in mid–August, Connor tallied seven hits, including two triples and a double, and scored four runs. Against Louisville in a 13–2 win on July 28, he collected two doubles and a triple. At Louisville in early August he knocked out two doubles and a triple, and in a 7–6 loss at Cincinnati he contributed three doubles to a losing cause. The next day he scored four runs and banged out three hits, including a home run.

When the Giants visited St. Louis in September, Manager Ward ruefully expressed "trader's remorse" for having let Connor go. "Roger Connor is as good a ball player as he ever was.... I cannot understand why I replaced him at first with [Jack] Doyle.... I question whether there is man of his size in the profession who can run the bases as well.... I appreciated the fact that the Giants were not winning and determined to introduce a new element in the team."[63] The significance of the Connor acquisition was apparent to all St. Louis fans as the season's end approached; "Roger Connor is much more valuable to the Browns now [September] than when he first joined them."[64]

Now the third-oldest player in the League, Connor finished the 1894 campaign hitting .316, with eight home runs, 35 doubles, a career-high 25 triples, and a .522 slugging percentage. His offensive heroics could not, however, save the Browns from ninth place, with a record of 56 wins and 76 losses. Despite withering criticism of Chris Von der Ahe both in the St. Louis and national press, Connor, in a carefully worded statement in late July, managed to find positive aspects of his role as team owner:

> A good many players find fault with Von der Ahe, but as far as I'm concerned he's treated me fairly and squarely. I like St. Louis and have made many friends there. If we had a winning team Chris couldn't do much for the players. As it is he has reason to feel dissatisfaction, as he is one of the hardest losers in the business. We have been crippled [by injuries] but you'll hear from us, I think....[65]

Things went from bad to worse for the St. Louis Browns and their owner in 1895. Over the course of the year, Chris Von der Ahe "managed to alienate his players, his fans, the National League and just about everybody else."[66] "*Der* Boss" was his own worst enemy. After a disagreement over real estate investments, Von der Ahe removed his son, Eddie, from the position of Treasurer of the Browns in August 1894, and then sued him and his business partner, James Noonan. Father and son never spoke to each other again. In January 1895, Chris's long-suffering wife, Emma, brought suit for divorce against him on grounds of physical abuse and adultery. Court proceedings revealed that Von der Ahe was a long-standing serial adulterer, who at the time of the suit was carrying on affairs with at least three women, including Anna Kaiser, his 22-year-old housekeeper. Missouri and national newspapers published all the lurid details.

In March, two weeks before the divorce proceedings concluded, Von der Ahe attacked a black man whom he had never met on a street corner near Sportsman's Park, pummeling him mercilessly and then shooting him in the heel with a pistol. Arrested for assault, the Browns owner's defense was that black men repeatedly robbed his saloons of cases of liquor. Chris Von der Ahe escaped a prison sentence for his deed only due to the fact that the victim, George W. Stevenson, "failed to give security for court costs."[67]

One morning in June at the ballpark, Von der Ahe ordered two of his injured players, George Miller and Denny Lyons, to stand at first and third base respectively, and announced to the frightened players, "I shoot at you and you tell me how close I come."[68] The players disarmed the owner before target practice began.

In July, Von der Ahe announced the construction of a ⅜-mile horse

THE ST. LOUIS BROWNS.

The Heroes of the Hour.

1895 St. Louis Browns team portrait that appeared on the front page of the *St. Louis Post-Dispatch* on April 18, 1895, with the title: "The Heroes of the Hour." The sketch features a rare portrait of Roger Connor without a moustache, which he grew back soon afterward (author's collection).

racing track *inside* the ballpark, a project that required removing portions of the left and right field bleachers and increasing the distance behind home plate to the stands to 150 feet. Upon his departure from St. Louis, Roger Connor, noting this great distance, wryly remarked, "There is one consolation about playing ball in St. Louis. The diamond is so far from the grandstand that the player can't hear the remarks discharged by the fans."[69] The proposed horse track prompted protests from all quarters, but did not deter Von der Ahe, and on September 30, the track opened for business. It closed for the season two weeks later.

Events on the diamond at Von der Ahe's park proved as chaotic as those of his personal life. "*Der* Boss" continued to take out his anger and frustration over his financial and family problems on his ballplayers, blowing his shrill whistle from the stands to signal his disappointment and fining or suspending players who committed errors or who were caught drinking after hours. Al "Buck" Buckenberger, who had managed the Pirates in 1894, was hired to manage the club, but resigned in June and was replaced by second baseman Joe Quinn. Quinn quit in August and was replaced by Lou Phelan, a saloon keeper with no baseball experience who was a relative of one of Von der Ahe's paramours. Phelan lasted six weeks; thereafter Von der Ahe himself managed until season's end.

The local press described the Browns as "Von der Ahe's misfits,"[70] and the "Done Browns."[71] Their owner's off-field exploits earned him the epithet "St. Louis Maggot"[72] [a play on the term "magnate"], and for his baseball dealings he was mocked as "Von der Ha! Ha!"[73] By late June, the *Washington Post* reported that

> Von der Ahe's peculiar actions lately have very nearly killed the interest of the game in St. Louis. He has sold so many players that with three men crippled, he has just enough players left to take the nine positions, thus working pitchers every day, making those who are not twirling go into the outfield. He seems to be making no effort to get new men and the St. Louis papers and patronage are roasting him thoroughly.[74]

The constant controversy and turmoil in St. Louis, and the "gruesome parody of baseball"[75] under Von der Ahe, eventually succeeded in unsettling the teams' pillar of stoic endurance — Roger Connor. Initially, however, he showed no signs of slowing down as he began his 16th major league season at spring training camp in Hot Springs, Arkansas. In his first exhibition game against a New Orleans squad on March 22, he rapped out three hits and stole three bases. A few days later in Montgomery, Alabama, he went 5-for-6 and scored two runs in a 14–8 win.

In the season-opening series against Chicago, Connor stroked five hits, including three doubles. He hit his first home run in early May off Boston's future Hall of Famer Kid Nichols. He hit a second four-bagger off Brooklyn's Brickyard Kennedy five days later, and a third followed in two weeks off Washington's Otis Stockdale in a 23–2 blowout in which he went 3-for-3. The home run, however, was not a feature in Connor's premier offensive performance of the season — and one of the greatest of his career — on

June 1. As so frequently occurred, Connor did this damage against the Giants at the Polo Grounds. "Connor was the hero of the day. His friends gave him a cordial welcome when he first came to bat and he repaid them. With seven times at the bat, he made six hits and got a base on balls. A triple and two doubles were among the lot. He also caught two foul flies which were of the sensational order."[76] Apparently Connor didn't find the historic hitting barrage against his former team too tiring. In his next game he connected for a home run and a double off Ad Gumbart in Brooklyn. Two weeks later against Cincinnati, he slammed two home runs in successive at-bats off Frank Dwyer.

After 70 games, Connor had collected 90 hits and was only two home runs shy of his previous year's total. His performance included 17 two-hit games, eight three-hit games, and one six-hit game. Every indication pointed to a banner season. Thus, it came as a shock when *The Sporting News* on July 20 reported that Connor had retired from the game. "Roger Connor called upon Von der Ha! Ha! Wednesday and requested his release. 'I am getting old now, and nervous,' said the grand old player, 'and I am better out of the game than in it. I have enjoyed a long and I think useful career and am ready to give way to the younger men. I will immediately return to my home in Waterbury, Conn., and take life easy for the balance of my time on earth.'"[77]

It is highly improbable that these words and sentiments were Roger Connor's. A man who claimed at this juncture to be "better off out of the game than in it," as Connor allegedly stated, would not, as he did, continue to play major league, minor league, and semi-pro ball for the next 15 years. Just two weeks after he headed home for Connecticut, for example, the *St. Louis Post Dispatch* reported that "Roger Connor has not retired from the diamond after all. You could not keep the veteran off the field with a derrick. Last Saturday he played first base for the Winsted [Connecticut] club."[78] Two years later, in 1897, in his definitive exit from the major leagues, he did not, as alleged in the aforementioned *Sporting News* article, concede the diamond to the young players. To the contrary, he stated, "All this talk of 'young blood' has failed to bear any fruit. The best men you have in the league are seasoned players and I am confident there are several years of old form ball playing in me yet."[79] Finally, the notion that the sanguine, 6'3", 230-pound "Sturdy Oak" Connor could attribute his departure from St. Louis to being "nervous," is so contrary to the Waterbury star's nature and temperament as to be inconceivable.

While the exact motivations of conscientious Connor's decision to take a five-week vacation from the Browns in the middle of the 1895 season remain unclear, his early departure from post-season exhibition tours in New Orleans and San Francisco, previously discussed, suggest that undisclosed family matters or simple distaste for events at the sites may have played a part in his decision. The chaotic and embarrassing state of affairs in St. Louis certainly offered him no incentive to stay.

On August 29, under the headline, "Roger Connor to the Rescue," the St. Louis press paid Connor a left-handed compliment in announcing his return to the Browns. "A telegram from Washington announces that Chris Von der Ahe has resigned Roger Connor and that the ex-first baseman will resume his place on the initial bag. The news may not be good for the St. Louis fans, but Connor will be better than nobody and everybody at first."[80] The next day Connor homered off Washington's Joe Corbett in the second game of a doubleheader that the Browns swept from the Nationals. It soon became apparent that Connor had negotiated more than his own return to the Browns; "Joe F. Connor [Roger's youngest sibling] will join the Browns in Boston and play third base for the team."[81]

Connor averaged nearly a hit per game in the final month of the season, and at Boston on September 7, hit an opposite-field home run that clinched a 4–3 win for the Browns. Joe Connor played in just two games for St. Louis before being sent back to the minors. The Browns ended the season in 11th place at 39–92, 48½ games behind Baltimore's first-place "rowdy boys." Playing in only 104 of the season's 135 games, Connor slugged 29 doubles, nine triples, and eight home runs, hit .329, and finished second to Baltimore's Scoops Carey on defense, posting a .986 average compared to Carey's .987. It was a record that most men who had played the full season would envy.

The 1896 season at Sportsman's Park was a replica of the previous year. Chris Von der Ahe added yet another new, non–baseball-related attraction — a shoot-the-chutes ride beyond the right-field fence. Harry Diddlebock, a Philadelphia sportswriter, was hired as the Browns' manager, only to be fired after three weeks for drunkenness. Arlie Latham, who had played for the Browns during their glory days in the American Association and who had been traded back to St. Louis, took over for Diddlebock. He lasted three days. Von der Ahe then took the reins himself for two contests before handing over control of the team to Roger Connor. He went 8–37, including a 15-game losing streak, before resigning as manager. Tommy Dowd finished out the year as team skipper.

As the season opened, the St. Louis fans and press had modest hopes:

"with good management we may hope to land eighth [place]."[82] Connor's hard hitting began early. His first home run, off Cleveland's Nig Cuppy in the second game of the season, cleared the right field fence and tied the game in the fourth inning. Nine days later against Louisville, he drove his second four-bagger an even greater distance in the same location: "The drive was one of the biggest ever made on the grounds. It cleared the fence by at least 50 feet and dropped in the middle of the 'shoot the chutes' lake."[83] In May, by permission of owner Von der Ahe, the St. Louis players elected Connor captain and manager by unanimous consent. *Sporting Life* noted that

> This is the first time that he [Connor] had or would accept authority. He is of a naturally retiring disposition and did not desire such honors.... Just how much Roger will do with so much on his broad shoulders is a question. He is not naturally aggressive in disposition, and yet he would always stand up for his rights.... What he will do now will be watched with interest. There is one thing, however, he will have the hearts and co-operation of his players in everything he does.[84]

Not even the "Hercules" of the old Giants, however, could resuscitate the dying Browns.

Connor's tenure was brief and painful. The frustration of managing a terrible team, and the belief that while on an eastern tour umpires showed favoritism to the home nine, prompted behavior that he had never previously exhibited on the diamond. "Since Roger Connor became manager of the St. Louis Browns he has developed into quite a kicker [complainer to the umpire]."[85] One month into his new role, Connor acknowledged the behavior and tried to explain the team's poor showing, saying, "Now you know, I'm no kicker, but the way in which the umpire gave it to us was simply awful.... We were robbed out of five games by deliberate umpiring.... I must say Chris [Von der Ahe] gave me a fair show. He has had a kick coming too because we should have won more games. Then the players got sick and we were in a bad fix."[86] However, rumors were already circulating regarding the possibility of Roger being relieved of his duties. "There is a feeling among the players that Roger will not be managing long. The big fellow himself admits that he is not in love with the job of trying to make a poor team play good ball."[87]

Ultimately, the Browns' poor play was not responsible for Connor's hasty retreat from managing. On June 30, Von der Ahe released Joe Quinn, one of the team's old guard, who fielded well but hit poorly. On hearing the news, "Roger Connor was wild. He was not consulted about the affair.

When he heard of it this morning, he rushed into Von der Ahe's office. A warm interview took place."[88] A few days later, Von der Ahe fined third baseman Bert Myers, who was sick, $100 for failing to show up at the ball-park. Then he suspended him. Von der Ahe "worked himself into a fit of passion last night and sent for Manager Roger Connor. Roger failed to show up and thus made Chris madder, and he announced that Connor would be released as manager and that he himself would manage the team."[89] The final straw for the old Player's League rebel, was not his poor showing in the won-lost column, but his concern for the rights of his players.

Despite such trials, the 39-year-old Connor slugged 11 home runs in 1896 — his best total in four years — including an inside-the-park four-bagger off Pittsburgh's Frank Killen on June 30. He hit 24 doubles and nine triples, and finished the season with a .284 average. His last league-leading honor of his career was a defensive award. In his final full season, he led all first basemen with a .988 fielding average.

Toward the end of the campaign, the St. Louis press suggested that Con-nor would not be returning in 1897 — not because management didn't want him, but rather, in the manner of his good friend, former teammate, and fellow Connecticut native Jim O'Rourke, because he was planning to buy a minor-league franchise.[90] Although Connor denied the rumor, he clearly was making plans for his post–major-league years.

Connor would indeed return to St. Louis in 1897, but only for a brief curtain call. Perhaps it was his failing eyesight, or the continuing chaos on the Browns. Perhaps it was the result of the slow but relentless effects of aging, or the thought of another year away from home, riding the rails from city to city. Perhaps it was a combination of all these factors. After 22 games of the young 1897 season, he was batting .229 and ranked fifth in the league defensively at his position. There were a few brief moments of glory — a home run, his last major league four-bagger, off Cleveland's Cy Young, and a fine overall performance in a 9–7 win at Chicago. "Three runs, four hits [one a triple], ten putouts and no errors was Roger's record. Not bad for an old man, is it?"[91] Nevertheless, in the main, it was not the old Roger Connor who showed up for the 1897 season.

On May 19, he was benched by manager Tommy Dowd, who observed, "He is not fast enough for high fouls, swift grounders, and wide throws from across the diamond."[92] It was the last straw for Connor.

> During the game with Boston yesterday Roger had an interview with Von der Ahe and the result was the honorable discharge with salary up to date and a railroad ticket that was five feet long when unfolded. Then Roger told

a few friends around the office good-bye, went to the dressing room for some belongings, and then started to his room to pack up. He will board a train to-night for New York City, the town he once owned, and if the temptation is not too great for him to stop off and see a few friends between Cortland Street and Grand Central Station, he will be at home Tuesday. If he stops off he will not reach Waterbury — but then he won't stop. Roger said yesterday, with a smile and a wink, "it would never do" for him to try such a thing. "I am glad I am going ... but understand me.... I have no complaint to make and no babyish excuses to offer.... It has been my wish all along to get away from St. Louis, and when I was told to take the bench I made up my mind to go if I had to buy my release.... As for the Browns as a team, I hope they'll win a game — many of 'em, I mean. I have nothing but the best of wishes for the club and hope that St. Louis may yet have a team of which the city may be proud. This is a great ball town and I am sorry to see it so deep in the hole."[93]

Connor took leave of the major leagues in the same matter in which he had played the game for nearly two decades — as the "Gentleman of the Diamond."

6

—m—

The Squire of Waterbury

"I love the game and intend to stick with it. If nobody wants me I'll play on the lots at home with the kids."
— Roger Connor, *St. Louis Post-Dispatch*, May 22, 1897

Although he retired from the major leagues and was home in New England permanently before his 40th birthday, professional baseball remained an integral part of Roger Connor's life for the next half-dozen years. There was much more time now, however, to spend with Angeline, nine-year-old Cecelia, and the many members of his extended family. Catherine Sullivan Connor, the family matriarch, and Connor's sisters Mary and Nellie, still lived just a block from Roger's home on South Main Street. Brothers Dennis and Daniel's businesses were located a short buggy ride away. Brother Matthew was a prizefighter, and Roger, an expert in the sport, could be found in his brother's corner providing advice and encouragement. Mortimer and Catherine Connor's eldest child, Hannah, married Robert Wilson of New Jersey, a man 16 years her senior, in 1883, and moved to Manhattan. In the late 1890s, Hannah, then a mother of four, found herself in financial straits when husband Robert became too ill to work. For several years, Roger and Angeline took in Hannah's second-oldest son, Roger's namesake, Roger Connor Wilson, at their Waterbury home.

Baseball fans discovered years earlier that Connor had talents other than those he displayed on the diamond. "Big Roger Connor's melodious 'tenor' voice takes the cake. Roger is a 'sweet singer.'"[1] Daughter Cecelia also possessed musical talent. She began piano lessons in the second grade, and although she never took singing lessons, she had a beautiful voice, and could hit high "C" in many songs. At Connor clan gatherings, "they [Roger and daughter Cecelia] would sing together many an evening."[2]

Connor maintained closest family contact with his youngest brother Joe, 17 years his junior, who, we recall, was born in 1874 during his older brother's absence from home. Roger used his influence to get his sibling a two-game trial with the St. Louis Browns in 1895, later signed him to contracts for Waterbury and Springfield of the Connecticut League, and also arranged for Joe to accompany him during his brief stay with the New England League's Fall River team.

As was the case with most baseball stars of the era, Connor's financial status was the object of intense interest and scrutiny by the press. Writing for the *Washington Post*, former player Sam Crane, for example, asserted that "Roger Connor owns enough real estate in Waterbury, Conn. to insure him a big income as long as he lives."[3] Frank "Red" Donohue, who, as we have seen, had spun yarns about Connor's physical strength and boxing abilities, added more details about the slugger's finances for *Sporting Life*.

> When the Giant first baseman from this city [Waterbury] was making those $4,000 and $5,000 salaries as first baseman of the New York team, he wasn't spending it in riotous living. Big Roger was putting about nine-tenths of it away for a rainy day. That day isn't quite here, but near it. Roger is now in a minor league but if he retires from the diamond this year his rent roll will bring him more every year than nine-tenths of [what] big leaguers now receive in the way of salaries. According to what [Frank] Donohue said the other day, big Roger has more money than any ball player in America. "I know what I am talking about," said Donohue. "Roger has a whole row of houses and they are worth over $50,000.... Every month of the year Connor receives $300 cash in rent. This means $3,600 a year. Roger invested his money wisely. He got hold of property that enhanced in value. Now, what need has a ballplayer with $300 a month coming in to worry whether he makes a base hit or gets through a game without an error?"[4]

By the time the story of Connor's finances was reported in the *Dallas Morning News* years later, it had acquired tall tale status. "Roger Connor has houses and lots in Waterbury that put him in the $100,000 class without the least doubt."[5] The facts, however, tell a different story. From 1881 to 1889, Connor made a total of $20,800, ranging from a low of $900 in 1881 to a high of $3,600 in 1889.[6] Although statistics are lacking for the later years in his career, it is doubtful that in the twilight of his career he earned more than his best years of the 1880s, and probable that he earned less. Prudent investments certainly had provided him and his family a comfortable lifestyle, but he did not possess fabulous wealth.

In addition to land and houses, Connor invested in another sport
that was regionally popular in the late 19th century, but which today is
unknown. Roller polo, a spinoff of the Victorian-era roller skating craze
and a progenitor of modern hockey, was a popular sport along eastern
seaboard states from New Jersey to Maine during the winter months.
Thanks to the popularity of roller skating that developed during the 1870s,
almost every town had a rink composed of hard maple floors. The venues
typically "had a gallery above where spectators could watch the show below.
New York's Casino Rink accommodated one thousand spectators and one
thousand skaters."[7]

In roller polo, two teams composed of seven skating players armed
with short, crook-end sticks competed by trying to knock a small, hard
ball through a goal. The contests proved a welcome diversion for gallery
spectators during the long New England winters prior to the invention of
television and radio. In the 1890s, the game's popularity helped move it
from an amateur to a professional pursuit. Considering the size of the
towns and the relative difficultly of simply getting to the rink on snowy
winter evenings, attendance at professional roller polo games was remarkable. In January 1896, 2,000 paying fans watched the home team Pawtucket, Rhode Island, squad defeat New Bedford.[8] In March 1898, a
similar-size crowd packed the Chapel Street Polo Rink in New Haven to
watch the home team defeat rival Fall River for the National Roller Polo
Championship.[9] Many New England–born baseball players, including
Arlie Latham and Billy Hamilton, grew up playing roller polo, and played
the sport professionally or managed teams in the off-season. Others, like
catcher Malachi Kittridge, became team owners.

In December 1898, a *Sporting Life* writer noted that "Roger Connor,
the veteran ball player, has branched into new fields, and this winter will
run a roller rink in Newark.... I wonder if Roger ... will make any money
out of his roller polo investment.... No one deserves it more for he is a
gentleman, all the time."[10] In its contemporaneous article on the new
American Polo Association, the *New York Times* listed the names of many
baseball men, including Connor, as roller polo investors, and at the same
time documented the great regional popularity of the sport.

> The New York polo team has cut loose from the Southern New England
> League and joined the newly organized American Polo Association. The
> other cities in the Association are Brooklyn, under the management of J.C.
> Chapman [former pitcher and manager of Louisville National League and
> American Association teams]; Jersey City, with William Barnie [former

catcher and Brooklyn manager] at the helm; Newark, with Roger Connor, formerly first baseman of the Giants, in charge, and Philadelphia, with Walter Burnham, a well-known baseball manager [Indianapolis, National League] at the head. All the teams are made up of New England players. The season will open tomorrow. Each team will play two games at home every week.[11]

While happy to be home in New England with family after 17 years on the road, baseball was never far from Roger Connor's mind. He played on two local minor league teams as manager-captain for the remainder of the 1897 season, all the while trying to lay the foundation for the purchase of a local franchise. In early June he played temporarily with Waterbury's Connecticut State League team. Later that month he signed with Fall River of the New England League and brought along his brother Joe to catch and play third base. The league fielded teams in Fall River, New Bedford, Brockton, Taunton, Pawtucket and Newport in 1897.

The net of interurban trolley lines that connected cities and towns in the region allowed the league to schedule many two-game series that started at one team's town on the first day and ended at the second team's field the next day. On these occasions, fans from both teams used trolley transportation to attend home and away games. During Decoration Day and Fourth of July matchups, teams often played the first game of a doubleheader at one home-team diamond, and the second game later the same day at the other team's field.

Joseph Francis Connor stood nearly as tall (6'2") as his oldest brother, but weighed 45 pounds less (185 pounds). After his two-game introduction to major league baseball with the St. Louis Browns in 1895, he played 14 minor league seasons for eight teams. During these years he was called up occasionally for brief periods by several major league teams, compiling a .199 batting average in 92 games. In the minors, Joe hit .267, with 1,049 hits in 1,091 games, and eventually played every position except pitcher and shortstop. Like his brother Roger, he had good speed on the base paths — he stole 51 bases with Bridgeport in 1900. Roger made sure wherever he played during his post–major league years that Joe was also offered a contract on the same team.

With the exception of his brief tenure as St. Louis Browns manager in 1896, Roger Connor had scrupulously avoided leadership roles in baseball, and as we have seen, even refused to serve as an occasional first- or third-base coach. In joining the Fall River team as manager-captain, he found himself in charge of scheduling, team travel, finances, grounds and equipment, recruiting, lineups, and on-field strategy. The new responsibilities initially took a toll on his hitting, but did not affect his fielding; "Roger Connor is playing a fine first base for Fall River."[12] After going hitless in his first five games, his bat warmed up. He cracked his first post–major league home run and stole a base in a June 22 win at New Bedford, and went 4-for-4 with a double and a four-bagger two days later at Taunton. When Joe joined the team in July, the brothers frequently led the Fall River attack. Against Pawtucket on July 6, Roger went 3-for-5, including two doubles and two runs scored, and Joe scored a run and went 3-for-4. In a blowout victory against the same opponent late in the month, the Connors accounted for five hits, including three doubles, and scored five runs. Roger added a sacrifice and Joe stole a base.

Near the end of the season Connor got the offer he wanted — a return to Waterbury's Connecticut League team as majority owner and manager-captain. Although under his leadership Fall River had gone just 20–27, the team had moved up from fifth to fourth in the rankings during his tenure, and his departure prompted the observation that "as Captain of the local team he has built it up from a poor one to a strong one, and he will greatly be missed by the base ball public."[13]

The Connecticut League owed its existence to Bridgeport-born Jim O'Rourke, Roger Connor's friend, fellow Brotherhood loyalist, and Giants teammate and roommate. Despite their dramatically different personalities — O'Rourke was gregarious and loquacious, and Connor retiring and quiet — their circumstances, interests, and philosophies were similar. Both were born in Connecticut of mid–19th century Irish immigrant parents of modest means, both were outstanding boxers — Boston boxer Patsey Sheppard nearly convinced O'Rourke to turn professional,[14] each was a devoted family man who disdained the rowdy-player lifestyle of drinking and gambling, and both espoused a standard of "manliness" that emphasized gentlemanly habits, but which did not rule out defending oneself or one's honor.

After being released by Giants manager Pat Powers in September 1892, O'Rourke spent a year as a much-criticized National League umpire and then ran unsuccessfully for a seat in the Connecticut legislature. With the arrival of spring in 1895, the Orator, then 44 years old, "began to pine for the crack of the bat, the scent of a well-oiled glove, and the feel of a shiny white ball."[15] He soon formed an independent Bridgeport team, the "Victors," and took on the task of organizing a new professional regional or state league. Thanks to O'Rourke's efforts, the Connecticut State League was born in March 1897, and the following year became an "official" league by signing the National Agreement. O'Rourke served as league Secretary and manager-captain of the Bridgeport team, which adopted the future Hall of Famer's own nickname for its own: the Orators. By the time Roger Connor assumed command at Waterbury, the Connecticut State League "had matured into a tight knit circuit of eight clubs [Derby, Bridgeport, New Haven, Meriden, Danbury, Waterbury, New Britain, New London], all contained within the borders of Connecticut. This helped to keep down travel costs, and made overnight hotel stays unnecessary."[16]

In his first full year as a professional-league manager in 1898, Roger Connor led the Waterbury Pirates to the Connecticut State League championship. With Joe Connor alternating between the catcher and third-base positions and Roger holding down first base, the Connor boys, as at Fall River, often worked in tandem to help achieve victory. In a mid–May win against Danbury, for example, "The Connor brothers' double steal was one of the features of the game."[17]

Nearly all of Roger's five home runs during the season were memorable. Two were walk-off four-baggers — the first in a July ten-inning, 6–5 win over New Britain, and the second a ninth-inning game-saver against New Haven. "Roger pasted the ball and when it dropped it struck the track on the back stretch near the electric light pole in right field, bounded over the fence, and was lost."[18] A third home run against Bridgeport in April was described as "a splendid home run over the fence,"[19]and a fourth against New Britain in May was even more unusual. "Roger Connor came in for his usual home run and made a most remarkable hit. The ball went from his bat like a shot to the right field fence and wedged in between the boards of the fence and a post, and while the New Britain fielder was trying to get it Roger made the circuit of the bases."[20]

Over the course of the season, Connor's managerial style received high praise around the league. The *Meriden Republican* affirmed that "The secret of Waterbury's success is team work"[21]; Connor "received great praise from Danburians [residents of Danbury] yesterday for the great control he has over his players."[22] The *Meriden Journal* noted that "The old National leaguer has drilled his men into playing clean baseball and he sets an excellent example for them."[23]

After a thrilling pennant race that ended on the last day of the season when Waterbury defeated Danbury to finish in first place, two percentage points ahead of New Haven, *Sporting Life* declared, "Hail to the King! Roger Connor and his band of Pirates have landed the 1898 pennant after one of the most exciting races known."[24] The *Waterbury American* credited the victory to "the old leaguer, [who] was the right hand man in all games. He directed the individual play of his men and brought them out on top.... His work at first has been of the steady, reliable kind and at the bat and the field has led his team."[25] Connor finished the season at .292, with 147 hits in 93 games, including 29 doubles and five four-baggers. His fielding average of .983 was 40 points above the next man on the team.

Twenty-two years earlier, a tall, slender, inexperienced Roger Connor put on his first uniform and made his debut in professional baseball with the hometown Waterbury Monitors. After his difficult final years in the major leagues with the disintegrating St. Louis Browns franchise, the triumphant return of the "old Leaguer" was doubly rewarding because of the presence of his brother Joe on the team and the regular participation of Angeline, Cecelia, Joe's wife Agnes and their daughters Catherine and Agnes in the everyday management of the ballpark. A brief note in *The Sporting News* captured the idyllic nature of the enterprise:

A Happy Family Arrangement
The Connor family is fully represented in Waterbury base ball, with Roger on first, Joe behind the plate, Mrs. Roger in the box office, and the Connor children scattered all around the ground.[26]

After the championship 1898 season, the Waterbury team changed its nickname to the Rough Riders in honor of Teddy Roosevelt's cavalry unit that fought during the recently-successful Spanish American War. It proved to be an apt nickname, since the team's path would be rough during the coming years. It was an unsettling time for minor league baseball. Plagued by chronic low attendance, Connecticut League teams regularly disbanded or moved to other cities, and numerous poorly-paid players preferred to take their chances in outlaw leagues where salaries were double that received in Connecticut. On off days, other players violated their league contracts by participating in rival leagues' games for extra pay. Seven 1899 Waterbury players, including Roger Connor, returned to the Rough Riders for the 1900 season, but only three from the 1900 squad returned for the following year's campaign. Even Joe Connor left the team, making a brief appearance for the National League Boston Beaneaters in 1900, and spending the remainder of the 1900 season with Jim O'Rourke's Orators in Bridgeport. In 1901 he played a few games for the American League Cleveland Blues and the Milwaukee Brewers before finishing the season with the Orators.

Only five teams returned for the 1899 Connecticut League season, and Roger Connor himself seriously considered moving the Waterbury franchise to Danbury. In early June, the old Leaguer went on an offensive tear, collecting 18 hits in eight games, stealing five bases, hitting two home runs, scoring 12 runs, and raising his batting average above .400. By the end of July he was up to .429, prompting the *Waterbury American* to observe that "there are some people in this town who want Roger Connor to quit the game. The old man ought to be in the big league. He's good enough."[27] At age 42, his pop-up slide remained a potent weapon on the base paths — he stole three bases in a game on two separate occasions, and in each of three other games he stole a pair.

In July, as the Rough Riders battled the New Haven Blues for first place, Connor added extra offensive power to the lineup by signing Louis "Chief" Sockalexis, whose meteoric rise with the Cleveland Spiders in 1897 was followed by an equally meteoric fall due to alcohol abuse. A member of Maine's Penobscot Indian tribe, Sockalexis was the first Native American to play in the National League. Signed by Spiders manager Patsy Tebeau after having been expelled from Notre Dame University for drunkenness, Sockalexis' presence on the Cleveland nine during spring training caused the local newspapers to refer to the team as "Tebeau's Indians."[28] Years later, the "Indians" moniker would be adopted as the team's official nickname. Starting the season in right field, Sockalexis' hitting and speed on the base paths made him a sensation in the press, but by the end of July he was suspended for drunkenness. He played infrequently the following year due to his illness, and was released by Cleveland in May 1899.

Sockalexis suited up with the Rough Riders in July after brief stints with Hartford of the Eastern League and with the Bristol Bell Makers of the Connecticut League. In his first game for Waterbury on July 24, his triple with the bases loaded in the seventh inning brought in the winning runs against the Derby nine, whose team nickname, ironically, was the "Lushers." Sockalexis controlled his drinking under manager Roger Connor, and hit over .300 with the Rough Riders for the remainder of the season. Thereafter he disappeared from sight, much to the chagrin of Connor, who sought to sign him to a contract for the following year. He surfaced infrequently in the next few years, and after several failed comeback attempts, returned to the Penobscot reservation in Maine, where he died of a heart attack at age 42.[29]

The efforts of Sockalexis and Connor of the Rough Riders were not enough to deny the New Haven Blues the pennant after compiling a 55–37 record in 1899. Waterbury finished second at 52–43. Playing in all but three games, Connor led the league in hitting at .392, with 28 doubles, 5 home runs, and 18 stolen bases.

Accounts of the Rough Riders' 1900 season are incomplete, since neither the Waterbury newspapers nor *Sporting Life* chose to publish Connecticut League box scores that year (*The Sporting News*, based in the mid-west, had never done so). Of the 29 players who donned a Waterbury uniform in 1900, 18 lasted less than a month, and five lasted only a day. Only three players on the team were local talent. Attendance, thus, was predictably poor. Similar circumstances caused both the Norwich and New Haven franchises to be transferred to other owners. After briefly leading the league in early June, the Rough Riders dropped to sixth place at season's end, with a record of 43–54. At age 43, his eyesight failing, Roger Connor continued to contribute, banging out 82 hits in 83 games, including two home runs and nine doubles, and stealing 20 bases.

As the 1901 season began, Roger, disappointed by the lack of fan support in his home town, secretly began looking elsewhere to start up a new team. In February, the Springfield, Massachusetts, Ponies, who had finished sixth of eight teams in the Eastern League in 1900, were expelled to make room for a Buffalo nine. The Ponies then belatedly applied for admission to the Connecticut League, but were informed that they would have to wait until the 1902 season for consideration. The prospect of being able to select a completely new roster of players for a team representing a city that would be hungry for baseball after a season without it appealed to Connor, and behind the scenes he began laying the groundwork to establish a franchise in Springfield.

Meanwhile, the rag-tag collection of Waterbury players got off to a poor start, losing 10 of their first 12 games. In classic Connor fashion, Roger got hot in early June, smacking 13 hits in five games, including two triples, and rallying the Rough Riders to a 24–32 record by mid–July. Word then came that the Squire of Waterbury had sold the Brass City team to local businessman George Harrington. This was followed by the news that "The famous Roger Connor has joined the New Haven team."[30] Connor's contributions to both the Blues and the Rough Riders in 1901 were significant — he hit .299 for the season, with 123 three hits, including 10 doubles, eight triples, and three home runs.

In 1902, with the help of Jim O'Rourke, Roger Connor's Springfield team was accepted in the League, which, conceding that it no longer exclusively consisted of teams from the *state* of Connecticut, dropped the word from its official title, becoming simply the Connecticut Baseball League. Connor chose a familiar figure for a partner in the Springfield enterprise; "Joe [Connor] is associated with his brother Roger in the ownership and management of the club, and believes that he can make more money than he would receive [playing] either in the American or National League."[31] In March a playing field was secured. 'Roger Connor has made a deal for the use by his new Springfield club of Hampden Park.... Nothing now stands in the way of a successful season."[32] As the season opened, *Sporting Life* reported that "The baseball cranks in this section [Springfield] are in a happy frame of mind now that they have real live base ball team in their midst.... From all sides one hears nothing but praise for the work of Manager Connor's men."[33]

Once again the Connor boys were back in action together. On May 10 at Hartford, both brothers stole two bases in a 15–6 win. In New London on May 20, they combined for three hits and three runs, with Roger registering a double and a sacrifice. Even though Joe was now 27, a June 12 encounter with former Boston first baseman Tom Tucker, now playing with Meriden, proved that Roger still felt it was his duty as Joe's older brother to protect him.

Tucker, a Holyoke native, was a solid offensive player whose offensive language directed toward fans and umpires almost cost him his life in a game at Philadelphia in 1894. In a mid–July contest in the City of Brotherly Love, Tucker, playing for Boston, loudly protested the umpire's safe call at second when Phillies speedster Billy Hamilton stole the base. After Hamilton later scored, Tucker began taunting and cursing the Philadelphia fans. Behind in the game, the Bostons, seeing a thunderstorm approaching, undertook a series of delaying tactics in the hope of having the game called due to the weather. After the umpire declared a forfeit in favor of Philadelphia, the fans converged on the field and headed for Tucker, who had been cursing them all afternoon. Staggered by a blow that broke his left cheekbone, Tucker was placed under the stands for protection until he could be escorted off the grounds.

During his last season of professional ball, Tucker once again received a pummeling on the ball field — this time not from the fans, but from Roger Connor:

> Satisfying a grudge dating back to old Brotherhood times [Tucker supported neither the Brotherhood nor the Players' League] old Roger Connor, now manager and owner of the Springfield club, landed on the neck of old Tom Tucker yesterday. Roger was playing first base for the Springfield nine in the game with the Meridens. Roger was offended because his brother Joe tried some horseplay in base running and was hurled into the grass by Tucker. There is a legend that the Tuckers don't like the Connors. Roger soon got his base on balls and directly he was pummeling Tucker in the neck. Tucker,

strange to tell, didn't resent it. Roger was removed from the field while Tucker was sent to the bench. It is Roger's first offense in all his ball life."[34]

After 26 years in organized baseball, it took a perceived slight to his younger brother to get Connor ejected from a game. Two weeks later, however, in a return contest against Meriden, he exacted his revenge. "The feature of the game was a steal home by [Roger] Connor."[35]

Serious confrontations between league enemies, however, were not the only unusual events that took place on minor league ball fields. During a Springfield-Waterbury matchup in mid-season, for example, "Lindeman [Waterbury's pitcher] hit the ball to deep centre [sic], and the ball rolled through a hole which boys had dug. Kennedy [Springfield's center fielder] tried to get through the hole after the ball but could not move one way or the other when half way through. It was necessary to dig him out."[36]

The Ponies were in first place in mid–June, but took a tumble when "two valuable men,"[37] a second baseman and pitcher, deserted the team and signed with outlaw clubs in Ohio and Kansas City respectively for twice ($200) what they received monthly from the Ponies. A month later the team lost the services of its manager-captain. After having gone 4-for-5 in the previous game at Waterbury, Connor sprained an ankle against Meriden on July 10. He played infrequently afterward until the end of August, and after that, not at all. It was the first time in 27 years that an injury had sidelined the Iron Giant for more than a few games. Playing in a total of 62 contests, Connor hit .259 and managed just seven doubles, a triple, and one home run. Even before the injury, he had let it be known that 1902 would be his last season as a player. The reports of his definitive retirement, however, were still a bit premature.

Although the Ponies finished second (65–46) to the New Haven Blues (70–39), Springfield fans were delighted with the result. "Roger Connor was induced to try Springfield and lo and behold! scored a winner and a heavy one at that, the very first season."[38] Near year's end, Connor disclosed publicly for the first time that his bad ankle was not his only physical ailment. "Dear Old Roger Connor, somewhat gray, was in attendance [at a meeting of minor league clubs] and in discussing the good old days said he would be good yet on the diamond were his 'lamps' [eyes] as bright as in the days gone by."[39]

After bench-managing during the first week of the 1903 season, Connor surprised the Springfield fans by donning glasses for the first time in his career and inserting himself in the Ponies lineup against Meriden on May 15.

When Roger Connor, the famous old New York first baseman stepped to the plate at Springfield ... the fans gasped. Roger had announced that he would never break into the game again. The first time up he cracked a three-bagger and he made two more hits during the game. Roger says he made the mistake of his life in not putting on glasses years ago. Had he done so he would have never left the big league, he says.[40]

Today, the refusal of a ballplayer to wear glasses if they were needed would be perceived as sheer foolishness. In Connor's era and for some time afterward, their use was considered a sign of weakness. As late as 1912, former major leaguer Sam Crane still considered Connor's use of glasses late in his minor league career as a handicap: "[In the Connecticut State League] he [Connor] made a big success as owner-manager, and also as a player, [and] although he found it necessary to wear spectacles while playing, even with this handicap he did not lose his great batting ability."[41] A year later, the *Hartford Courant*, reporting on Connor's play in the Connecticut Elks League, found it necessary to include the fact that while the former Giant still played well, he needed glasses to do so. "Roger Connor, at the head of the Waterbury team, cleaned up the league. Roger played first base with goggles on."[42]

Connor played good baseball for the rest of May 1903, but he was not putting up the power numbers of old. The sacrifice, the steal, and an occasional two-bagger now took the place of the triple or the tape-measure home run. His progress was further hampered by a chronic charley-horse, and by an embarrassing off-field confrontation with another player.

During a game at New London on June 4, Whalers first baseman Scott Hardesty tripped Connor as he was running to the base. Hardesty and the press claimed it was an accident, but Connor thought otherwise. "Hardesty accidentally tripped Connor as the latter attempted to reach first base during the game to-day [*sic*] and the Springfield man got a bad fall. Tonight Connor met Hardesty on the street and it is alleged assaulted him."[43] After the confrontation, Connor was arrested and then released on bond prior to an appearance at Police Court.

Although there is no press record of the adjudication of the charge, it soon became apparent how the matter was settled. A week later, Hardesty, "late of [the] New London [team],"[44] was signed by Springfield's owner-manager, Roger Connor. There are two possible explanations for this course of action — either the 33-year-old Hardesty's price for not pressing charges was a spot on Connor's team, or Connor, regretting his intemperate action of assaulting Hardesty, had offered him a Rough Riders contract as an apology for his own conduct. Given Connor's gentlemanly reputation in the game and his general good character, the second explanation seems the more plausible. However, a month later, Hardesty was released by the Ponies, and *Sporting Life* reported that in Springfield "Roger Connor is again covering the bag."[45]

While there were flashes of the old brilliance in Connor's on-field performance, it was clear that donning glasses could not overcome the effects of age and deteriorating reflexes. He went 3-for-4 against Holyoke on July 16, but his four errors against New Haven two weeks later cost the Ponies the game. Although he continued to find a way to get on base, to steal and to sacrifice, a late season batting slump (two for 23 in six games) pulled his average down to .291. On the next-to-last day of the season at Bridgeport, September 11, he went hitless in four at-bats and committed an error at first. On that date 17 years earlier, the giant of the Giants smacked the only home run ever hit out of the old Polo Grounds, added another four-bagger and two other hits for good measure, fielded flawlessly at first base, and became the toast of New York and the baseball world.

Perhaps at Bridgeport on September 11, 1903, the old Leaguer recalled his day of glory in New York 17 years earlier. Perhaps he did not. He removed himself from the lineup for the final game of the year on the following day, a 6–3 win against Hartford. Springfield finished the season in seventh place with a record of 41–64. Holyoke, a newcomer to the Connecticut League and representing the town where Connor began his professional career a quarter-century earlier, won the league championship with a 66–37 mark.

On October 26, *Sporting Life* reported that "After the last game of the season Roger Connor announced that he had sold his Springfield club to Dan O'Neil of Holyoke and would permanently retire after 25 years of service on the diamond."[46]

This time he meant it. More or less.

In the spring of 1876, six years after baseball's first professional team, the Cincinnati Red Stockings, completed its two-year exhibition tour with only one defeat, Roger Connor donned his first baseball uniform and joined his hometown Waterbury Monitors. The National League was born that same spring, and played its first game in Philadelphia on April 22. During the ensuing years, as Connor plied his trade with different teams, other leagues challenged the National League's baseball monopoly. Two of them failed in that endeavor, a third was absorbed by the Senior Circuit, and a fourth, the American League, successfully established itself as its predecessor's equal.

A few weeks after Roger Connor finished his professional career in 1903, the bi-partite major league structure that we know today was ceremoniously ratified when the Boston Americans played the National League Pittsburgh Pirates in the first modern World Series. The timeline of Connor's playing career thus corresponds exactly to the birth, growth, and consolidation of what we know today as major league baseball.

When Connor started with the Monitors, home plate was a 12-inch square, fielders didn't wear gloves, it took nine balls to earn a walk, and pitchers threw underhanded at a distance of 45 feet from the batter. By the time Connor played in his last game, every major modern regulation except those that established the designated hitter and abolished the spitball was in place. The same evolution occurred in equipment, with one exception: the "dead ball" that Connor nailed for his first major league home run in 1880 off Tommy Bond, was essentially the same "dead ball" that he slugged out of the park against Cy Young for his last big league four-bagger. Clubs were not required to provide two balls for a game until 1896, Connor's last full year in the big leagues. Prior to that, regardless of how scuffed, stained or water-logged the original ball became, it remained in play. Connor's history on the "diamond green," therefore, is as much the history of a sport in transition as it is one man's ability to adapt to such transitions.

Three other factors must be considered in contextualizing Roger Connor's offensive and defensive statistics: season length, playing and traveling conditions, and playing strategy. In the first decade of Connor's major league career, he had the possibility of playing in 1,100 games (he actually played in a remarkable 1,083 of them). Seasons during those years ranged from a low of 81 games (1882) to a high of 131 games (1889). The modern player, in contrast, has the possibility of playing in 1,620 games in a decade. One would not expect even the hardiest of modern players to participate in all such contests, but if he were to play in 80 percent of them (1,296 games), he would play 200 more games than Roger Connor had the opportunity to play over the same time period. The statistical implications of such disparity are self-evident.

Connor played in every game in his first two major league seasons — a total of 168, or, just six more contests in two years than the total for a single season in our era. Viewed in this context, his 113 hits in 1880 and 107 in 1881 combine to represent approximately 220 hits in a modern 162-game season. His 53 and 55 runs scored totals in these years equate to approximately 100 scored in a 162-game season. His doubles total would be 35, his triples 14, and his home runs 5.

While the effect of playing and traveling conditions on performance cannot be quantified in the same manner in which differing game totals required to constitute a season can be, such factors were daunting in the Connor era. Clubhouses and dugouts were non-existent — players dressed at their hotel and sat during the game on uncovered wooden benches halfway between the bleachers and the foul line, exposed day-in-and-day-out to the sun, rain, and bottles and rotten vegetables thrown from the stands. Playing fields were muddy in the spring and fall, and baked solid in the summer. Infields rarely were flat or graded, and grass was so tall and overgrown in some outfields that home team players customarily hid spare balls there, substituting the spare when the ball in play got beyond them. Road trips to play western clubs could last a month, and travel was in wooden, non-air conditioned Pullman railroad cars with no shower facilities. The one-way journey from New York to Chicago could last nearly two days, and "the prospect of spending 15–20 hours in a wooden rail car traveling across the mid–West in mid-summer heat must have tested the mettle of the hardiest team member."[47] Food, water, and sanitary conditions on the road were at best unpredictable, and at worst atrocious.

Game strategy during the Connor era can properly be described as the survival of the fittest. "Dirty. Very, very dirty. The tactics of the eighties were aggressive; the tactics of the nineties were violent. The game of the eighties was crude; the game of the nineties was criminal. The baseball of the eighties had ugly elements; the game of the nineties was just ugly."[48] Such is the context of Roger Connor's career statistics.

The record for which Connor is remembered, the record that ultimately qualified him for selection to the Hall of Fame, remained unknown until the latter half of the twentieth century. As late as 1966, David Quentin Voigt, whose *American Baseball* remains a classic in the field, had conceded the 19th-century home run title to another player, writing, "[Sam] Thompson achieved a career [home run] total of 127, a record that stood until Babe Ruth's day."[49]

Connor's belated recognition as the premier home run hitter before Ruth, with a total of 138, was a double-edged sword, however, for it promoted a tendency to view him as a one-dimensional player, which he decidedly was not. He led his league once in home runs, and at least once each in hits, doubles, triples, RBI, walks, batting average, slugging, and on-base percentage. He ranks fifth all-time in career triples, and despite never playing a season that equaled today's number of games, still ranks 38th in runs scored (1,620). In 1885 he made 506 plate appearances and struck out just eight times. He hit for the cycle once, and if a Troy newspaper account of the era is correct, may have done it twice and also been the first to do so. He hit safely six times in a game (1895), and made nine consecutive hits over two games (1895). Besides ranking first among all 19th-century players in home runs, he ranks first in triples (233), second in walks (1,002), hits (2,467) and total bases (3,788), fourth in runs (1,620) and seventh in slugging (.486). He was the first player to hit an ultimate grand slam, the only man to hit a ball out of the original Polo Grounds, and was credited with hitting the longest home run in numerous ball parks of his era.

Former player Sam Crane, as previously mentioned, asserted that Connor despised the bunt, but Connor himself, in an 1896 interview, set the record straight. "Another thing I want to call your attention to is this: There is less bunting today, and bunting, to my mind, is one of the most scientific points in baseball. It develops base running and fielding, and sharpens the work of the infielders."[50] He was adept at the sacrifice bunt, and found it a particularly useful tool in his post–major league career. He stole 43 bases in 1887, averaged over 20 steals a year in the years after stealing was formally recognized in scoring accounts, and is credited with having invented the pop-up slide. The frequency and success of his thievery throughout his major and minor league years strongly suggests that it was a weapon in his arsenal long before it figured in official game accounts. From the 1870s to the 1890s, Connor switch-hit under specific circumstances, namely unfavorable wind conditions for hitting left-handed or when facing certain left-handed pitchers. At least four of his home runs were hit right-handed; future research may reveal more. Although he is traditionally listed as a left-handed hitter, a more appropriate designation for Connor would be that of "situational switch-hitter."

The most overlooked aspect of Connor's play was his defense. After spending only one full year at first base in his first five seasons, he subsequently led his league at that position in total chances four times and in fielding percentage four times. In 1887 and in 1890, he led in both categories in the same year, a feat accomplished by no other 19th-century first baseman except Cap Anson. Connor's 1887 posed studio photograph shows him not wearing a glove. That year he led the league with a .993 fielding percentage, the best of the gloveless era. In 1896, at the age of 39, he became the oldest 19th-century first baseman to lead the league in fielding.

While most historians concede first place among the era's first basemen to Cap Anson, William Curran, author of *Mitts: A Celebration of the Art of Fielding*, demurs:

If I had to name the best first baseman of the Victorian era on evidence available — and it is scanty — I would have to say the Giants' Roger Connor. A left handed thrower, Connor was as large as Anson, but by all accounts significantly more agile and sure-handed.... Like Anson, Connor is in the Hall of Fame, and like Anson he's there because he was a heavy hitter. Connor happens to have been an excellent fielder as well, not as imaginative and daring at first base as his contemporary, Charlie Comiskey, perhaps, but steady and reliable.... I can't determine whether he ever wore [a glove]. Judging from the size of his hands, he didn't need one. If you tanned Roger's right hand and tied an thong around the fingers, it could pass for the fielder's glove your kid got last Christmas.[51]

Retired from the professional game at age 46 and freed from the responsibilities of team ownership, Connor now spent his time with family — which would soon include grandchildren — and traveling — both abroad and to sunny Florida during the winter months. There was time for a new job with the City of Waterbury, and time to organize benefit programs for his beloved Elks Club.

There was even time for a little more baseball.

7

The Forgotten Star

"I used to nail the horsehide over the fence into the tall grass and that would tickle some of the old stockbrokers."
— Roger Connor, *Waterbury American*, January 5, 1931

It was not at all certain that Connor would stay retired. As soon as the New Year, 1904, dawned, a report noted that "Roger Connor, the veteran, is considering a proposition to take the Fitchburg franchise of the New England League."[1] That opportunity passed, and Connor for the time being contented himself with playing in an Old Timers' game at the Polo Grounds after John McGraw's Giants won the 1905 National League pennant. Dan Brouthers and members of the Giants' 1888 championship team, including Connor, Jim O'Rourke, Mickey Welch, and George Gore, gave McGraw's men a good fight but lost, 10–8.

In February of the following year, Connor, Gore, Welch, and John Ward organized a benefit for their former manager, Jim Mutrie, who had been experiencing hard times. After being fired by the Giants at the end of the 1891 season, Mutrie was hired to manage the Eastern League's Elmira, New York, team, but his inability to stay sober led to his release in April, just prior to the start of the season. Thereafter, "Truthful Jeems" had been living in genteel poverty with wife Kate and daughter Grace on Staten Island, and he reportedly was too ill to work.

In July 1905, Connor's mother, Catherine, passed away at age 72. His generosity had freed her from the struggles of her early life, and she had outlived her husband Mortimer by more than three decades.

The Old Timers' game experience at the Polo Grounds the previous year inspired Connor to organize a team, "Connor's Veterans," to challenge

155

town clubs around the state, a venture that proved so successful that the team's games far outdrew those of the old Troy National League team of his youth. "The Waterbury Veterans, known as Roger Connor's team, went to Stamford today and before a crowd of 2,500 people defeated Stamford 4 to 3. Wallace and Gaffney was the battery for Waterbury. Paul Corcoran of the New Havens pitched for Stamford and Jones caught. Roger and Joe Connor and Fitzpatrick played with the Veterans."[2]

Although tales of old-time players who were down on their luck were common in the national sports journals of the time, the scant news that appeared about "Old Waterbury" was positive. After a February 1906, encounter between Connor and former National Association player and National League manager Jack Chapman, it was reported that "Jack engaged in a game of pool with that other well known youngster, Roger Connor.... 'Nothing the matter with the way Connor is fixed,' said the veteran. 'He's all right. Don't ever worry about him.'"[3] This judgment was proven sound when Roger announced he would make a second trip to Europe, and in particular, to Ireland; "Roger has been over before and says he likes the 'old sod.'"[4]

The Connor clan increased by one in 1907, when 19-year-old Cecelia married Waterbury resident James F. Colwell, a recently graduated pharmacist. Eventually, five grandchildren would be added to the Connor family, the eldest of whom, Roger, was named after his famous grandfather.

The old slugger, however, was still looking for a place in the baseball business. A July report on a game between the Waterbury Brass Company team and Bristol's town club noted that "The contest was made more interesting by the presence of Roger Connor ... the former crack first baseman of the New York National Team, who acted as coach for the Waterbury men. He did grand work and impressed the audience with the undisputable fact that he is still master of the game, even if his legs are stiff and his hair gray."[5] The following summer, Connor and a half-dozen other members of Connecticut Elks Club Lodges organized the Elks Baseball League, consisting of teams from Hartford, Waterbury, Meriden, Middleton, Bristol and New Britain. Connor co-managed Waterbury's entry and played first base. Although the league only had a six-week, 12-game schedule, clubs wore uniforms emblazoned with B.P.O.E. (Benevolent Protective Order of Elks) and each town's lodge number on the shirt, and home teams were required to "pay all the local expenses, furnish an umpire who must be a member of the order, supply the balls, and each team will pay its own traveling expenses abroad and other incidentals, such as cigars, etc."[6]

Three weeks into the season Waterbury held the league lead, and 51-

year-old Connor's play was praised after a 15–3 blowout win against Hart-ford. "The finest work of the afternoon was performed by the former National Leaguers Roger Connor and John M. Henry. The latter was not as fresh as usual ... but Connor was in great condition and played the bag with all his old time skill. The old man's eyesight is not as good as it was in the last century and he did not get a hit until the last time he was up."[7] The game's box score reveals that "Old Waterbury" had also taken part in two double plays.

One year later, Connor briefly played for yet another team. "Roger Connor feels jealous because Jim O'Rourke is getting back into the game and Roger has decided to take a backward leap into baseball. Roger has joined the Clintons [the team from Clinton, Connecticut]. Roger is sum-mering on the East Shore and yesterday he accepted an invitation of Man-ager Lively to join the ranks of that club for today's game with the Milfords. Roger will be placed at first base."[8] The 58-year-old O'Rourke's return to the playing field, however, like Connor's, was brief: "Jim played in only one ballgame in 1909, on August 21.... It was the first game of a double header against Holyoke."[9] While it appears that Connor's stay on the Clin-ton team was also only for a day, he made the most of it. "Roger Connor, the former first baseman on the Giants, played for several innings at first base for Clinton against Milford yesterday afternoon and put one of his old-time hits over the stone wall. The score was 7–3 in favor of Clinton."[10] This is the last known record of a Roger Connor home run, occurring 31 years after his first, which he hit while with the Waterbury Monitors in 1878.

In 1910, Connor assumed his old position at third base for a New London club that played in a four-team Connecticut league. In a July 2– 0 win against Willimantic, he doubled, and at the age of 53, stole a base.[11] The following month he was injured in a game, the account of which pres-ents a scene that approximates the chaos of a Keystone Cops silent movie:

> Roger Connor was laid out in the third inning by a bad bound. Paddy O'Mara was waiting at the plate in the fourth for a ball thrown to the plate. Patsy Sul-livan had plenty of room to hook slide, but instead, most rudely and ungentle-manly ran plumb into O'Mara.... The water boy fell through the grandstand in the fifth inning. A dog fight in the sixth under the third base bleachers called off everything for a few minutes until the two Brunos were pulled apart. The eighth inning was the limit. Lefty Smith had the ligaments of the little finger of his salary wing [arm] snapped and his knuckles knocked out. Umpire Sul-livan was banged in the arm by a foul tip and Griffith met the same fate. Everybody mentioned took the count and Roger Connor, O'Mara and Smith were fixed up by doctors. Say, can any town beat that?[12]

At the end of the season, after playing organized baseball in five decades, Roger Connor called it a career.

In the fall of 1910, Connor took in a game at the Polo Grounds with old Brotherhood friend Dan Brouthers, and the pair passed on their views of the "modern" game to a *New York Sun* reporter.

> "I can't see where the game has improved, Dan!" said Connor. "In fact, I don't believe there's anybody excepting Lajoie, Cobb, Wagner, and others who can hit the ball any harder that we did!" "That's been my argument all along," replied Brouthers. "And furthermore, the pitchers and fielders aren't a bit better. You don't see any greater stars than Ewing, Keefe, Clarkson, Ward, Anson, Hardie Richardson, Radbourne, Kelly and Williamson, do you?" "You can bet your life on that!" said Connor, with a grim smile.[13]

In 1913, the Connecticut League changed its name to the Eastern Association in order to reflect the fact that it now had three teams, Holyoke, Springfield, and Pittsfield, from outside the borders of the Nutmeg State. That year the Association's President, Jim O'Rourke, called his old Giants teammate out of retirement for a new assignment at the ballpark.

> Roger Connor, who a decade ago was regarded as one of the greatest long distance hitters in the business, is still tied up in the game. Connor is acting as general supervisor of the umpires in this league for President O'Rourke. Roger's chief duties are to look an umpire over from the stand [*sic*] during the game, then point out to him what mistakes he made after the contest is over. So far the idea has worked like a charm and many umpires have developed considerably under Connor's advice and coaching.[14]

At season's end, Roger and Angeline celebrated their 30th wedding anniversary with a vacation cruise to Bermuda.

Connor had the unusual habit of changing his residence every few years, and after selling his Springfield ball club at the end of the 1903 season, he sold his house on South Main and moved first to East Liberty Street, and then in 1907, the year of Cecelia's marriage, to a three-story brick house on Crescent Street in Waterbury. In the next few years Cecelia gave birth to two children while living in crowded circumstances at the home of husband James's mother. In 1913, Connor purchased a three-story house on South Waterville Street that was large enough to accommodate the Connors and the growing Colwell clan. This arrangement allowed the doting grandfather to spend more time with his grandchildren. "Grandpa's lap was always available to us and we loved to climb up. He'd raise his knees up and down and tell us we were riding horsey-back."[15]

Management of his real estate holdings, however, soon wasn't enough to occupy the Squire of Waterbury. In January 1914, he assumed a position that was intended to be purely honorary, but which he took quite seriously; "Roger Connor, a famous demon batsman of old, who was a favorite of the fans at the Polo Grounds, has just been made an inspector of schools in his home city of Waterbury, Conn."[16] *Sporting Life's* need to clarify the identity of the old slugger in its report was both a telling lesson on the fleeting nature of fame and a portent of the future. The new appointment included a bonus that the old slugger deeply enjoyed: "Roger Connor, one time an idol of the Polo Grounds fans, is now engaged as coach of the high school team at Waterbury, Conn., where he has made his home for years. Roger is connected with the school department in the capacity of inspector."[17]

As the rigors of the New England winter became harder to bear with the passing years, Connor recalled his spring training days in Florida decades earlier, and resolved to make a change in his life. In the early Twenties, he and Angeline began spending their winters in Miami, bringing with them Cecelia's oldest son and Roger's namesake, Roger Colwell, who was enrolled in a Catholic school in the area. Once again, as in the case of his brother Joe and his nephew Roger Connor Wilson (his sister Hannah's oldest son), Connor was extending a helping hand to his family. The annual Florida stay was the adventure of a lifetime for young Roger Colwell, and likewise gave Cecelia, now with four other children, a chance to catch her breath back in Waterbury.

During this period Connor and Angeline sold their Waterville Street property after stipulating to the new owners that the Colwells continue to be allowed to rent one floor of the house. They then moved into a smaller home on Calumet Street, a short walk from Connor's beloved Elks Club and St. Margaret's Church, where the couple attended mass. The old Leaguer, who turned 60 in 1917, settled into a comfortable lifestyle centered on family and close friends. He kept busy in Waterbury as school inspector, and annually enjoyed the mild winters of Florida.

The Connors' yearly sojourn in the Sunshine State coincided with the great Florida land boom. After World War I, an increasingly mobile and well-to-do U.S. populace became fascinated with Florida's balmy weather and ocean shoreline. The state's business-friendly legislature abolished income and inheritance taxes, automobile drivers there enjoyed the highest speed limit in the country, 45 miles per hour, without the bother of having to secure a driving license, and rum runners from Cuba made it easy to circumvent Prohibition. Population growth was rapid and new cities and towns blossomed overnight. By the early 1920s, the Waterbury couple owned a house and property in the Miami area. A 1922 "Notice of Realty Changes" listed him as the seller of a land parcel to a Thomas McDougall.[18] In this time of prosperity Connor did not forget his family. He bought Cecilia a spacious, three-story house on Willow Street, just a block from his own house. "One spring on their return from Florida we were pleasantly surprised when Grandpa bought the Carmody house on Willow Street for us. We were crowded now with five children on Waterville Street. Our new one family home had plenty of room for us."[19]

One day in early 1922, a New York baseball fan discovered one of his old-time idols watching a pickup game of baseball in a Miami park.

> I was strolling 'round Royal Palm Park the other day when a ball player asked me if I knew Roger Connor. "I certainly do," I said. "Well there he stands." Looking in the direction the player pointed, I noticed a gentleman wearing glasses and his hair and moustache almost white. I knew the veteran many years ago, but I failed to recognize him with that make-up — but it sure enough was good old Roger Connor, and you would know him in a minute after you talked to him even half that long. He is still the ardent baseball fan, for there he was, standing up behind home plate watching the twirlers swish them over the pan. "When did you get here?" I asked. "Well, you see, I have a nice political position up in my home town, Waterbury, Conn. but am able to take a trip to this city to spend the winters. In fact, I am almost a resident here, for I own a home and spend all the cold months down this way. I suppose about one more year up north will be my last, for I contemplate moving to Miami. I have never seen such climate. I think it will add a few years to my life."[20]

As the interview progressed, the topic naturally turned to baseball. In response to a question about his thoughts on the modern game, Connor spoke at length:

> But I would like to see some of the boys of today play the game we did without gloves or any other thing to help. Why, the catchers did not even wear masks when I began to play back in the late seventies. Even back in the early nineties, there was a catcher, George "Doggie" Miller, who never wore a chest protector.... In those days they had better pitchers than they have now.... Many will dispute this, but we have no Radbournes [sic], Tim Keefs [sic], Mickey Welchs, Jimmy Galvins, the Only Nolans [nickname for Edward Sylvester Nolan], Jim McCormicks and other old timers like John Clarkson ... Tom Bond ... and many others that could be mentioned.[21]

At this point in the interview, like an old Civil War soldier making peace with a former opponent years after the battles, Connor praised the baseball skills of Buck Ewing, whom he felt had betrayed the Brotherhood cause in 1890, and who had died in 1906.

We have no "Buck" Ewings to catch today, and he was the greatest ball player of all times, in my estimation, for he could do everything, bat, catch, run the bases, and no catch [catcher] ever lived who could throw to the bases with his accuracy. Then we had to play with no gloves, even the first baseman had to catch them barehanded. When a catcher, and there was generally but one on each team, had his finger broken, and his hands so badly bunged up, that he could not hold a fork at the table, he never laid off to have his hands repaired. No siree, he just put some tape around them and back he went. I tell you the players are not as game and sturdy as they were in my days.[22]

News reports soon made it apparent, however, that Connor was doing more than watching Miami ballgames as a simple spectator. "Arison Turner, one of the best young ballplayers turned out on the local diamond, has signed a contract to play first base with the Waterbury Conn., team of the Eastern League. Turner was recommended to that club by Roger Connor, the old New York first baseman, who makes his home in this city during the winter, and who was born and raised in the city where Turner is to play."[23] Turner was a farm boy who attended an agricultural high school. He must have looked very familiar to the Old Leaguer, since he was "a left-handed fielder who bats both ways."[24]

In May 1925, Connor, along with other old-timers, gathered at the Polo Grounds prior to an early-season Giants game.

Good, gray old timers who were baseball heroes forty years back were there to help celebrate the National League's Golden Jubilee.... It was something of a thrill to the generation of baseball fans to gaze upon the green carpet of the Polo Grounds and behold such celebrities as Jim Mutrie, the first manager of the Giants, Amos Rusie, who had more smoke than Walter Johnson or Dazzy Vance put together, and Roger Connor, the Squire of Waterbury, who used to play first base for the old Giants.[25]

The event was Connor's last hurrah in baseball.

By the time the Connors again headed south late that fall, the Florida Land Boom was beginning to go bust. For the better part of the year,

Property prices soared, and some people got rich. One woman who had bought a Miami lot for $25 sold it during the boom, reportedly for $150,000. Many prices tripled or quadrupled within a year. Buyers often obtained lots solely in order to unload them quickly on someone else; in many cases they could barely afford the 10 percent "binder" that locked in the sale, let alone the property's full price. Sometimes, a parcel changed hands several times in a single day.[26]

By early 1926, the limit on property values had been reached and demand disappeared. Individuals lost their savings, Florida towns that had

Roger Connor, age 68, and future Hall of Famer Leon "Goose" Goslin, age 25, of the Washington Senators, 1925. The size contrast between Goslin —not a small man himself (5'11½", 185 pounds), and Connor suggests how imposing Connor must have been on the ball field four decades earlier (courtesy Library of Congress).

invested heavily in infrastructure went broke, and banks that lent them money followed suit. Later that year, Mother Nature added physical destruction to the financial devastation in Florida. In September a powerful hurricane came on shore north of Miami, killing 100 in that city and destroying thousands of dwellings.

Present-day photograph of the Willow Street, Waterbury, home purchased by Roger Connor for his daughter, Cecelia, and her family in the mid–1920s. After their financial setbacks during the Florida Land Boom/Bust of 1926, Roger and Angeline sold their own house and moved in with their daughter's family here, displacing two of their grandsons on the third floor. Angeline died here in 1928, as did Roger in 1931 (courtesy Gary Laios).

While it is unclear how much the Connors lost in the Florida real estate bust and subsequent hurricane, family members reported that the couple was significantly affected. Their house on Calumet Street in Waterbury was sold, and they moved in again with Cecelia's family, displacing two of their grandsons from the third floor of the Willow Street home. Nevertheless, Connor and Angeline wintered in Florida again in 1927, and were there in February 1928, when Angeline, now 68, became seriously ill and had to return home. There her health continued to fail, and she died at her daughter's house on March 17. She had been experiencing chest pains for three months, and on St. Patrick's Day suffered a fatal heart attack. Her obituary noted that Angeline had "won the friendship and love of a great many people. In various neighborhood gatherings, she was a prominent figure in all the activities of the community."[27] Most revealing and touching, however, was the observation that "Mrs. Connor was a real comrade to her husband in all [of] his business incident [*sic*] to his long service as a professional ballplayer. And later, when Roger became a magnate, Mrs. Connor played an important part in the successful operation of such a risky venture for those days."[28]

Connor's own health gradually deteriorated after the loss of his "angel." Diagnosed with cancer of the larynx in the winter of 1929, he was asked to choose between two treatments: the first operation would leave a hole in the throat through which a tube could be inserted to produce sounds; the second was the partial removal of the voice box. He chose the latter, and after a month's recovery in a New Haven hospital, he returned home able to talk in a raspy voice loud enough to be heard.

In his last years, Connor was a man of regulated habits. As his granddaughter put it, "Grandpa's routine never changed."[29] He rose at 8:30, ate breakfast at 9:00, read the newspaper, took a light lunch, walked to the Elks Club, and spent the afternoon there chatting with old friends. On Sundays he attended 11 o'clock mass at St. Margaret's church, just a few blocks up Willow Street. "Then he'd be ready to chat with his nieces and nephews who came to visit him regularly. If no one was coming that day, he'd nap until five and have supper and be ready to listen to Jack Benny on the radio. He enjoyed that program."[30] At 8:30 in the evening, he drank his customary night-cap — cider brandy and milk — and retired to his room, where he read late into the night.

In the fall of 1930, Connor developed what was later described euphemistically by the press as a "stomach condition" that gradually worsened. Four days into the New Year, 1931, he passed away at the home he had purchased for Cecelia, at 215 Willow Street. It was neither throat cancer nor stomach ailments, however, that brought down the giant of the Giants. His death certificate lists two causes: chronic myocarditis, and sepsis caused by the removal of his prostate three weeks earlier. In death, as in life, Roger Connor's complete story remained untold.

On Wednesday, January 7, 1931, the great slugger was laid to rest at Old St. Joseph's Cemetery in Waterbury. Interment was preceded by a solemn high Mass of requiem at St. Margaret's, his parish church. There, a special musical program was provided by the church quartet, which included Joseph Connor, bass, Roger's youngest sibling, whose ballplaying career had always received support from his oldest brother. Floral tributes arrived from the National League office, the New York Giants, and the New York police department. Written tributes fittingly included a letter from a player from the old state-league Derby club, H.D. Hedrick, who used the occasion to report yet another long-ago Connor tape-measure home run. At a game at Derby's Housatonic Park, Connor "hit the ball over the right field fence, far up a side hill, among a cluster of trees, the longest hit ever made on the Derby grounds."[31]

Former Connecticut Governor Charles A. Templeton's comments recognized Connor as "the greatest hard hitting first baseman of all time," but placed major emphasis on how Connor led his life off the field. "He had the good sense to utilize his athletic ability in such a way that it was profitable for him, and at the same time he had sound judgment which taught him to save his money so that he became an outstanding figure in the baseball world, in other words, he knew how to play ball and he knew how to save his money.... I always admired the devotion which was so apparent between Mrs. Connor and Roger.... He was a great ball player, a good fellow, and a fine citizen."[32]

Reporting on the funeral, the *Waterbury Republican* sadly noted that "Roger Connor made his last 'home run' yesterday. The famous star first baseman of the New York Giants of the 80's completed his round of the bases of life and took his exit amid the sorrowful utterances of friends and admirers instead of the plaudits and cheers of idolizing fans who had watched him perform on the diamond."[33]

Fame is fleeting. Soon after the tributes to him ended, the life and accomplishments of the old Leaguer, the "Babe Ruth of the 80's," faded from the memory of all but a few. New stars arose, and in the age of the "lively ball" began hitting home runs at a previously inconceivable pace. While other great players of his era eventually were enshrined in the newly-established Hall of Fame after World War II, the true record of Roger Connor's baseball career remained entombed in the crumbling, yellowed pages of half-century-old newspapers and sports journals.

The remains of the man once revered as "the Big Fellow, "the Oak of New York, "the "Rajah of Waterbury," and the "King of the Baseball Diamond," were buried in an unmarked grave. There they lay forgotten for seven decades.

8

—⁓—

The Past Recaptured

"I doubt if Ruth ever heard of Roger Connor. A lot of people haven't."
— Tommy Holmes, retired sportswriter, *New York World
Journal Tribune*, quoted in the *New York Times*, September
5, 1973

Sam Crane's 1912 *New York Evening Journal* article, the 26th in a
series entitled "The Fifty Greatest Ballplayers," was the first press retrospective of Roger Connor's career. Crane, a former shortstop and second-
baseman, played for seven major league teams in a seven-year career,
compiling a .203 batting average. He earned the enmity of Connor teammate and friend Jim O'Rourke for electing to play for the National League
during the Brotherhood War of 1890, his last major league season. "I know
Crane of old and would not willingly cooperate with him in anything....
I'm afraid that he has borne the reputation of being a sower of discord
wherever he was connected with ball players."[1]

Crane's article, while citing no statistics and making several factually
incorrect assertions that were repeated in later Connor biographies, nevertheless views Connor's career in a very positive light. He has high praise
for Connor's "nimble and agile" fielding, and for his running and sliding.
His assertion that Connor became a "bona fide professional player" in 1878
with Holyoke, is, as we have seen, incorrect — he lasted two weeks with the
team in April before being released, and he played the remainder of the season
with the Waterbury Monitors. While playing for Holyoke, Crane claims
that "Home run drives into the adjoining Connecticut River were common
with him."[2] Connor hit three home runs at his home field, Riverside Park,
in his only season (1879) with Holyoke, and while the field was located

adjacent to the Connecticut River, game accounts give no indication that any of these blows reached the river. Crane neglects to mention that Connor played a season — one of his most productive — with Philadelphia, and once again renews the claim that Connor's worth was over $100,000.

In 1918, an anonymous *Philadelphia Inquirer* article named Connor the runner-up to Sam Thompson in the all-time home run department, erroneously asserting that Big Sam, who spent 10 years with the local Phillies, had hit 120 four-baggers, while Roger had hit just 111. Ed Delahanty, another famous Phillie, was listed as having captured third place with 105 home runs.[3] All three figures are incorrect.

A second Connor retrospective, penned by Fred Lieb, who later gained fame by co-authoring the histories of seven major league teams, appeared in the *Hartford Courant* in 1923, and was titled "Roger Connor, Once Giant in Big Show Twenty Years."[4] Lieb began reporting on baseball in 1908, and thus never saw Connor play. He was the first to note Connor's exceptional ability to score runs — he declared him fourth all-time in this category — and also mentioned his six-hit performance against his old teammates, the Giants, in 1895. Then, after first stating that "Perhaps we had better not mention this,"[5] Lieb noted that Connor is one of six players who made five errors in a game (May 7, 1882). He failed to mention that Connor at the time was playing one of just 14 games that season at third base, and that he was suffering from the effects of a dislocated shoulder, an injury from which he which would not completely recover until the 1883 season. Lieb apparently was also unaware that Connor's fielding average during his brief stint at third base position in 1882 was .862, third-best in the league. He made no mention of the fact that after being shifted permanently to first base in 1885, Connor led the league in defense at that position four times.

Lieb did note Connor's three home runs in a game and provided a statistical sheet showing games, at-bats, runs, hits, stolen bases, and batting average. His statistics, however, varied widely from those accepted today for Connor, and unaccountably tacked on three years of service with Chicago's National League teams (1897 with the Colts; 1898–1899 with the Orphans) to Connor's career. Connor's stigma of being known as a poor fielder, which surfaced again in later years, is in all probability attributable to Lieb — a man who claimed Connor spent three years with a team for which he never played.

Six years after Lieb's article was published, a brief half-page Connor retrospective written by sports editor Albert W. Keane appeared in the *Hartford*

Courant. Keane's report combines comments on Connor's record with the old star's opinion of the lively or "jack rabbit" ball of the late twenties.

> Roger Connor, one of the grand old men of baseball, believes that if the jack rabbit ball had been in use in his day that the swatting records now being established in the major leagues would not approach those of the good old days.... Roger does not like the lively ball, but he does like to imagine what he and his slugging mates would have done to it with their heavy ash bats of the gay nineties. He believes that Ruth and Gehrig are super hitters, but not a bit better, if as good as Jim [*sic*] Delehanty, Dan Brouthers, or Pop Anson.[6]

It is inconceivable that Connor would have referred to his former Phillies teammate (1892) and future Hall of Famer, Ed Delahanty, as Jim Delahanty. Additionally, Keane states that for 11 consecutive seasons, 1883–1893, "Roger toiled at first base for the Giants. He played in every game but one in those [11] seasons."[7] In reality, Connor missed 14 games with the Giants between 1883 and 1894, and did not play for them either in 1890 (Brotherhood Giants) or in 1892 (Phillies). Keane, however, writing in 1929, appears to have been one of the first to link Connor with Babe Ruth: "Connor, who in his day was the Babe Ruth of that time...."[8]

While in the main complimentary, the reports of Crane, Lieb, and Keane, all written during Connor's retirement years, contain serious inaccuracies. The anonymous *Philadelphia Inquirer* article mistakenly awards the home-run crown to another player. That such uneven and inaccurate accounts were written while Connor was alive did not bode well for his baseball reputation after his death.

Only a handful of 19th-century players were inducted into the Hall of Fame during the first nine years of its existence (1936–44). A Veterans' Committee was established in 1939, but did not meet during World War II, prompting concerns that pioneer-era players either were being ignored or deliberately excluded from consideration. Although 21 men from earlier eras were selected in 1945–1946, one-fourth of them were early twentieth-century players, and two-thirds of those selected from the 19th century had either managed or coached in the major leagues after their playing years ended. The Veterans' Committee, citing the lack of reliability of 19th century records, chose a majority of 19th-century players in 1945 and 1946 not on the basis of their playing records, but on the basis of their later coaching and managing records, which were deemed more reliable. Prior to 1960, 19th-century Hall of Fame inductees who had no subsequent major league coaching or managing experience included only Jim O'Rourke, Ed Delahanty, Dan Brouthers, Hoss Radbourn, Tommy McCarthy, and Hugh Duffy.

In 1945, 14 years after Roger Connor's death, two of his supporters began a campaign to encourage consideration of him for a plaque at Cooperstown: former umpire Bill Klem, who, as we have seen, was encouraged by Connor nearly a half-century earlier when he was a fledgling umpire in the Connecticut League, and *New York Daily Mirror* sports reporter Dan Parker, a native of Waterbury.

After the Committee on Old-Timers announced its 1945 selections, which included only two players whose careers ended before 1901 (Mike Kelly and Jim O'Rourke) Parker penned an article, "Roger Connor Belongs in the Hall of Fame," in which he agreed with Klem that "Roger Connor ... should have been among the old timers selected for baseball's Hall of Fame."[9] Parker's piece is a masterpiece of persuasion that includes facts about Roger's hitting — although his home run leadership was as yet unknown — and details of his Waterbury roots, all offered from the perspective of someone who actually had met the former Giant star. Although Connor had reached his peak as a major leaguer before Parker was born, he regarded him as "one of the last survivors of a legendary race of diamond heroes."[10] While covering education issues for a Waterbury newspaper as a cub reporter, Parker often saw Connor on his rounds as a school inspector. Although there was nothing glamorous about Connor's post — he oversaw school janitors and tradesmen — Parker noted that "such was Roger's regal dignity and majestic aloofness that his commonplace job didn't diminish his effulgence by a single candlepower. The horse and buggy he drove around on his tours of inspection might have been a Roman Emperor's chariot."[11]

Parker also knew how to impress and (hopefully) influence in much more subtle ways. Aware that Roger Bresnahan, former catcher for the Giants, had just been selected by an Old-Timers Committee that had included Connie Mack, the *New York Mirror* journalist was quick to note a special bond between the recent inductee, one of the men who selected him, and Roger Connor:

> Roger came from solid Irish stock which originated in County Kerry. Undoubtedly his ancestors played hurling with the forebears of Roger Bresnahan, a native Kerryman who became a big league star when the other Roger was fading out of the baseball firmament. The McGillicuddy Reeks, [the] highest mountains in Kerry, were named for the progenitors of another great baseball figure, now popularly known as Connie Mack.[12]

A year later, Klem and Parker received some assistance in their attempt to lobby Connie Mack from a Connor family member and a former U.S. Senator from Connecticut. In December 1946, Roger Connor Wilson, the nephew that Roger Connor, a half-century earlier, had taken in after Wilson's family experienced financial difficulties, wrote to former Senator John A. Danaher, asking his help to enlist Connie Mack's support for Connor's Hall of Fame candidacy. Danaher's father, Cornelius "Con" Danaher, owned the Connecticut League's New Haven club early in the century, and knew Mack and Connor personally.

During the interim between Dan Parker's column and Roger Connor Wilson's letter to Senator Danaher, the Old Timers' Committee had voted in another 11 early-era players for 1946, only two of whom, Tommy McCarthy and Jesse Burkett, had played primarily in the 19th century. Danaher supported Wilson's request, and sent a correspondence to Connie Mack, suggesting that "it is entirely possible that some of the great sportswriters in the East can recall Roger Connor — and you surely will. Therefore, Mr. Mack, I would like very greatly if some day you can take the time to write me a letter expressing your views and your recollections about the abilities and the record of Roger Connor."[13] A week later, Danaher received this response from Mack:

> The Hall of Fame Committee has overlooked many great players, among them Roger Connor [who] in those days was as noted as Babe Ruth of today. You can use my name in saying that Roger Connor should have his name in the Hall of Fame. Roger was of a grand character and an honor to his profession, and above all, should have his name in the Hall of Fame.[14]

Despite Mack's support, neither Connor nor any other 19th-century players was elected to the Hall of Fame until Kid Nichols received the honor in 1949. By 1951, 20 years after Connor's death, even Waterbury natives needed to be reminded of his identity. *Waterbury Republican* sportswriter Hank O'Donnell found it necessary in June of that year to reintroduce him to modern fans from his own home town.

> We remember him as a big man quietly sitting in the stands at Reidville and old Brassco Park watching the Eastern Leaguers. He was a school inspector and he was pointed out to you by elders as the ex-great first baseman of the New York Giants. He came before the days of the lively ball, but he was a tremendous hitter by all accounts. We have heard of his prowess as a slugger and recall that when Babe Ruth was playing for the Yankees in the Polo Grounds [*sic*] some of his circuit drives were compared to Roger Connor's.[15]

Over the next 20 years, six more 19th-century players received plaques at Cooperstown, among them Connor's teammates John Ward and Tim Keefe. After the 1971 election, which brought Joe Kelley, one of Baltimore's original "Rowdy Boys," into the Cooperstown fold, Don Harrison, a *Waterbury Republican* sportswriter, picked up where Don Parker had left off a quarter-century earlier, in an article entitled "Hall Overlooks Connor." Parker's polite approach, however, was shunned by Harrison, whose frustration over what he perceived as an injustice added fire to his argument.

He began by faulting the Veterans' Committee for its now obvious preference for twentieth-century ballplayers. "If Waterbury-born Roger Connor had played during the past 25 years or even during the first half [of the twentieth] century, there's little doubt he would be enshrined along with baseball's other greats in the museum at Cooperstown, N.Y."[16] After providing the names of the Committee members (which included Fred Lieb, whose 1923 article on Connor had mistakenly placed him on the National League's Chicago team for three years), Harrison chided the group for not availing itself of the modern research, such as the *Encyclopedia of Baseball*, to review Connor's record, concluding that "only a few minutes study would be necessary to appreciate his [Connor's] greatness."[17] After citing some of Connor's achievements, which "seem awesome even today,"[18] Harrison focused on the home run record (still in dispute at the time between 136 and 131, and not the currently accepted number of 138), noting, "For the first 45 years of big league play Roger Connor was the reigning home run king.... This distinction alone should merit his selection to the Hall of Fame."[19]

The following year, the Veterans' Committee ignored Harrison's passionate plea. It elected a Giant to the Hall of Fame, but not Giant Roger Connor. Ross Youngs, who roamed the Polo Grounds outfield under John McGraw from 1917 to 1926, was the early-era selection for 1972 — once again a choice from the twentieth century. In 1973, Smiling Mickey Welch got the nod, Connor's fifth teammate from the 1888–1889 championship Giants seasons to be so honored. Events occurring on the ball field, however, soon would do as much to help bring Connor's name and accomplishments back from the past as did the sporadic press reports about him over the previous three decades.

In the waning weeks of the 1973 season and the first days of the 1974 campaign, the nation's attention focused on another quiet slugger who infrequently led the league in four-baggers, but whose steady home run production enabled him to overtake Babe Ruth's record on April 8, 1974. "When Henry Aaron eclipsed the all-time home run record of Babe Ruth in 1974, it sent baseball historians diving into the record books in search of home run lore. That's when they discovered Roger Connor, baseball's greatest player in the dead ball era and at one time the most fabled athlete in New York City ... during his glory years with the New York Giants."[20] In September 1973, for example, the *Washington Star-News* asked the question, "With all the excitement over Henry Aaron closing in on Babe Ruth's career home run mark, did you ever stop to wonder whose record Ruth broke?"[21] The brief article credited Connor with 131 four-baggers and a lifetime .325 average (both marks are inaccurate), and described him as "long since relegated to obscurity and old record books."[22] Most significantly, however, it countered for the first time the long-standing notion that Connor was a poor fielder by noting that "he led National League first baseman a couple of times [actually, four times] in fielding average."[23]

Members of the Veterans' Committee, however, had yet to receive the message. In what must have seemed to many a cruel irony, in 1974 it selected Sam Thompson, runner-up to Connor among 19th century home run hitters, for the Hall of Fame.

At this juncture, Jack "Peerless" McGrath, retired editor of the *Troy Times* and a friend of the now-deceased Dan Parker, took up the Connor crusade. McGrath found Connor at an unfair disadvantage simply because he played in an earlier era. "The nine decades and more since he was powering the greatest output of home runs known up to then in baseball have denied him the eyewitness acclamation that rolls out the red carpet to immortality to those of more recent diamond vintage."[24]

In lieu of such spectator support, McGrath pleaded for a consideration of his case that would be based not on anecdotal remembrances, but on the statistical record. "The records will have to speak out, and they do, very eloquently, on behalf of his admission to the Hall of Fame,"[25] he wrote, citing specifically Connor's home runs, triples, and stolen base totals, and dismissing the lingering issue of alleged poor fielding that Fred Lieb had suggested 50 years earlier "the continued refusal to admit Connor to his rightful place in the Hall of Fame on ground of poor fielding."[26] McGrath concluded his defense by citing liberally from Dan Parker and Sam Crane's portraits of Connor from the 1940s and 1920s respectively.

The Veterans' Committee's response? In 1975, it selected two 20th-century players and a manager for induction.

Just prior to the 1976 selection process, however, the Connor crusade picked up a powerful ally. In the January 31, 1976, edition of *The Sporting News*, the journal's editors noted that "a number of pre–1900 players who rate serious consideration for the Hall of Fame never have received it."[27] Among all those overlooked, *The Sporting News* singled out one old timer, noting, "Perhaps one of those to be chosen in 1976 will come from the pre–1900 era. We think the committee could not go wrong selecting Roger Connor."[28]

This time the committee listened. On February 3, Don Harrison informed his Waterbury readers of its decision. "Injustice, in any form, should be rectified, and so it was Monday. Finally, after years of being bypassed in favor of players with inferior records, after seemingly being forgotten, Waterbury's Roger Connor was elected to the Baseball Hall of Fame."[29] In a follow-up story, *The Sporting News* noted that "Not even the members of the Veterans' Committee knew much more about Connor than what appears in the record books.... The committee saw fit to elect him at long last even though he has been eligible since first it met in 1937."[30]

Connor shared Hall of Fame honors in 1976 with two others elected by the Veterans' Committee — umpire Cal Hubbard, already in the National Football Hall of Fame and the College Football Hall of Fame, and Fred Lindstrom, a Giants third baseman/outfielder who played in the 1920s and 1930s. In the *New York Times'* 14-paragraph story on the awards, Hubbard and Lindstrom were mentioned in the headline, but Connor, who received only 11 lines of coverage, was not.

In its brief mention of Connor, the *Times* did, however, manage to do something that evoked a century-old habit of the press with regard to the Waterbury slugger: it misspelled his name: "Connors [*sic*], who batted .325 and hit 131 home runs during a 15-year career in the 1880s and 1890s, died in 1931."[31] Just before Connor was enshrined on August 9, 1976, the *Waterbury Republican* reported that "three researchers recently found [that] seven other circuits [Connor home runs] were not duly recorded."[32] One hundred years after he first stepped to the plate for the Waterbury Monitors, Connor's correct home run total (138) was finally entered into the record books.

Connor's re-entry into the mainstream of baseball consciousness was brief. Shortly after his Hall of Fame selection, his accomplishments were once again filed away in the record books, and he resumed a position of relative anonymity in discussions of the game's history. A quarter-century later, however, some Connecticut residents were making plans to insure that such anonymity would never again extend to his home town. In July 2000, two members of Waterbury's Monuments Committee visited Babe Ruth's grave in Westchester County, New York, and "noticed the array of memorabilia left by adoring fans."[33] After then discovering that Roger Connor was the only man in the Hall of Fame without a gravesite memorial, they decided that "something needed to be done for Waterbury's own baseball legend."[34]

Due to Connor's financial losses in Florida and the expenses incurred by Angeline's final illness and his own cancer and prostate surgeries, no money was left from his estate to erect a gravestone at his burial site. In the midst of the Great Depression, his only child Cecelia, with five children of her own, likewise was unable to erect a cemetery marker to her father. As a result, Connor had lain in an unmarked grave at Old St. Joseph's Cemetery for nearly 70 years.

During a year-long campaign, Monument Committee members raised $5,000 to purchase a four-foot tall, polished red granite stone for the gravesite. The stone features an etched portrait of Connor, his name and reference to his Hall of Fame status, and includes the names of Angeline and of his grandson and namesake, Roger Colwell, who, as a teenager, accompanied the couple on their annual Florida trips in the 1920s. Both Colwell and Angeline also had been buried in unmarked graves next to Connor.

On June 30, 2001, Connor's tombstone was unveiled and dedicated in a ceremony attended by about 100 people, including Society for American Baseball Research representative Mark Alvarez. "As the dedication began, men in old-time uniforms, holding thick wooden baseball bats walked into view from the hill overlooking the stone,"[35] like the baseball ghosts in the film "Field of Dreams," who materialized out of an Iowa cornfield to play ball. The ceremony concluded at a local ball field with a baseball game played under 1860s rules, between the Middletown (Connecticut) Mansfields and the Huntingdon Suffolks of Long Island, New York. Connor would have been pleased to know that his native state's Mansfields team defeated the Suffolks, 10–1.

During Barry Bonds' quest to surpass Henry Aaron as baseball's all-time home run leader, Roger Connor's name again resurfaced in the sports columns. In the main, such reports were both complimentary in nature and historically accurate. In his May 2007, "Going Deep Before Bonds, Aaron and Ruth," for example, *New York Times* writer George Vecsey countered the old argument that Roger was a one-dimensional player: "Roger Connor was a complete player — a deft first baseman and an agile base runner who hit 233 triples and stole 244 bases."[36] Nevertheless, the old slugger's invisibility still exists in surprising enclaves, as Waterbury's Joe Palladino noted in 2006: "Here is what the AP [Associated Press] said when Barry Bonds tied the Babe's all-time homer total last week: 'Ruth passed Sam Thompson ... on June 20, 1921, when he hit his 127th home run.'"[37]

Connor family members at Roger Connor's grave, Old St. Joseph's Cemetery, Waterbury, Connecticut, 2009. Right, Roger's grand-niece, Gerry Laios, grand-daughter of Roger's sister, Hannah; left, Gary Laios, Roger's great-grand-nephew (author's collection).

Looking to the northwest across Interstate 84 from atop the steep rise behind Roger Connor's grave at Old St. Josephs' Cemetery in Waterbury, one can easily spot the Abrigador in the distance — the looming granite hill that in Connor's day served as the boundary between the city's Irish shanty town and its respectable neighborhoods. Connor's gravestone is placed in such fashion that its smooth, unmarked rear surface faces this direction. The stone's engraved front, which displays his Hall of Fame status, is positioned in the opposite direction, toward the southeast, on the path to New York City, where, nearly 130 years ago, Connor rose to fame, both for his feats on the ball field and for his character as a man. He sleeps here now in the quiet shadows, the stone on his resting place serving as a symbolic marker between his humble origins and his future glory.

Epilogue:
The Giants of New York

"I can see the old boys now. Tim Keefe on the mound, John Montgomery Ward at shortstop. Buck Ewing behind the plate. Roger Connor on first base ... [a]nd Jim Mutrie, with his high hat, walking around with a great air of importance and authority."
— John Kieran, *New York Times*, April 25, 1933

Like Roger Connor, the two men who brought major league baseball to Manhattan, and Connor's five future Hall of Fame teammates who brought New York City its first two pennants and national championships, took divergent paths on their journeys later in life.

John B. Day, the Massachusetts tobacconist and semi-professional pitcher who created the American Association Metropolitans and the National League New Yorks, later nicknamed the Giants, never recovered from the financial chaos brought about by the Brotherhood revolt of 1890. After the 1892 season he sold his remaining shares of stock in the Giants to lawyer and financier Edward B. Talcott, and returned to his cigar factory. Soon afterward his business went bankrupt. Day made a brief reappearance in baseball as the Giants' manager in 1899, leading the club to an unimpressive 29–35 start before being replaced in July, after which he disappeared from the public eye until the fall of 1921, when the Giants organized a benefit game for Day and Jim Mutrie, after which the pair were awarded modest, life-long pensions by the team.

In a speech given in early 1893, just after Day's retirement from the Giants, John Ward, referring to the team's former owner, stated, "In my opinion he has done more to elevate the grand game than any one man connected with it."[1] As Ward finished, "every man in the room was affected. The great ball player, who has faced thousands of spectators and on the ballfield was never known to lose his head or grow excited, was overcome and he turned his head to hide the tears that trickled down his cheeks."[2] In 1925, shortly after the death of his wife, Day passed away in Cliffside, New Jersey, at age 77, of a paralytic stroke.

After being released as the skipper of Elmira's Eastern League club in late April 1892, Jim Mutrie, the manager under whom the New Yorks became the Giants, spent his remaining years in poverty in the New Brighton community of Staten Island. From time to time his former players and friends arranged benefits for "Old Jim," and the Giants established a modest pension for him. In August 1936, 84-year-old Mutrie returned to the Polo Grounds for his last hurrah, during an Old Timers' event that commemorated the 60th anniversary of the National League's founding. He died of throat cancer at the New York Free Cancer Hospital on Welfare Island, New York City, on January 25, 1938. Mutrie was 86.[3]

John Montgomery Ward played for and managed the Brooklyn and New York National teams until 1894, and then devoted all his time to his law practice. He returned briefly to baseball in December 1911, when he became part-owner and President of the Boston Braves, then the National League's perennial last-place team. Nine months later, he resigned his position and sold his stock in the cellar-dwelling club. Ward served for a year as the business manager of the Federal League's Brooklyn club, the Brook-feds, in 1914, and then withdrew permanently from baseball, dedicating himself to golf, hunting and fishing. He excelled on the links, winning the New Jersey amateur championship in 1905 and competing regularly in Europe. In 1903 he married Kathleen Waas, an athletic tomboy who enjoyed all of Ward's pastimes and was the complete opposite of his refined, French-speaking first wife, actress Helen Dauvray. Content at last, Ward spent his final years as a gentleman farmer on his 200-acre North Babylon, New Jersey, estate. In 1921, a bout of pneumonia weakened his lungs, and four years later he again contracted the disease while on a hunting trip in Georgia. The founder of the Brotherhood movement and the Players' League died of acute lobar pneumonia in Augusta, Georgia, on March 4, 1925.[4]

After Tim Keefe was released by the Giants in 1891, he liquidated his New York sporting goods business and signed on with Philadelphia, where he registered a 29–23 record before retiring after the 1893 season. Following three difficult years as a much-maligned National League umpire, Keefe walked off the field in the middle of a game in St. Louis in July 1896, announcing that he was severing his "connection with the National game forever."[5] He kept his word. Happily married to the sculptor Clara Helm, sister of John Ward's first wife, Helen Dauvray, Keefe lived comfortably off his real estate investments in his native Cambridge, Massachusetts. He died of a heart attack at age 76, in April 1933.

After being released by the Giants in 1892, Tim Keefe's pitching mate, Mickey Welch, spent a year in the minor leagues with Troy's Eastern League team before retiring from baseball. For the next 20 years he tended bar in Holyoke, Massachusetts, and served as a steward for that city's Elks Club. In 1912, John McGraw, who had a soft spot for Giants old-timers, hired Welch as a "watcher" at the Polo Grounds bleacher entrance, where the old pitcher regularly regaled the fans with tales of baseball's early years. Smiling Mickey was 82 when he died of unspecified causes in 1941.[6]

After completing his major league career, Jim O'Rourke practiced law, owned, managed and played for his hometown Bridgeport Orators, and held numerous administrative positions in the Connecticut State League. In September 1904, the 54-year-old O'Rourke, who in 1876 made the first hit in National League history, became the oldest player to hit safely in a major league game and the oldest player to play a complete major league game. Invited back for a curtain call by Giants manager John McGraw, O'Rourke banged out a single and caught nine innings in a contest against Cincinnati. Orator O'Rourke died of pneumonia in 1919.

Buck Ewing returned to his native Ohio in 1893, playing two seasons for Cleveland after being traded to the Spiders by John Ward. Ewing managed the Cincinnati Reds from 1896 to 1899, never finishing higher than third place in the standings. He returned to New York in 1900 to manage the Giants, but was released before mid-season after compiling a 21–41 record. Financially well-off, Ewing coached amateur teams in the Cincinnati area until three weeks before his premature death. He was diagnosed with Bright's disease (kidney failure) in the spring of 1906, and that disease and paralysis ended his life at age 47.[7]

None of the six future Hall of Fame members who played on John B. Day's and Jim Mutrie's 1888-1889 New York Giants teams ever played on a championship major league team again.

Appendix A:
Connor's Nicknames

Presented in chronological order:

"The Giant Third Baseman," *Holyoke Transcript*, July 23, 1879.

"Megatherian Connor," *Albany Argus*, quoted in the *Troy Daily Times*, May 17, 1882 [*Megatheria* was a giant prehistoric sloth].

"The Jumbo of the Field," *Albany Express*, quoted in the *Troy Daily Times*, May 17, 1882.

"The Hercules of the New York Team," *New York Times*, February 15, 1885.

"The Giant of the Home Team," *Sporting Life*, June 18, 1885.

"Big Roger Connor," *New York Times*, July 24, 1885.

"The Giant of the Giants," *New York Times*, August 1, 1885.

"The Gigantic First Baseman," *Daily Inter-Ocean* (Chicago), February 26, 1888.

"Gigantic Connor," *Sporting Life*, October 17, 1888.

"The Giant of the Team," *New York Times,* May 30, 1889.

"The Biggest of the Giants," *New York Times*, May 30, 1889.

"The Rajah of Waterbury," *Los Angeles Times*, January 1, 1889.

"Home Run Roger," *St. Louis Post-Dispatch*, June 2, 1894.

"The Celebrated First Baseman," *The Sporting News*, June 19, 1894.

"Old Roger," *New York Times*, August 15, 1894.

"King of First Basemen," *The Sporting News*, June 15, 1895.

"The Grand Old Player," *St. Louis Post-Dispatch*, July 20, 1895.

"Old Waterbury," *Sporting Life*, May 3, 1896.

"The Big Fellow," *St. Louis Post-Dispatch*, April 18, 1896.

"Dear Old Roger," *Sporting Life*, May 3, 1896.

"The Gentleman of the Diamond," *St. Louis Post-Dispatch*, June 24, 1896.

"The Old Reliable," *Naugatuck Daily News*, August 9, 1897.

"Big Connor," *Sporting Life*, January 5, 1898.

"The Brass Nutmeg," *Sporting Life*, February 2, 1898 [*Brass*: reference to Waterbury, "The Brass City"; *Nutmeg*: reference to Connecticut, "The Nutmeg State"].

"The Old National Leaguer," *Sporting Life*, June 28, 1898.

"The Old Leaguer," *Sporting Life*, September 13, 1898.

"The Old Man," *Waterbury American*, August 3, 1899.

"King of the Baseball Diamond," *Naugatuck Daily News*, March 23, 1900.

"Dear Old Roger Connor," *Sporting Life*, November 6, 1902.

"The Sturdy Oak," *Sporting Life*, May 23, 1903.

"The Famous Demon Batsman of Old," *Sporting Life*, January 24, 1914.

"The Idol of Polo Grounds Fans," *Sporting Life*, May 2, 1914.

"The Old Oak," *Hartford Courant*, January 13, 1916.

"Good Old Roger Connor," *Miami Herald*, March 7, 1922.

"The Squire of Waterbury," *New York Times*, May 15, 1925.

"The Babe Ruth of the 1880s," *Waterbury Republican*, January 5, 1931.

"The Oak," *Hartford Courant*, July 21, 2001.

"Baseball's Original Giant," *Boston Globe*, July 29, 2001.

"The Oak of New York," undated, unattributed clipping, Roger Connor player file, National Baseball Hall of Fame Library, Cooperstown, New York.

Appendix B:
Connor's Major and
Minor League Statistics

Major League

Year	Club	League	G	AB	R	H	2b	3b	HR	RBI	SB	BA
1880	Troy	NL	83	340	53	113	18	8	3	47	–	.332
1881	Troy	NL	*85*	367	55	107	17	6	2	31	–	.292
1882	Troy	NL	81	349	65	115	22	*18*	4	42	–	.330
1883	New York	NL	98	409	80	146	28	15	1	50	–	.357
1884	New York	NL	*116*	477	98	151	28	4	4	82	–	.317
1885	New York	NL	110	455	102	*169*	23	15	1	65	–	*.371*
1886	New York	NL	118	485	105	172	29	*20*	7	71	17	.355
1887	New York	NL	127	471	113	134	26	22	17	104	43	.285
1888	New York	NL	134	481	98	140	15	17	14	71	27	.291
1889	New York	NL	131	496	117	157	32	17	13	*130*	21	.317
1890	New York	PL	123	484	133	169	24	15	*14*	103	22	.349
1891	New York	NL	129	479	112	139	29	13	7	94	27	.290
1892	Philadelphia	NL	*155*	564	123	166	*37*	11	12	73	22	.294
1893	New York	NL	*135*	511	111	156	25	8	11	105	24	.305
1894	New York	NL	22	82	10	24	7	0	1	14	2	.293
1894	St. Louis	NL	99	380	83	122	28	25	7	79	17	.321
1895	St. Louis	NL	104	401	78	131	29	9	8	78	9	.327
1896	St. Louis	NL	126	483	71	137	21	9	11	72	10	.284
1897	St. Louis	NL	22	83	13	19	3	1	1	12	3	.229
18 yrs			1998	7797	1620	2467	441	233	138	1323	*(244)*	**.316**

Bold italics = league leader; *(italics)* = records incomplete

World's Series

1888 vs. St. Louis Browns (AA)
1889 vs. Brooklyn Bridegrooms (AA)

Year	G	AB	R	H	2b	3b	HR	RBI	SB	BA
1888	7	23	7	7	1	2	–	3	–	.333
1889	9	35	12	9	2	2	–	12	–	.343

Minor League

Year	Club	League	G	AB	R	H	2b	3b	HR	RBI	SB	BA
1876	Waterbury	Ind	–	–	–	–	–	–	–	–	–	
1877	Waterbury	Ind	–	–	–	–	–	–	–	–	–	–
1878	New Bedford	NA	11	46	6	8	–	–	–	–	–	.174
1879	Holyoke	NA	45	210	49	77	–	–	–	–	–	.367
1897	Fall River	N.Eng.	47	171	32	49	9	1	4	–	–	.287
1898	Waterbury	Conn.	95	–	–	–	–	–	–	–	–	.319
1899	Waterbury	Conn.	92	347	79	136	28	2	5	–	–	***.392***
1900	Waterbury	Conn.	83	286	54	82	9	3	2	–	–	.287
1901	Waterbury/ New Haven	Conn.	107	411	–	123	10	8	3	–	–	.299
1902	Springfield	Conn.	62	224	–	58	7	1	1	–	–	.259
1903	Springfield	Conn.	75	279	–	76	12	3	0	–	–	.272
11 Seasons			522	1974	*(220)*	609	*(75)*	*(18)*	*(15)*			.308

Bold italics = league leader; *(italics)* = records incomplete

Sources
The Baseball Encyclopedia; baseball-reference.com; retrosheet.org
World's Series statistics: David Nemec, *The Great Encyclopedia of 19th Century Major League Baseball*

Notes

Prelude

1. *New York Times*, September 12, 1886.
2. *Bridgeport Telegraph*, June 21, 1927.
3. *New York Times*, September 12, 1886.

Chapter 1

1. "The History of Brass Making in the Naugatuck Valley," www.copper.org/publications/newsletters/innovations/1990/03/naugatuck.html.
2. *Ibid.*
3. *Ibid.*
4. *Indian Names in Connecticut*, by James Hammond Trumbull, 1.
5. U.S. Census, Waterbury, Connecticut, 1870.
6. Margaret Colwell, "Roger Connor: A Moving Tribute," *Waterbury Sunday Republican*, August 8, 1976, 37.
7. *Ibid.*
8. Harold and Dorothy Seymour, *Baseball: The Early Years*, 84.
9. David Quentin Voigt, *American Baseball*, 3–22.
10. Peter Morris, *But We Had Fun, Didn't We?*, 155.
11. *Ibid.*, 157.
12. Colwell, 37.
13. *Waterbury Democrat*, January 5, 1931.
14. *Naugatuck Daily News*, March 23, 1900.
15. Charles Alexander, *John McGraw*, 10–14.
16. Robert Obojski, *Bush League*, 11.
17. *Waterbury American*, July 11, 1876.
18. William J. Ryczek, *Blackguards and Red Stockings*, 15.
19. *Ibid.*, 21.
20. "Lipman Emmanuel Pike," by Joseph M. Overfield, in *Nineteenth Century Stars*, 103.
21. "Robert V. Ferguson (Old Fergy)," by Frank V. Phelps, in *Nineteenth Century Stars*, 43.
22. *Waterbury American*, May 10, 1876.
23. *Waterbury American*, August 14, 1876.
24. David Block, *Baseball Before We Knew It*, 146.

25. *Ibid.*
26. *Ibid.*, 147.
27. *Waterbury American*, July 9, 1877.
28. *Waterbury American*, May 3, 1878.
29. *Ibid.*
30. *Waterbury American*, July 5, 1878.
31. *Waterbury American*, July 8, 1878.
32. *Waterbury American*, July 19, 1878.
33. *Waterbury American*, August 5, 1878.
34. *Waterbury American*, October 6, 1878.
35. John Richmond Husman, "Francis Carter Bancroft," in *Nineteenth Century Stars*, 9.
36. *Sporting Life*, May 4, 1897.
37. Husman, 9.
38. *Manitoba Free Press*, July 4, 1889.
39. Obojski, 5.
40. *Holyoke Transcript*, April 16, 1879.
41. *Holyoke Transcript*, May 31, 1879.
42. *Holyoke Transcript*, April 30, 1879.
43. *Holyoke Transcript*, August 16, 1879.
44. *Holyoke Transcript*, July 23, 1879.

Chapter 2

1. Don Rittner, *Troy: A Collar City*, 88.
2. *Ibid.*, 95.
3. *Ibid.*, 98.
4. *Ibid.*
5. Richard A. Puff, ed., *Troy's Baseball Heritage,* unpublished.
6. "Haymakers and Daisycutters," in *Troy's Baseball Heritage*, 8.
7. *Ibid.*, 9.
8. Robert L. Tiemann and Jose de Jesus Jimenez, Jr., "Esteban Enrique Bellán," in *Nineteenth Century Stars,"* 11.
9. Warren N. Wilbert, *Opening Pitch: Professional Baseball's Inaugural Season, 1871*, 68.
10. Puff, 12.
11. David Nemec, *The Great Encyclopedia of 19th-Century Major League Baseball*, 27.
12. Joseph M. Overfield, "Dennis Joseph Brouthers," in *Baseball's First Stars*, 11.
13. Irv Bergman, "William Ewing," in *Baseball's First Stars*, p. 60.
14. Quoted in Peter Morris, *A Game of Inches*, 131.
15. *The Sporting News*, March 2, 1933, reprinted in Morris, 162.
16. *Saint Louis Post-Dispatch*, June 19, 1886, reprinted in Morris, 150.
17. Harold and Dorothy Seymour, *Baseball: The Early Years*, 107.
18. *Troy Press*, May 25, 1880.
19. *Troy Daily Times*, May 25, 1880.
20. *Ibid.*
21. *Troy Daily Times*, July 20, 1880.
22. *Ibid.*
23. *Troy Daily Times*, September 15, 1880.
24. *New York Clipper*, July 7, 1880.
25. *Troy Daily Times*, July 15, 1880.
26. *Troy Press*, June 5, 1880.
27. *New York Clipper*, June 12, 1880.
28. *Hartford Courant*, July 30, 1910.
29. *New York Clipper*, October 2, 1880.

31. *Troy Daily Times*, October 7, 1880.

32. *New York Times*, October 30, 1880.

33. Nemec, 139.

34. Margaret Colwell, "Roger Connor: A Moving Tribute," *Waterbury Sunday Republican*, August 8, 1976.

35. Joseph Anderson, et al., *The Town and City of Waterbury, Connecticut*, 1105.

36. U.S. Census, Otsego County, New York, 1870.

37. U.S. Census, Warren County, New York, 1880.

38. Colwell, 37.

38. *Ibid.*

39. *Ibid.*

40. *Ibid.*

41. *Ibid.*

42. *Ibid.*

43. *New York Clipper*, March 26, 1881.

44. *New York Clipper*, July 16, 1881.

45. *New York Clipper*, April 30, 1881.

46. John R. Husman, "Lee Richmond," www.bioproj.sabr.org.

47. *Troy Press*, May 17, 1881.

48. *Troy Press*, October 12, 1881.

49. *Troy Daily Times*, May 17, 1882.

50. David L. Fleitz, "Walk-Off Grand Slams," www. wcnet.org/~dfleitz/gs.htm.

51. Nemec, 168.

52. *Troy Daily Times*, May 17, 1882.

53. Richard A. Puff, "Haymakers and Daisycutters," in *Troy's Baseball Heritage*, 15.

54. *Troy Daily Times*, May 15, 1882.

55. *Troy Daily Times*, May 17, 1882.

56. *New York Clipper*, July 10, 1882.

57. *Waterbury Democrat*, January 5, 1931.

58. Quoted in *Troy Daily Times*, October 14, 1882.

59. *Troy Daily Times*, August 17, 1882.

60. *Troy Daily Times*, August 2, 1882.

61. *Troy Daily Times*, August 14, 1882.

62. *Troy Daily Times*, October 27, 1882.

63. *Troy Daily Times*, October 23, 1882.

64. *Troy's Baseball Heritage*, 18.

65. Thomas M. Blair, "A Reminder of Troy's Proud Baseball History," *Troy's Baseball Heritage*, n.p.

Chapter 3

1. Peter Mancuso, "Jim Mutrie," www.bioproj.sabr.org.

2. *Ibid.*

3. *Newark Daily Advocate*, June 29, 1889.

4. *Philadelphia Inquirer*, April 28, 1892.

5. *Sporting Life*, September 12, 1891.

6. *Ibid.*

7. Sam Crane, *New York Evening Journal*, April 6, 1912.

8. "The Sacrifice Fly," by John Schwartz, SABR Research Journals Archive, research.sabr. org./journals/sacrifice-fly.

9. *St. Louis Post and Gazette*, June 2, 1894.

10. Ed Koszarek, *The Players League*, 97.

11. *New York Times*, July 14, 1885.

12. *Ibid.*
13. *New York Times*, July 26, 1886.
14. *Sporting Life*, May 22, 1890.
15. *Boston Globe*, November 22, 1891.
16. *St. Louis Post and Gazette*, October 13, 1894.
17. *Sporting Life*, April 25, 1885.
18. *Sporting News*, March 16, 1895.
19. *New York Times*, May 17, 1893.
20. Red Smith, *New York Times*, September 5, 1973.
21. *New York Clipper*, October 2, 1880.
22. *St. Louis Post Dispatch*, April 4, 1896.
23. *St. Louis Post Dispatch*, May 22, 1897.
24. *Sporting News*, August 23, 1890.
25. *Sporting Life*, May 3, 1896.
26. Lyle Spatz, "John Joseph Doyle (Dirty Jack)," in *Baseball's First Stars*, 53.
27. *Ibid.*
28. *Sporting News*, June 10, 1894.
29. Larry R. Gerlach, "John H. Gaffney (Honest John)," in *Baseball's First Stars*, 64.
30. *St. Louis Post Dispatch*, July 2, 1894.
31. Dan Parker, *New York Daily Mirror*, May 9, 1945.
32. *Sporting News*, September 27, 1886.
33. *Sporting Life*, August 29, 1896.
34. *Sporting Life*, June 2, 1886.
35. *St. Louis Post Dispatch*, July 15, 1896.
36. *Sporting Life*, May 8, 1889.
37. Mike Higgins, *The Victorians and Sport*, 74.
38. Stew Thornley, *New York's Polo Grounds*, 74.
39. *Ibid.*, 18.
40. Thomas Gilbert, *Superstars and Monopoly Wars*, 103.
41. J. Thomas Hetrick, *Chris Von der Ahe and the St. Louis Browns*, 21.
42. *New York Herald*, May 6, 1883.
43. *New York Tribune*, June 17, 1883.
44. *New York Herald*, June 7, 1883.
45. *New York Times*, May 2, 1883.
46. *Ibid.*
47. *New York Times*, May 4, 1883.
48. *Sporting Life*, June 7, 1883.
49. Di Salvatore, 166.
50. *Ibid.*, 167.
51. David L. Porter, *Biographical Dictionary of American Sports*, 906.
52. James D. Hardy, Jr., *The New York Giants Base Ball Club*, 20.
53. *New York Times*, October 21, 1884.
54. Tom Melville, *Early Baseball and the Rise of the National League*, 109.
55. Hardy, 46.
56. *Ibid.*
57. *Ibid.*
58. *Sporting Life*, December 31, 1884.
59. Quoted in Frank Graham, *The New York Giants: An Informal History*, 6.
60. Howard B. Tuckner, "Giants First Batboy Not Entirely Alone," *New York Times*, September 29, 1957, S.3.
61. Mike Roer, *Orator O'Rourke: The Life of a Baseball Radical*, 142.
62. Hardy, 62.
63. Mancuso, 7.
64. *Sporting Life*, June 10, 1885.

65. *Sporting Life*, May 27, 1885.
66. *Sporting Life*, June 24, 1885.
67. Hardy, 63.
68. *New York Times*, April 25, 1885.
69. *New York Times*, June 14, 1885.
70. Derby Gisclair, *Baseball in New Orleans*, 9.
71. *Sporting Life*, November 18, 1885.
72. *Sporting Life*, February 17, 1886.
73. *Sporting Life*, January 6, 1886.
74. Graham, 7.
75. *New York Times*, letter to the Sports Editor, February 17, 1938.
76. *Sporting Life*, March 10, 1886.
77. *Sporting News, October 4, 1886.*
78. *Ibid.*
79. *Waterbury Democrat*, January 5, 1931.
80. *Sporting Life*, May 25, 1887.
81. *Sporting Life*, June 22, 1887.
82. *Hartford Courant*, August 2, 1929.
83. *Sporting Life*, November, 1887.
84. *Sporting Life*, December 21, 1887.
85. *Sporting Life*, December 28, 1887.
86. *Sporting Life*, December 21, 1887.
87. Frederick Ivor-Campbell, "Charles J. Sweeney," in *Nineteenth Century Stars*, 123.
88. *Sporting Life*, January 18, 1888.
89. *Sporting Life*, July 25, 1888.
90. *Ibid.*
91. *Sporting Life*, April 4, 1888.
92. *Sporting Life*, April 25, 1888.
93. David Nemec, *The Great Encyclopedia of 19th Century Major League Baseball*, 340.
94. *Sporting Life*, August 8, 1888.
95. *Boston Daily Globe*, August 3, 1888
96. *Sporting Life*, July 25, 1888.
97. Hardy, 80.
98. *New York Times*, May 10, 1888.
99. *Sporting News*, October 20, 1888.
100. Margaret Colwell, "Roger Connor: A Moving Tribute," *Waterbury Sunday Republican*, August 8, 1976.
101. "Little Lulu, the Fragile Girl Who Overpowered All Challengers," anonymous article, *Blithering Antiquity*, Volume 1, Number 6, June, 2003, http:/www.hornpipe.com/ba/babd.htm.
102. *Ibid.*
103. *Ibid.*
104. *Ibid.*
105. *Ibid.*
106. *Sporting Life*, October 31, 1888.
107. *Ibid.*
108. *Sporting Life*, November 7, 1888.
109. Quoted in Di Salvatore, 227.
110. *Sporting Life*, May 1, 1889.
111. Thornley, 41.
112. *Sporting Life*, May 15, 1889.
113. *Chicago Daily Tribune*, July 17, 1889.
114. Quoted in Di Salvatore,. 255.
115. Nemec, 370.

116. *Sunday Waterbury Republican*, August 8, 1976.
117. *New York Times*, June 29, 1889.
118. *Sporting Life*, July 17, 1889.
119. *New York Times*, June 14, 1889.
120. *Sporting Life*, October 6, 1889.
121. *Sporting Life*, October 30, 1889.

Chapter 4

1. Bryan Di Salvatore, *A Clever Base-Ballist: The Life and Times of John Montgomery Ward*, 175.
2. *Players' League Baseball Guide, 1890*, quoted in *Early Innings*, Dean A. Sullivan, editor, 196.
3. Mike Roer, *Orator O'Rourke: The Life of a Baseball Radical*, 134.
4. John Montgomery Ward, "Is the Base Ball Player a Chattel?" in *Early Innings*, 164.
5. *Ibid.*, 169.
6. Roer, 134.
7. Di Salvatore, 283–284.
8. "The Brotherhood Manifesto," in *Early Innings*, 188–89.
9. *Sporting Life*, November 13, 1888.
10. *Chicago Daily Tribune*, February 26, 1890, quoted in Roer, 154.
11. *Sporting Life*, January 8, 1890.
12. *Ibid.*
13. *Sporting Life*, January 29, 1890.
14. Brian McKenna, "John Clarkson," 3.
15. *Ibid.*, 7.
16. Dick Thompson, "John Clarkson," in *Baseball's First Stars*, 32.
17. *Sporting Life*, April 26, 1890.
18. James D. Hardy, Jr., *The New York Giants Base Ball Club, 1870 to 1900*, 107.
19. *Sporting Life*, April 12, 1890.
20. *The Sporting News*, March 1, 1890.
21. *Ibid.*
22. *The Sporting News*, March 15, 1890.
23. *New York Times*, April 20, 1890.
24. *Boston Daily Globe*, April 27, 1890.
25. *Boston Daily Globe*, April 30, 1890.
26. Philip Lowry, *Green Cathedrals*, 108.
27. *Boston Daily Globe*, June 3, 1890.
28. *New York Times*, July 22, 1890.
29. *Sporting Life*, August 2, 1890.
30. *Chicago Daily Tribune*, August 3, 1890.
31. *Sporting Life*, July 28, 1890.
32. *Sporting Life*, March 10, 1890.
33. *Sporting Life*, June 4, 1890.
34. *The Sporting News*, July 12, 1890.
35. *Ibid.*
36. *The Sporting News*, August 16, 1890.
37. *Sporting Life*, August 16, 1890.
38. *Sporting Life*, August 9, 1890.
39. *Ibid.*
40. *Sporting Life*, November 29, 1890.
41. *The Sporting News*, May 24, 1890.
42. David Quentin Voigt, *American Baseball*, 165.

43. *Ibid.*, 166.
44. *Ibid.*, 168.
45. *Ibid.*, 169.
46. *Sporting Life*, August 16, 1890.
47. *Sporting Life*, September 6, 1890.
48. *The Sporting News*, November 8, 1890.
49. *Sporting Life*, October 4, 1890.
50. *The Sporting News*, quoted in *Sporting Life*, October 4, 1890.
51. Ed Koszarek, *The Players League*, 357.

Chapter 5

1. Richard Puff, "Amos Wilson Rusie (The Hoosier Thunderbolt)," in *Baseball's First Stars*, 143–44.
2. James D. Hardy, Jr., *The New York Giants Base Ball Club, 1870 to 1900*, 137.
3. Stew Thornley, *New York's Polo Grounds: Land of the Giants*, 50.
4. *The Sporting News*, August 1, 1891.
5. *Boston Daily Globe*, April 25, 1891.
6. *Boston Daily Globe*, July 14, 1891.
7. *Chicago Daily Tribune*, July 14, 1891.
8. *The Sporting News*, March 25, 1891.
9. *The Sporting News*, August 22, 1891.
10. *The Sporting News*, September 5, 1891.
11. *Ibid.*
12. *Bismarck Daily Tribune*, September 30, 1891.
13. Harold and Dorothy Seymour, *Baseball: The Early Years*, 251.
14. *Ibid.*, 252.
15. *Ibid.*, 256.
16. *New York Times*, April 6, 1892.
17. Margaret Colwell, "Roger Connor: A Moving Tribute," *Waterbury Sunday Republican*, August 8, 1976.
18. *Waterbury Republican*, March 18, 1928.
19. Colwell, 38.
20. *Mansfield Ohio News*, May 14, 1904, reprint from the *Cleveland Press*.
21. *Sporting Life*, October 7, 1911.
22. *New York Times*, April 6, 1892.
23. *Sporting Life*, February 20, 1892.
24. *Sporting Life*, February 27, 1892.
25. Norman L. Macht, "Sam Luther Thompson (Big Sam)," in *Baseball's First Stars*, 165.
26. *Philadelphia Inquirer*, July 19, 1892.
27. *Philadelphia Inquirer*, April 13, 1892.
28. *Philadelphia Inquirer*, April 28, 1892.
29. *Dallas Morning News*, July 5, 1908.
30. Hardy, 145.
31. *Ibid.*, 149.
32. David Nemec, *The Great 19th Century Major League Baseball Encyclopedia*, 492.
33. *Ibid.*
34. *Sporting Life*, March 18, 1893.
35. David Quentin Voigt, *American Baseball*, 102.
36. *New York Times*, April 5, 1893.
37. *Ibid.*
38. *New York Times*, April 27, 1893.
39. *New York Times*, May 1, 1893.

40. *New York Times*, May 10, 1893.

41. *New York Times*, May 23, 1893.

42. *New York Times*, May 26, 1893.

43. *New York Times*, June 1, 1893.

44. *New York Times*, April 19, 1893.

45. *New York Times*, August 17, 1893.

46. *New York Times*, August 8, 1893.

47. *New York Press*, August 8, 1893.

48. *New York Press*, May 6, 1893.

49. *New York Press*, June 7, 1893.

50. *New York Times*, July 27, 1893.

51. *Philadelphia Inquirer*, February 11, 1894.

52. *Philadelphia Inquirer*, May 27, 1894.

53. *The Sporting News*, May 19, 1894.

54. *The Sporting News*, June 1, 1894.

55 Bryan Di Salvatore, *A Clever Base-Ballist: The Life and Times of John Montgomery Ward*, 352.

56. *St. Louis Post Dispatch*, June 6, 1894.

57. J. Thomas Hetrick, *Chris Von der Ahe and the St. Louis Browns*, 193.

58. *Ibid.*, 188.

59. *The Sporting News*, June 9, 1894.

60. *St. Louis Post Dispatch*, June 16, 1894.

61. *The Sporting News*, July 21, 1894.

62. *St. Louis Post Dispatch*, July 12, 1894.

63. *St. Louis Post Dispatch*, September 13, 1894.

64. *St. Louis Post Dispatch*, September 3, 1894.

65. *St. Louis Post Dispatch*, August 21, 1894.

66. Hetrick, 168.

67. *Ibid.*, 169.

68. *Ibid.*, 175.

69. *Sporting Life*, July 25, 1896.

70. *The Sporting News*, April 20, 1895.

71. *The Sporting News*, May 4, 1895.

72. *St. Louis Post Dispatch*, September 17, 1895.

73. *Sporting News*, July 20, 1895.

74. Quoted in the *St. Louis Post Dispatch*, June 28, 1895.

75. Peter Morris, Keynote Speech, SABR 19th Century Baseball Conference, National Baseball Hall of Fame, Cooperstown, New York, April 17, 2010.

76. *St. Louis Post Dispatch*, June 2, 1895.

77. *St. Louis Post Dispatch*, July 20, 1895.

78. *St. Louis Post Dispatch*, August 12, 1895.

79. *St. Louis Post Dispatch*, May 22, 1897.

80. *St. Louis Post Dispatch*, August 29, 1895.

81. *St. Louis Post Dispatch*, September 6, 1895.

82. *St. Louis Post Dispatch*, April 13, 1896.

83. *St. Louis Post Dispatch*, April 26, 1896.

84. *Sporting Life*, May 3, 1896.

85. *Sporting Life*, June 13, 1896.

86. *St. Louis Post Dispatch*, June 15, 1896.

87. *St. Louis Post Dispatch*, June 18, 1896.

88. *St. Louis Post Dispatch*, July 1, 1896.

89. *St. Louis Post Dispatch*, July 11, 1896.

90. *St. Louis Post Dispatch*, August 6, 1896.

91. *St. Louis Post Dispatch*, May 6, 1897.

92. *St. Louis Post Dispatch*, May 19, 1897.
93. *St. Louis Post Dispatch*, May 22, 1897.

Chapter 6

1. *Sporting Life*, November 7, 1888.
2. Margaret Colwell, "Roger Connor: A Moving Tribute," *Waterbury Sunday Republican*, August 8, 1976.
3. *Washington Post*, December 12, 1904.
4. *Sporting Life*, April 16, 1898.
5. *Dallas Morning News*, March 31, 1907.
6. *Baseball Magazine*, xxi, no.3(1918), 291–92.
7. Thomas J. Schlereth, *Victorian America: 1876–1915*, 219.
8. *Boston Daily Globe*, January 14, 1896.
9. *Boston Daily Globe*, March 2, 1898.
10. *Sporting Life*, December 18, 1898.
11. *New York Times*, December 18, 1898.
12. *Sporting Life*, June 19, 1897.
13. *Sporting Life*, August 7, 1897.
14. Mike Roer, *Orator O'Rourke: The Life of a Baseball Rebel*, 39.
15. *Ibid.*, 203.
16. *Ibid.*, 217.
17. *Waterbury American*, May 16, 1898.
18. *Waterbury American*, September 7, 1898.
19. *Waterbury American*, April 7, 1898.
20. *Waterbury American*, May 18, 1898.
21. Quoted in the *Waterbury American*, August 17, 1898.
22. Quoted in the *Waterbury American*, May 19, 1898.
23. Quoted in the *Waterbury American*, June 28, 1898.
24. *Sporting Life*, October 15, 1898.
25. *Waterbury American*, September 13, 1898.
26. *Sporting Life*, 31, no. 22 (August, 1898), 15, quoted from the original in the *Meriden Journal*, n.d.
27. *Waterbury American*, August 3, 1899.
28. David Fleitz, "Louis Sockalexis," www.sabrbioproj.com
29. *Ibid.*
30. *Sporting Life*, July 27, 1901.
31. *Sporting Life*, February 8, 1902.
32. *Sporting Life*, March 1, 1902.
33. *Sporting Life*, May 10, 1902.
34. *Sporting Life*, June 14, 1902.
35. *Ibid.*
36. *Ibid.*
37. *Sporting Life*, June 28, 1902.
38. *Sporting Life*, November 15, 1902.
39. *Sporting Life*, November 15, 1902.
40. *Sporting Life*, May 23, 1903.
41. *New York Evening Journal*, February 6, 1912.
42. *Hartford Courant*, January 11, 1913.
43. *Hartford Courant*, June 5, 1903.
44. *Sporting Life*, June 21, 1903.
45. *Sporting Life*, July 25, 1903.
46. *Sporting Life*, September 26, 1903.

47. Roy Kerr, *Sliding Billy Hamilton: The Life and Times of Baseball's First Great Leadoff Hitter*, 35.

48. Bill James, *The New Bill James Historical Baseball Abstract*, 52.

49. David Quentin Voigt, *American Baseball*, 276.

50. *Sioux City Journal*, May 24, 1896.

51. William Curran, *Mitts: A Celebration of the Art of Fielding*, 119.

Chapter 7

1. *Sporting Life*, February 27, 1904.

2. *Hartford Courant*, October 2, 1905.

3. *Sporting Life*, February 24, 1906.

4. *Sporting Life*, June 16, 1906.

5. *Hartford Courant*, July 1, 1907.

6. *Hartford Courant*, June 10, 1908.

7. *Hartford Courant*, July 24, 1908.

8. *Hartford Courant*, July 24, 1909.

9. Mike Roer, *Orator O'Rourke: The Life of a Baseball Radical*, 245.

10. *Hartford Courant*, July 26, 1909.

11. *Hartford Courant*, July 30, 1910.

12. *Hartford Courant*, August 22, 1910.

13. *Sporting Life*, November 12, 1910.

14. *Sporting Life*, May 24, 1913.

15. Margaret Colwell, "Roger Connor: A Moving Tribute," *Waterbury Sunday Republican*, August 8, 1976.

16. *Sporting Life*, January 24, 1914.

17. *Sporting Life*, May 2, 1914.

18. *Miami Herald Record*, June 2, 1922.

19. Colwell, 38.

20. *Miami Herald Record*, March 7, 1922.

21. *Ibid.*

22. *Ibid.*

23. *Miami Herald Record*, June 2, 1922.

24. *Ibid.*

25. *New York Times*, May 15, 1925.

26. Kenneth Silber, "When Florida Sizzled," *Research Magazine*, August 1, 2009 (online edition).

27. *Waterbury Republican*, March 18, 1928.

28. *Ibid.*

29. Colwell, 38.

30. *Ibid.*

31. *Waterbury Republican*, January 7, 1931.

32. *Ibid.*

33. *Ibid.*

Chapter 8

1. Mike Roer, *Orator O'Rourke: The Life of a Baseball Rebel*, 211.

2. Sam Crane, "Roger Connor," *New York Evening Journal*, February 6, 1912, Laios clipping and photograph file.

3. *Philadelphia Inquirer*, May 12, 1918.

4. Frederick G. Lieb, "Roger Connor, Once Giant, in Big Show Twenty Years," *Hartford Courant*, February 20, 1923.

5. *Ibid.*

6. Albert W. Keane, "Calling 'Em Right," *Hartford Courant*, August 2, 1929.

7. *Ibid.*

8. *Ibid.*

9. Dan Parker, "Roger Connor Belongs in the Hall of Fame," Unattributed article, Roger Connor player file, National Baseball Hall of Fame Library, Cooperstown, New York.

10. *Ibid.*

11. *Ibid.*

12. *Ibid.*

13. John A. Danaher letter to Connie Mack, December 27, 1946, Laios clipping and photograph file.

14. Connie Mack letter to John A. Danaher, January 4, 1947, Laios clipping and photograph file.

15. Hank O'Donnell, "Roger Connor, Waterbury's Greatest Player," *Waterbury Republican*, June 23, 1951.

16. Don Harrison, "Hall of Fame Overlooks Connor," *Waterbury Sunday Republican*, February 21, 1971.

17. *Ibid.*

18. *Ibid.*

19. *Ibid.*

20. Joe Palladino, "It's Only Happened 21 Times, Waterbury Hero Was 1st," *Waterbury Republican American*, July 11, 2004.

21. "Whose Record Did Babe Ruth Break?" *Washington Star-News*, September 5, 1973.

22. *Ibid.*

23. *Ibid.*

24. Jack McGrath, "A Hall of Fame Vote for an Ex-Troy Ballplayer." Unattributed article, Roger Connor player file, National Baseball Hall of Fame Library, Cooperstown, New York.

25. *Ibid.*

26. *Ibid.*

27. "Stars Too Long Ignored," *The Sporting News*, January 31, 1976.

28. *Ibid.*

29. Don Harrison, "Roger Connor, Hall of Famer," *Waterbury Republican*, February 3, 1976.

30. *The Sporting News*, February 14, 1976.

31. *New York Times*, February 3, 1976.

32. *Waterbury Republican*, August 10, 1976.

33. *Waterbury Republican-American*, June 2, 2001.

34. *Ibid.*

35. *Waterbury Republican-American*, July 1, 2001.

36. *Waterbury Republican-American*, May 13, 2007.

37. *Waterbury Republican-American*, May 28, 2006.

Epilogue

1. *New York Times*, February 10, 1893.

2. *Ibid.*

3. Peter Mancuso, "Jim Mutrie," www.bioproj.sabr.org.

4. Bryan Di Salvatore, *A Clever Base-Ballist: The Life and Times of John Montgomery Ward*, 397.

5. *New York Times*, July 7, 1896.

6. *New York Times*, July 31, 1941.

7. *New York Times*, October 21, 1906.

Bibliography

Articles

Attiyeh, Mike. "Roger Connor: The 19th Century HR King." http://baseballguru.com.

Fleitz, David L. "Walk-Off Grand Slams." www.wcnet.org/~dfleitz/gs.htm.

Fleitz, David L. "Louis Sockalexis." http://bioproj/sabr.org.

"The History of Brass Making in the Naugatuck Valley." www.copper.org/publications/newsletters/innovations/1990/03/naugatuck.html.

Husman, John R. "Lee Richmond." http://bioproj/sabr.org.

Kim, Ray. "When Troy Was a Major-League City." www.empireone.net.

"Little Lulu, the Fragile Girl Who Overpowered All Challengers." *Blithering Antiquity*, Volume 1, Number 6, June 2003. Online edition.

McKenna, Brian. "John Clarkson." http://bioproj.sabr.org.

Mancuso, Peter. "Jim Mutrie." http://bioproj/sabr.org.

Schwartz, John. "The Sacrifice Fly." SABR Research Journals Archive, http://research.sabr.org./journals/sacrifice-fly.

Silber, Kenneth. "When Florida Sizzled." *Research Magazine*, August 8, 2009. Online edition.

Baseball Periodicals

Baseball Magazine   *Sporting Life*   *The Sporting News*

Books

Alexander, Charles C. *John McGraw.* New York: Penguin Books, 1989.

Anderson, Joseph, et al. *The Town and City of Waterbury, Connecticut.* Waterbury: Price and Lee, 1896. Online edition.

Block, David. *Baseball Before We Knew It: A Search for the Roots of the Game.* Lincoln: University of Nebraska Press, 2005.

Curran, William. *Mitts: A Celebration of the Art of Fielding.* New York: William Morrow, 1985.

Di Salvatore, Bryan. *A Clever Base-Ballist: The Life of John Montgomery Ward.* Baltimore: Johns Hopkins University Press, 2000.

Fleitz, David L. *Ghosts in the Gallery at Cooperstown,* Jefferson, NC: McFarland, 2004.

Gilbert, Thomas. *Superstars and Monopoly Wars: Nineteenth-Century Major-League Baseball.* New York: Franklin Watts, 1995.

Gisclair, Derby S. *Baseball in New Orleans.* Mt. Pleasant, SC: Arcadia, 2004.

Graham, Frank. *The New York Giants: An Informal History of a Great Baseball Club.* Carbondale: Southern Illinois University, 2002. Reprint of the original edition published by G.P. Putnam's Sons, 1952.

Hardy, James D. *The New York Giants Baseball Club, 1870 to 1900.* Jefferson, NC: McFarland, 1996.

Harrison, Don. *Connecticut Baseball: The Best of the Nutmeg State.* Charleston, SC: History Press, 2008.

Hetrick, J. Thomas. *Chris Von der Ahe and the St. Louis Browns.* Lanham, MD: Scarecrow Press, 1999.

Higgins, Mike. *The Victorians and Sport.* London: Hambledon and London, 2004.

Ivor-Campbell, Frederic, Robert L. Tiemann and Mark Rucker, editors. *Baseball's First Stars.* Cleveland: SABR, 1996.

James, Bill. *The New Bill James Historical Baseball Abstract.* New York: Free Press, 2001.

Kerr, Roy. *Sliding Billy Hamilton: The Life and Times of Baseball's First Great Leadoff Hitter.* Jefferson, NC: McFarland, 2010.

Koszarek, Ed. *The Players' League: History, Clubs, Ballplayers and Statistics.* Jefferson, NC: McFarland, 2006.

Lowry, Philip J. *Green Cathedrals.* Reading, MA: Addison-Wesley, 1992.

Melville, Tom. *Early Baseball and the Rise of the National League.* Jefferson, NC: McFarland, 2001

Morris, Peter. *But We Had Fun, Didn't We? An Informal History of Baseball's Pioneer Era, 1843–1870.* Chicago: Ivan R. Dee, 2008.

____. *A Game of Inches: The Game on the Field.* Chicago: Ivan R. Dee, 2006.

Nemec, David. *The Great Encyclopedia of 19th Century Major League Baseball.* Chicago: Ivan R. Dee, 2006. (Donald I. Fine Books, 1997.)

Obojski, Robert. *Bush League: A History of Minor League Baseball.* New York: Macmillan, 1975.

Porter, David. *Biographical Dictionary of American Sports.* Santa Barbara, CA: Greenwood Press, 2000.

Rittner, Don. *Troy: A Collar City History.* Charleston, SC: Arcadia, 2002.

Roer, Mike. *Orator O'Rourke: The Life of a Baseball Radical.* Jefferson, NC: McFarland, 2005.

Ryczek, William J. *Blackguards and Red Stockings: A History of Baseball's National Association, 1871–1875.* Jefferson, NC: McFarland, 1992.

Schlereth, Thomas J. *Victorian America: Transformations in Everyday Life.* New York: Harper Collins, 1991.

Seymour, Harold, and Dorothy Seymour. *Baseball: The Early Years.* New York: Oxford University Press, 1960

Sullivan, Dean A., ed. *Early Innings: A Documentary History of Baseball, 1825–1908.* Lincoln: University of Nebraska Press, 1995.

Thornley, Stew. *New York's Polo Grounds: Land of the Giants.* Philadelphia: Temple University Press, 2000.

Tiemann, Robert L., and Mark Rucker, editors. *Nineteenth Century Stars.* Cleveland: SABR, 1989.

Trumbull, James Hammond. *Indian Names of Places etc., in and on the Borders of Connecticut, with Interpretation of Some of Them.* Hartford, CT: Press of the Case, Lockwood and Brainard Co., 1888. Online edition.

Voigt, David Quentin. *American Baseball: From the Gentleman's Sport to the Commissioner System.* Volume 1. State College: Pennsylvania State University Press, 1983.

Wilbert, Warren. *Opening Pitch: Professional Baseball's Inaugural Season, 1871.* Lanham, MD: Scarecrow Press, 2008.

Newspapers

Bismarck Daily Tribune
Boston Daily Globe
Bridgeport Telegraph
Chicago Daily Tribune
Daily Inter-Ocean
  (Chicago)
Dallas Morning News
Hartford Courant
Holyoke Transcript
Manitoba Free Press
Mansfield Ohio News

Miami Herald Record
Naugatuck Daily News
Newark Daily Advocate
New York Clipper
New York Daily Mirror
New York Evening Journal
New York Herald
New York Press
New York Times
New York Tribune
Philadelphia Inquirer

St. Louis Post Dispatch
Sioux City Journal
Troy Daily Times
Troy Press
Washington Post
Washington Star News
Waterbury American
Waterbury Democrat
Waterbury Republican
Waterbury Republican-
  American

Online Resources

baseballalmanac.com
baseball-reference.com
baseballindex.org

retrosheet.org
baseballhalloffame.org
research.sabr.org.journals

bioproj.sabr.org
19Cbaseball.com

Census and Archives

U.S. Census, Waterbury, Connecticut, 1860, 1870.
U.S. Census, Otsego County, New York, 1870.
U.S. Census, Warren County, New York, 1880.
Medical Certificate of Death for Catherine Connor, Connecticut State Department of Health, Bureau of Vital Statistics, 1905.
Medical Certificate of Death for Angelina [sic] M. Connor, Connecticut State Department of Health, Bureau of Vital Statistics, 1928.
Medical Certificate of Death for Roger Connor, Connecticut State Department of Health, Bureau of Vital Statistics, 1931.

Special Publications

Troy's Baseball Heritage, Richard A. Puff, editor, Albany, NY: Committee to Preserve Troy's Baseball Heritage, Troy Local Development Corporation, 1992.

Conference Proceedings

Morris, Peter. Keynote Speech, SABR 19th Century Baseball Conference, National Baseball Hall of Fame Library, Cooperstown, New York, April 17, 2010.

Unpublished Sources

Silas Bronson Library, Waterbury, Connecticut, Connor, Roger, clipping file.
National Baseball Hall of Fame Library, Cooperstown, New York. Connor, Roger, clipping file.
National Baseball Hall of Fame Library, Cooperstown, New York, Connor, Roger, photograph file.
Laios, Gary, Damascus, MD, Connor, Roger, clipping, letter and photograph file.
Waterbury Republican. Connor, Roger, clipping file.

Index

Aaron, Henry 171–72, 174
Abrigador district, Waterbury, Connecticut 9, 175
Alvarez, Mark 174
Anson, Adrian "Cap" 32, 40, 43–44, 66, 72, 85–87, 104, 107, 118, 121, 153–54, 158, 167–68

Bagley, Ed 67–68
Baldwin, Mark 103
Bancroft, Frank "Banny" 18–19, 22, 49, 66, 82, 103
Barnie, William "Billie" 112, 140
Bell, Alexander Graham 88
Bellán, Esteban "Steve" 26–27
Bennett, Charlie 100
Bierbauer, Lou 111–12
Block, David 16
Bond, Tommy 15, 33, 151
Bonds, Barry 174
Boyle, "Handsome Henry" 87, 100
Boyle, Jack 110
Bradley, George 28
Breitenstein, Ted 128
Bresnahan, Roger 15, 169
Brice, Fanny 85
Brouthers, Dennis "Big Dan" 28–29, 32, 44, 47–48, 51, 53, 62–63, 76, 82, 92, 96, 105, 155, 158, 168
Brown, Willard "Big Bill" 109
Browning, Pete 104–5
Buckenberger, Al 132
Burkett, Jesse 170
Burnham, Walter 141

Carey, George "Scoops" 167
Cartwright, Alexander J. 4

"Casey at the Bat: A Ballad of the Republic" 86–87, 121
Caskin, Ed 57, 62
Chadwick, Henry 64
Chapman, Jack 140, 156
Chesbro, Jack 30
Clapp, John 72, 76, 78, 83
Clarkson, John 57–58, 61–63
Cobb, Ty 158
Cody, "Buffalo Bill" 3
Cogswell, Ed 40
Colwell, James F. 156, 158
Colwell, Margaret 7, 38–39, 88, 93
Colwell, Roger Connor 159, 174
Comiskey, Charlie 60, 66, 98, 126, 154
Commeyer, A.J. 4
Conan Doyle, Sir Arthur 96
Connor, Agnes 144
Connor, Angeline 64, 74–75, 83, 93, 112, 138, 144, 158–59, 163–64, 174
Connor, Catherine Sullivan 8–9, 75, 138, 155
Connor, Cecelia 112, 138, 144, 163–64, 174
Connor, Daniel 75, 138
Connor, Dennis 75, 138
Connor, Hannah 9, 13, 138
Connor, Joseph 11–12, 134, 138, 141–43, 146–47, 164
Connor, Lulu 93, 112
Connor, Mary 9, 75, 138
Connor, Matthew 138
Connor, Mortimer 8, 11, 138
Connor, Nellie "Nettie" 12, 75, 138
Coogan, James J. 91
Coogan's Bluff 91
Corbett, Joe 134
Corcoran, Larry 21, 32, 69

199

Crane, Ed "Cannonball" 85, 92, 109, 138
Crane, Sam 51, 153, 166–67, 172
Creighton, Jim 10
Cross, Lave 116
Cummings, Arthur "Candy" 15
Cuppy, George "Nig" 135
Curran, William 153

Daley, Bill 102–3
Dalrymple, Abner 32, 34, 43
Danaher, Cornelius "Con" 170
Danaher, John 170
Dauvray, Helen 59, 89, 168
Davis, George 120
Day, John B. 49–50, 57–58, 65–68, 70,
    72, 83, 85, 89, 90–91, 94, 98, 101, 104,
    106–7, 112, 177
Delahanty, Ed 52, 104, 117, 167–68
Denny, Jerry 100
Diddlebock, Harry 104
Donohue, Frank "Red" 56, 113, 127, 139
Dorgan, Mike 57, 62, 79
Dowd, Tommy 56, 128, 136, 170
Doyle, John "Dirty Jack" 55, 125
Duffy, Hugh 168
Durocher, Leo 70
Dwyer, Frank 133

Ely, Bill "Bones" 128
Engle, Fred 70
Esper, Charles "Duke" 122
Esterbrook, Thomas "Dude" 71–72, 79
Evers, Johnny 48
Ewing, John "Long John" 105, 110
Ewing, William "Buck" 30, 40, 45, 47–
    48, 57–58, 61–64, 66, 69, 71–73, 80,
    84, 88, 91–92, 94, 98, 101, 103–8, 110–
    11, 120, 158, 160–61, 171, 179

Ferguson, Bob 15, 20, 22, 29, 32, 34,
    36–40, 43, 51
Flint, Frank "Silver" 32
Foley, Tom 73
Force, David "Wee Davy" 27
Frank, Charlie 128
Freedman, Andrew 109

Gaffney, "Honest John" 55
Galvin, James "Pud" 65, 120
Ganzel, Charlie 100
Garfield, James 39
Gehrig, Lou 168
George, Bill 80
Gerhardt, Joe 72, 79
Geronimo 3
Getzein, 43, 52, 57, 69, 72, 78

Glassock, "Pebbly Jack" 100–1, 108, 110
Gleason, William "Kid" 52
Goldsmith, Fred 32
Gompers, Samuel 97
Gordon, Joseph 101
Gore, George 32, 34, 43, 79, 84, 92, 109,
    119, 155
Goslin, Leon "Goose" 162
Gould, Charley 42
Grilley, Henry 7
Grilley, Samuel 7
Grilley, Silas 7
Guiteau, Charles 39
Gunter, Archibald Clavering 86

Haggard, H. Rider 4
Hallman, Bill 116
Hamilton, Billy 52, 79, 117–18, 140
Hankinson, Frank 40, 57, 62
Hardesty, Scott 149–50
Harrison, Don 171, 173
Hatfield, Gil 92, 104, 109
Healy, John "Egyptian" 87
Hearst, William Randolph 86
Hedrick, H.D. 165
Helm, Clara 178
Henry, John M. 157
Henschel, Alexander 76
Hetrick, J. Thomas 126
Higgins, Mike 57
Holbert, Bill 40
Holmes, Thomas 166
Hopper, De Witt 86–88
Hotchkin, A.L. 44, 46
Hoy, Ellwood "Dummy" 106
Hubbard, Cal 173
Hulbert, William 37
Hurst, Lulu 88–89
Hutchinson, Billy 110–11, 118

Johnson, Albert 103, 106
Johnson, Byron "Ban" 99
Johnson, Walter 161

Kaiser, Anna 130
Keane, Albert W. 81–82, 167–68
Keefe, Tim 30–31, 40, 43–44, 46, 48,
    56–57, 65, 71–72, 77, 80, 83–85, 88,
    91–94, 96, 101, 104–5, 107, 109–10, 122,
    158, 160, 170, 177–79
Kelley, Joe 170
Kelly, John 39
Kelly, Mike "King" 43, 57, 64, 80, 92,
    104, 120–22, 158, 169
Kennedy, William "Brickyard" 132
Kieran, John 70, 177

Killen, Frank 123, 136
Kilroy, Matt 102–3
King, Steve 27
Kitteridge, Malachi 140
Klem, Bill 55
Knight, Alonzo 71
Koszarek, Ed 108

Lajoie, Larry "Nap" 158
Latham, Arlie 134, 140
Lieb, Fred 167
Lindstrom, Fred 173
Lucas, Henry Van Noye 64–65
Lyons, Denny 130

Mathewson, Christy 30
McCalpin, E.A. 106
McCarthy, Tommy 168
McCormick, Jim 160
McDougall, Thomas 159
McGeachy, Jack 87
McGillicudy, Cornelius (Connie Mack)
    99, 106, 169–70
McGrath, Jack "Peerless" 172
McGraw, John 12, 123, 155, 179
McKeon, James 26
McKinnon, Alex 67–68
Meir, Addie 38
Meir, Angeline 38
Meir, Apoline 38
Meir, Jakob 38
Miller, George "Doggie" 128, 130, 160
Montague, Hannah Lord 24
Morris, Peter 10
Mullane, Tony 123
Murnane, Tim 53
Mutrie, Grace 155
Mutrie, Jim 19, 39, 49–50, 58, 64, 69–
    72, 78–80, 85, 90, 92, 94, 100, 107,
    109, 112, 119, 155, 161, 171, 177–78
Mutrie, Kate 155
Myers, Burt 155

Nichols, Charles Augustus "Kid" 66, 110,
    132, 170
Nolan, Edward "The Only" 160
Noonan, James 130

O'Day, Hank 92, 109
O'Donnell, Hank 170
O'Mara, Paddy 157
O'Neil, Dan 150
O'Neil, James "Tip" 63
O'Rourke, Jim "Orator" 33–34, 70–71,
    73, 84, 91, 107, 109, 119, 136, 142, 146,
    155, 158, 166, 168, 179

O'Rourke, John 33
Orr, Dave 105–6

Palladino, Joe 174
Palmer, Billy 73
Parker, Dan 169–70, 172
Pattison, Edward 7
Pattison, William 7
Peitz, Henry "Heine" 128
Phillips, Horace 28
Pike, Lipman "Lip" 15
Powers, Pat 119–20, 142
Price, James L. 67

Quigley, John 28
Quinn, Joe 132, 135

Radbourn, Charles "Old Hoss" 5, 19, 52,
    61, 63, 65, 68–69, 87, 92, 105, 158,
    160, 168
Radbourn, George 63
Reach, Al 116
Reilly, "Long John" 114
Rice, Fanny 85
Richardson, Danny 68, 78, 84, 107, 109–
    15
Richardson, Hardie 158
Richmond, Lee 34, 40–42
Rogers, John I. 119
Roosevelt, Theodore 144
Rusie, Amos "the Hoosier Thunderbolt"
    60, 109–110, 161
Ruth, George Herman "Babe" 2, 165,
    168, 171, 174

Selee, Frank 66, 110
Sharrot, George 119
Sheppard, Patsey 142
Shire, Moses 106
Shugart, Frank 128
Slattery, Mike 84, 92, 109
Smith, Charles "Pop" 100
Smith, Lefty 157
Sockalexis, Louis "Chief" 145
Soden, Arthur 31
Spalding, Albert G. 10, 90, 92, 104
Stern, Aaron 103
Stevenson, George W. 130
Stith-Pemberton, John 4
Stockdale, Otis 165
Stovey, Harry 79, 111–12
Sullivan, Johanna Slattery 8
Sullivan, John L. 56, 113
Sullivan, Patsy 157
Sullivan, Ted 60
Sweeney, Charley 82–83

Talcott, Edward B. 106–7, 120, 125, 177
Taylor, Jack 125, 129
Tebeau, Oliver "Patsy" 145
Templeton, Charles A. 165
Terry, William H. "Adonis" 92
Thayer, Ernest Lawrence 85–86
Thompson, "Big Sam" 57, 117, 172, 174
Tiernan, "Silent Mike" 79, 84, 98, 100, 108–9
Titcomb, Ledell "Cannonball" 80, 85
Tolstoy, Leo 4
Troy, Dasher 58
Tucker, Tom 123, 147–48
Turner, Arison 203–4

Vance, Clarence "Dazzy" 161
Van Rensselaer, Stephen 23
Vecsey, George, 174
Voigt, David Quentin 10–11, 152
Von der Ahe, Chris 89, 98, 125–28, 130, 132–36
Von der Ahe, Eddie 130
Von der Ahe, Emma 130

Waas, Kathleen 178
Wagner, Honus 158

Ward, John Montgomery 53, 58–62, 64, 66–67, 69, 71, 80, 83–84, 89–98, 104–7, 109–10, 118, 123, 125, 129, 155, 158, 177–79
Watkins, Bill 128
Welch, "Smiling Mickey" 21–22, 29–30, 40, 44, 46, 57–58, 63, 68, 69, 70, 72, 77, 80, 84, 88, 92, 94, 98, 100, 107–10, 119–20, 122, 155, 160, 170–71, 178–79
Weyhing, Gus 105, 116, 129
White, Jim "Deacon" 76, 106
White, Will 114
Whitney, Art 84, 104, 109
Wilde, Oscar 96
Williams, Ted 118
Williamson, Ned 32, 35, 158
Wilson, Robert 138
Wilson, Roger Connor 138, 169
Wright, Harry 25, 66, 90, 115–16

Young, Cy 66, 136, 151
Youngs, Ross 171

Zettlein, George 27, 42